Trustworthy Reconfigurable Systems

Thomas Feller

Trustworthy Reconfigurable Systems

Enhancing the Security Capabilities of Reconfigurable Hardware Architectures

Thomas Feller
Darmstadt, Germany

Dissertation Technische Universität Darmstadt

D17

ISBN 978-3-658-07004-5   ISBN 978-3-658-07005-2 (eBook)
DOI 10.1007/978-3-658-07005-2

The Deutsche Nationalbibliothek lists this publication in the Deutsche Nationalbibliografie;
detailed bibliographic data are available in the Internet at http://dnb.d-nb.de.

Library of Congress Control Number: 2014948339

Springer Vieweg
© Springer Fachmedien Wiesbaden 2014
This work is subject to copyright. All rights are reserved by the Publisher, whether the whole or part of the material is concerned, specifically the rights of translation, reprinting, reuse of illustrations, recitation, broadcasting, reproduction on microfilms or in any other physical way, and transmission or information storage and retrieval, electronic adaptation, computer software, or by similar or dissimilar methodology now known or hereafter developed. Exempted from this legal reservation are brief excerpts in connection with reviews or scholarly analysis or material supplied specifically for the purpose of being entered and executed on a computer system, for exclusive use by the purchaser of the work. Duplication of this publication or parts thereof is permitted only under the provisions of the Copyright Law of the Publisher's location, in its current version, and permission for use must always be obtained from Springer. Permissions for use may be obtained through RightsLink at the Copyright Clearance Center. Violations are liable to prosecution under the respective Copyright Law.
The use of general descriptive names, registered names, trademarks, service marks, etc. in this publication does not imply, even in the absence of a specific statement, that such names are exempt from the relevant protective laws and regulations and therefore free for general use.
While the advice and information in this book are believed to be true and accurate at the date of publication, neither the authors nor the editors nor the publisher can accept any legal responsibility for any errors or omissions that may be made. The publisher makes no warranty, express or implied, with respect to the material contained herein.

Printed on acid-free paper

Springer Vieweg is a brand of Springer DE.
Springer DE is part of Springer Science+Business Media.
www.springer-vieweg.de

To my beloved ones

> The most exiting phrase to hear in science, the one that heralds new discoveries, is not "Eureka!" ("I found it!") but rather, "Hmmm ... That's funny ..."

Isaac Asimov

Abstract

Almost invisible to the user, many computer systems are embedded into everyday artifacts, such as cars, ATMs, and pacemakers. The significant growth of this market segment within the recent years enforced a rethinking with respect to the security properties and the trustworthiness of these systems. On the one hand, the security-sensitive data stored on these devices has to be kept secret and on the other hand access to security-sensitive information shall only be granted to trustworthy applications.

In general, hardware-based approaches are favored for the implementation of trust anchors, since the malicious modification of hardware modules is more difficult in comparison to software applications. Today, virtually every commercially used computer is equipped with a hardware-based trust anchor allowing for the assessment of system integrity. Although these hardware-based trust anchors exist, the strict constraints for embedded systems require adapted approaches using only a minimal amount of resources.

The trustworthiness of a system in general equates to the integrity of its system components. Cryptographic hash functions are exploited to generate checksums of executed programs, enabling the comparison to reference measurements being considered trustworthy. Moreover, digital signatures are used to guarantee the authenticity of the conducted measurements.

Reconfigurable architectures represent a special case in this regard, as in addition to the software implementation, the underlying hardware architecture may be exchanged, even during runtime. Hence, the system integrity measurement is expanded to include the active hardware configuration. The fundamental concepts and an analysis of various realizations of reconfigurable trust anchors is conceived as the major contribution of this Thesis. A generic approach supporting the trustworthy reconfiguration of hardware modules is presented and is further extended by a novel architecture implementing authenticated encryption. This generic approach is broadened to support scenarios, which require to make trust anchors available for multiple stakeholders.

In conclusion, three application scenarios supporting the feasibility and effectiveness of the herein proposed concepts and implementations are presented.

Kurzfassung

Beinahe unsichtbar für den Benutzer liegen eingebettete Systeme in den Dingen des täglichen Lebens versteckt, wie z. B. in Autos, Geldautomaten und Herzschrittmachern. Das signifikante Wachstum dieses Marktsegments in den letzten Jahren erfordert ein Umdenken bezüglich der Sicherheitseigenschaften und der Vertrauenswürdigkeit solcher Systeme. Zum einen müssen auf den Geräten gespeicherte, sensitive Daten geheim gehalten werden und zum anderen ist es notwendig, dass der Zugriff auf sensitive Daten nur vertrauenswürdigen Anwendungen erlaubt ist.

Im Allgemeinen werden Hardware-basierte Ansätze zur Realisierung von Vertrauensankern bevorzugt, da im Vergleich zu Software-basierten Lösungen, die gezielte Manipulation von Hardware Modulen einen höheren Schwierigkeitsgrad aufweist. Hardware-basierte Lösungen, die eine Bewertung der Systemintegrität erlauben, sind bereits heute in beinahe jedem kommerziell genutzten Computer verfügbar. Obwohl diese Hardware-basierten Vertrauensanker verfügbar sind, erfordern die starken Beschränkungen eingebetteter Systeme jedoch angepasste Ansätze, die mit den vorhandenen Ressourcen sparsam umgehen.

Die Vertrauenswürdigkeit eines Systems wird im Allgemeinen mit der Integrität der Systemkomponenten gleichgesetzt. Unter Verwendung kryptographischer Hash-Funktionen, werden Prüfsummen der ausgeführten Programme erstellt, die einen Vergleich mit den als vertrauenswürdig eingestuften Referenzmessungen erlauben. Des Weiteren werden digitale Signaturen verwendet, um die Authentizität der durchgeführten Messungen sicherzustellen.

Rekonfigurierbare Architekturen stellen einen Spezialfall der eingebetteten Systeme dar, da sich zusätzlich zur Softwareimplementierung die zugrunde liegende Hardware, auch dynamisch zur Laufzeit, verändern lässt. Demzufolge erweitert sich die Messung der Systemintegrität auf die aktive Hardwareimplementierung. Die grundlegenden Konzepte und die Analyse der Realisierungen für rekonfigurierbare Vertrauensanker bilden den Kernbeitrag dieser Dissertation. Ein generischer Ansatz zur Unterstützung der vertrauenswürdigen Rekonfiguration von Hardware Modulen wird vorgestellt und im Folgenden um eine neuartige Realisierung für die authentifizierte Verschlüsselung erweitert. Dieser generische Ansatz wird anschließend auf

Szenarien ausgeweitet, die es erfordern Vertrauensanker für mehrere Interessenvertreter bereitzustellen.

Abschließend werden drei Anwendungsfälle dargestellt, die die Machbarkeit und die Wirksamkeit der hier vorgestellten Konzepte und Realisierungen untermauern.

Acknowledgements

A PhD thesis is an endeavor which requires support, opinions, and constructive criticism from others. During the time at the *Center for Advanced Security Research Darmstadt* and the *Integrated Circuits and Systems Lab* many people have contributed to the results presented in this thesis in one form or another.

I am very grateful to Prof. Dr.-Ing. Sorin A. Huss, for his support during the tougher times of this work and his unending optimism. He was always supporting my selection of research topics and guiding me to get the best out of them.

Further I would like to thank Prof. Dr. rer. nat. Claudia Eckert for her interest in this thesis and for taking the responsibility as the second reviewer.

I am indebted to the staff of the Integrated Circuits and Systems Lab for their open ears, great ideas, and also fun times. Tolga Arul, Tom Assmuth, Alexander Biedermann, Lijing Chen, Annelie Heuser, Adeel Israr, Attila Jaeger, Zheng Lu, Felix Madlener, Sunil Malipatlolla, H. Gregor Molter, André Seffrin, Abdulhadi Shoufan, Marc Stöttinger, Hagen Stübing, Qizhi Tian, Maria Tiedemann, and Michael Zohner were continuously stimulating discussions and giving useful suggestions for my work.

Further I would like to thank the members of CASED, especially Tobias Ackermann, Sami Alsouri, Sheikh Mahbub Habib, Matthias Hollick, Michael Kasper, Stefan Katzenbeisser, Ünal Kocabas, Richard Lindner, Leonardo Martucci, Sascha Mühlbach, Stefan Nürnberger, Michael Schneider, and Christian Wachsmann for coauthoring papers, sharing their expertise, and their useful comments.

The students supporting the projects presented within this thesis, deserve many thanks for their hard work, Mehmet Ariman Zuhaib Ahmed Chohan, Suraj Das, Felix Deichmann, Aziz Demirezen, Christopher Huth, Octavio Gamero, Norman Göttert, Mahmoud Kamar, Minakshi Karwa, David Meister, Joel Njeukam, Leonardo Solis Vasquez, and Erik Victorsson.

Finally, I would like to thank my remarkable family for their unconditional support, concern, strength, and love all these years. Without their constant encouragement this thesis would not have been possible.

Darmstadt, Thomas Feller

Contents

1 Introduction   **1**
    1.1 Reconfigurable Computing 2
    1.2 Trustworthy Reconfiguration 4
    1.3 Summary of Contributions 6
    1.4 Limitations 6
    1.5 Remainder of this Thesis 7

2 Trustworthy Computing   **9**
    2.1 The Meaning of Trustworthiness 11
    2.2 Trusted Computing Group 13
       2.2.1 Trusted Computing Limitations 13
       2.2.2 Trusted Platform Module Specification 14
       2.2.3 Platform Integrity Measurements 19
       2.2.4 Measured Boot 21
       2.2.5 Secure Boot 22
       2.2.6 Authentication Protocols 22
       2.2.7 System Integrity Reporting 23
    2.3 Supporting Multiple Stakeholders 25
       2.3.1 Reference Integrity Metric Certificates 26
    2.4 Beyond TCG Specifications and Related Products 27
       2.4.1 Intel Trusted Execution Technology 29
       2.4.2 ARM TrustZone 30
       2.4.3 Texas Instruments M-Shield 31
    2.5 Trustworthy Systems using FPGAs 31
       2.5.1 Software-based Attestation 32
       2.5.2 Hardware-based Attestation 33

3 Requirements for Trustworthiness   **35**
    3.1 Key Storage and Certificate Management 36
       3.1.1 Cryptographic Memories 38
       3.1.2 Storing Cryptographic Secrets 40
       3.1.3 Certificate Management 44

	3.2	Identification and Authentication	47
		3.2.1 Requirements for Cryptographic Keys	48
		3.2.2 Device Identifiers	49
		3.2.3 Physically Unclonable Functions	49
	3.3	A Notion of Time	52
	3.4	Measurements for Security	53
		3.4.1 The Orange Book	54
		3.4.2 Common Criteria for IT Security Evaluation	55
		3.4.3 NIST-FIPS 140-2	58

4 Design Security and Cyber-Physical Threats — 61
- 4.1 Design Security Goals ... 63
- 4.2 Vendor Specific Design Security ... 66
  - 4.2.1 Tamper Protection ... 71
- 4.3 Generic IP-Protection ... 71
- 4.4 Cyber-Physical Threats ... 72
  - 4.4.1 Cloning, Overbuilding and Counterfeiting ... 74
  - 4.4.2 Physical Attacks ... 75
- 4.5 Common Security Scenarios ... 82
  - 4.5.1 Trusted Computing Group ... 82
  - 4.5.2 FPGA Vendor ... 82
- 4.6 TPM Specific Attacks ... 83

5 Towards Trustworthy Cyber-Physical Systems — 85
- 5.1 Reconfigurable System Challenges ... 87
  - 5.1.1 Storage of Security-Sensitive Data ... 87
- 5.2 Trustworthy Reconfigurable Systems ... 88
  - 5.2.1 The Use of Partial Reconfiguration ... 90
  - 5.2.2 System State Reporting ... 91
  - 5.2.3 Freshness of Configuration Data ... 92
  - 5.2.4 TinyTPM Architecture ... 93
  - 5.2.5 Life-Cycle ... 96
  - 5.2.6 Bootstrapping ... 97
  - 5.2.7 Update Protocol ... 99
  - 5.2.8 Proof-Of-Concept Implementation ... 102
  - 5.2.9 Evaluation ... 103
- 5.3 TinyTPM Optimizations ... 110
  - 5.3.1 Authenticated Encryption ... 110
  - 5.3.2 Partial Reconfiguration Performance ... 118

5.4	Physical Attack Resistance	120
	5.4.1 Side-Channel Aware TinyTPM Architecture	120
	5.4.2 Evaluation	121
	5.4.3 Tamper Protection	121
5.5	Supporting Multiple Stakeholders	123
	5.5.1 Dynamic Context Management Concept	124
	5.5.2 dcTPM Proof-of-Concept	129
	5.5.3 Context Authorization Protocol	133
	5.5.4 dcTPM-Commands	134
	5.5.5 Multi-Context Trust/Live Migration	135

6 Application Scenarios — 137
- 6.1 IP-Protection for Partial Reconfiguration — 137
  - 6.1.1 Trustworthy Reconfiguration enforcing IP-Protection — 138
  - 6.1.2 Configuration Management — 141
- 6.2 Hard Disk Encryption — 141
  - 6.2.1 Proof-of-Concept Implementation — 142
  - 6.2.2 Multi-User Environments — 145
- 6.3 Pay TV Content Protection — 146
  - 6.3.1 Reconfigurable Security — 147
  - 6.3.2 Proof-of-Concept Implementation — 149

7 Summary — 151

A Cryptographic Primitives — 155
- A.1 Selection of Algorithms — 155
  - A.1.1 Providing Integrity — 157
  - A.1.2 Providing Authenticity — 157
  - A.1.3 Providing Confidentiality — 158
  - A.1.4 Providing Non-Repudiation — 158
  - A.1.5 Providing Long-Term Security — 158
- A.2 Secure Hash Algorithm — 159
- A.3 Advanced Encryption Standard — 160
  - A.3.1 Low Latency AES Implementation — 160
  - A.3.2 Sub-Bytes Implementations — 161
- A.4 Message Authentication Codes (MAC) — 163
  - A.4.1 Hash-based Message Authentication Codes (HMACs) — 164
- A.5 Authenticated Encryption — 164
  - A.5.1 AES Counter Mode with CBC-MAC – AES-CCM — 165
  - A.5.2 Hardware Implementation — 166

	A.6 Random Number Generators	168
B	**FPGA Technology**	**171**
	B.1 Configuration Technologies	171
	B.2 Partial Reconfiguration	172
	B.2.1 Workflow	173

List of Publications   **175**

List of Supervised Theses   **177**

List of Figures

2.1 Conventional TPM Architecture [TCG11c, p. 17] 14
2.2 Initialization Procedure of a TPM 16
2.3 Simplified TPM Life Cycle [TCG11b] 18
2.4 Measured Boot Procedure [TCG07, GKMB09] 21
2.5 Object-Specific Authorization Protocol (OSAP) [TCG11c] . . 23
2.6 TPM Remote Attestation Protocol [TCG07] 24

3.1 Generic Memory Authentication Protocols 42
3.2 Generic Key Hierarchy for Hardware Security Modules 43
3.3 Certificate Chain-of-Trust 45
3.4 Arbiter PUF Construction [SD07] 50

4.1 Authenticated Non-Volatile Memory [Alt07, Xil10] 70

5.1 TinyTPM Architecture [FMMH11] 93
5.2 System View of TinyTPM Architecture [FMMH11] 95
5.3 TinyTPM Life-Cycle 97
5.4 Bootstrapping Scheme [FMMH11] 98
5.5 TinyTPM Update Protocol [FMMH11] 99
5.6 Hardware Configuration Update Flowchart [FMMH11] 101
5.7 TinyTPM Resource Utilization on Virtex5 FPGAs 107
5.8 Frequency Histogram TinyTPM for Virtex5 Devices 108
5.9 AES-CCM-based TinyTPM Architecture 112
5.10 Datapath of the AES-CCM Architecture 115
5.11 Reconfiguration Time Comparison AES-CCM and TinyTPM 117
5.12 Resource Utilization on Virtex5 122
5.13 dcTPM System Architecture [FMKH11] 126
5.14 Simplified View of the dcTPM Proof-of-Concept
     Implementation [FMKH11, Dei10] 130
5.15 Context Authorization Protocol [Dei10] 133

6.1 Y-Diagram of Cyber-Physical Design Security 140
6.2 System Overview of Transparent Hard Disk Encryption . . . 143

6.3	System Architecture of Transparent Hard Disk Encryption [Hut12]	144
6.4	Functional View of Reconfigurable Set-Top-Box Architecture	147
A.1	Timing Diagram of Low Latency AES Implementation.	161
A.2	AES-CCM Timing Diagram	169
B.1	Module Structure for Partial Reconfiguration	172

List of Tables

2.1 The Designated Purpose of Platform Configuration Registers (PCRs) [TCG12b] 20

3.1 Comparison of Volatile and Non-Volatile Key Storage Properties 39
3.2 Trusted Computer System Evaluation Criteria Classification [DoD85] 54
3.3 Common Criteria Evaluation Assurance Levels [CC09c, CC07] 56
3.4 Cryptographic Module Requirement for Compliance to NIST-FIPS140-2 Security Levels [NIS02] 59

4.1 Available Protection Mechanisms for FPGA Configuration Data 68
4.2 Extended Hierarchy of Cyber-Physical Attacks (based on [VS07]) 73
4.3 Top-5 Semiconductor Counterfeits in 2011 (Percentage of Overall Reported Counterfeit Parts) [IHS12] 75

5.1 Comparison of SHA-1 and AES-based Hardware Implementations of Cryptographic Hash Functions [FMMH11] 104
5.2 TinyTPM Hardware Resource Utilization Separated into Individual Components [FMMH11] 105
5.3 Proof-of-Concept Parameter Values 110
5.4 Typical Size of Virtex-5 Configuration Data [Xil11d] and Estimated Reconfiguration Times (TinyTPM@100MHz). . . . 111
5.5 Comparison between Authenticated Encryption Schemes . . . 113
5.6 AES-CCM Parameter Values 114
5.7 Comparison of AES-CCM Hardware Implementations on Various Xilinx Device Families 116
5.8 Partial Reconfiguration Throughput for Xilinx Devices 118

5.9	Resource Utilization of dcTPM Prototype Implementation [FMKH11, Dei10]	132
5.10	Requirements for the dcTPM Commands [FMKH11]	135
5.11	Composition of the dcTPM_RES-Response [FMKH11]	135
6.1	Security Services Provided by the TinyTPM (based on [GKST07])	139
6.2	Resource Utilization of the Transparent Hard Disk Encryption Proof-of-Concept [Hut12]	146
6.3	Proof-of-Concept Resource Utilization [Sol12]	150
A.1	Comparison of SHA-1 Hardware Module Implementations.	159
A.2	AES Hardware Implementation Variants	161
A.3	Resource Utilization of Different SBox Implementations for Virtex-5 Devices	162
A.4	Scheduling of Internal Operations in AES-CCM Implementation	167

1 Introduction

The embedded systems market has grown significantly within the last decade. Currently, embedded and mobile systems far outnumber commodity computer systems. The research company IDC predicted that more than one third of all major electronic devices in 2015 will be "intelligent [embedded] systems" as stated in [Jac11]. Our daily life is increasingly depending on intelligent devices, guiding us the way through the urban environment or serving our diverse communication needs.

Current computer systems have to handle more and more sensitive data and thus are demanding sophisticated protection mechanisms. Not only data has to be protected, but also data processing algorithms and thereby the computer system itself requires protection. However, most users are not questioning the trustworthiness of devices they are using, but adversaries are actively manipulating these systems, e.g. ATMs.

Many intelligent computer systems are embedded into everyday artifacts making them almost invisible to the user. The fact that these systems are beginning to control entities of the physical environment, lead to the term cyber-physical systems. Moreover, for various applications the communication between cyber-physical systems is imperative to provide a greater good. Power grid management of decentralized renewable energy production facilities and inter-vehicle communication improving road safety are typical applications [Lee06].

Taking a closer look at SmartGrids, a continuous monitoring of system integrity is of utmost importance. In many countries, the energy sector is part of the critical infrastructure and hence, additional security mechanisms protecting this sector are crucial to governments. The Federal Office for Information Security (BSI) in Germany requires the use of a Hardware Security Module (HSM) (e.g., a SmartCard) in related metering technologies [BSI11].

The connection of cyber-physical systems to the physical surrounding can be extremely close. Medical implants, such as pacemakers and insulin pumps, represent the most lethal tip of the iceberg. Radcliffe has presented in [Rad11] severe vulnerabilities of currently available medical devices, by wirelessly disabling an insulin pump. Disabling a medical device is only one part of the story; if the adversary is issuing malicious modifications, it may lead to immediate fatal results. Hence, protection mechanisms against malicious modification shall be included in most of the cyber-physical systems.

The trustworthiness of cyber-physical systems is becoming more and more important, as these systems are influencing large areas of our society. The increasing complexity and performance of cyber-physical systems make them attractable targets to attackers. A shift in the current paradigm to protect only Personal Computers (PCs) and server systems shall be envisioned[1].

Some of these cyber-physical systems – mostly in industrial automation – may leverage the same technology available for commodity computers and may apply similar mechanisms. Many commodity computing platforms are already equipped with secure hardware components enabling the assessment of their configuration. The Trusted Platform Module (TPM) [TCG11c] provides means for authentication and software integrity measurement. Trustworthiness of a computing platform can be derived from these two basic services as they enable identification and substantiate integrity measurement to determine known-good configurations. Confidentiality is often an additional security goal, but for trustworthiness alone it is not required.

For the majority of cyber-physical systems the situation is dramatically different, as the operating conditions are subject to much tighter constraints. This includes smaller memories, lower processing power, larger operating temperature ranges, or lower energy consumption. Hence, novel solutions accommodating a generic computational environment with additional capabilities for establishing trustworthy relationships are required.

Reconfigurable devices using Field Programmable Gate Arrays (FPGAs), are providing means for application specific hardware implementations. Optimized hardware implementations are harnessing a high level of parallelism and thus, are relaxing some the aforementioned constraints. In addition to highly optimized implementations of the exploited algorithms, the overall platform can be customized to only include functions required by the particular application.

1.1 Reconfigurable Computing

Product piracy is a serious threat for both manufacturers and consumers alike [FS12]. Mostly companies have to deal with the negative effects of counterfeits. These effects range from economical losses to a damage to

---

[1] http://www.thefirewall.co.uk/news/54/now_is_the_time_to_secure_mobile_devices/

1.1 Reconfigurable Computing

the company's image. Customers are also affected by product piracy if the counterfeit does not meet the quality standards of a genuine product, especially when used in safety critical applications.

FPGAs are versatile devices for the implementation of cyber-physical systems. Systems benefit from the flexibility given by the reprogrammable hardware implementation. With this, the system architecture can be efficiently composed of the required modules by simply programming the FPGA. Moreover, FPGAs often feature numerous interfaces providing common functions. These interfaces range from a huge amount of generic input/output ports, analog to digital converters, > 10Gb transceivers, to digital signal processing blocks to name a few.

Vendors additionally support the dynamic partial reconfiguration of FPGA resources while the device is in use. This adds another layer of flexibility to the system design and allows the system designer to time-slice different hardware implementations similar to the execution of multiple software tasks. As a result, the system design may virtually exploit more of the FPGA's resources then there are actually available (see Appendix B).

This flexibility is a benefit on the one hand but it also imposes a risk on the other. FPGA-based systems have to face serious threats, such as device *cloning* and *overbuilding* (cf. Section 4.4). For volatile (Static Random Access Memory (SRAM)-based) FPGAs cloning of the device is simple if no additional protection is applied. The configuration of these FPGAs is stored in an external non-volatile storage and may be directly copied. FPGAs are standard equipment that can be purchased off-the-shelf in large quantities. Hence, most FPGA vendors do at least provide basic measures for Intellectual Property (IP) protection, but the implementation of trust enabling technologies is still missing.

The major issues of current FPGAs, with respect to security, are key storage, authenticated configuration, and trustworthy reconfiguration. Drimer surveys on available measures protecting FPGA configuration data in [Dri08]. For the mere protection of configuration data, the vendor supported measures may be sufficient. If the system designer needs to exploit partial reconfiguration, these features are not available for all commercially available devices.

In [Dri07], Drimer further stresses on the necessity to authenticate configuration data prior to configuration. Even if the configuration data is encrypted, a small modification in the configuration may lead either to a faulty behavior or it may destroy the system (cf. [HUS99]). Please note that, only the most recent reconfigurable devices support the authentication of configuration data.

The remote update of FPGAs configuration data has been addressed in [DK09]. Within this protocol the configuration is transmitted over an insecure channel to the FPGA. The roll-back of configurations is mitigated by using monotonic counters stored within an external non-volatile Memory (NVM). However, the trustworthiness of the device configuration is never questioned, leading again the requirement of trustworthy reconfiguration. A single modified device may otherwise be exploited to extract valuable IP from the overall FPGA's configuration data.

1.2 Trustworthy Reconfiguration

The Trusted Computing Group (TCG) TPM specification is a widely accepted technological solution for secure commodity computers. Today, virtually every laptop in enterprise environments is equipped with a TPM and makes this kind of technology available to most enterprises. According to [Bri12] already "[...] tens of millions of enterprise-class devices [...]" are equipped with TPMs. Usually, TPMs come as standard equipment at very little or no additional cost on enterprise-level platforms.

Trusted Computing platforms can be used to protect enterprise assets by denying access to company's resources, if the platform fails to attest its known-good configuration. The infrastructure needs to support private networks protecting the assets and a process defining known-good configurations on a regular basis. Given this management overhead, the TPM specification is mostly applicable for enterprise environments.

Infineon advocates the use of Trusted Computing to enhance embedded platforms with extensive cryptographic capabilities in [Inf06]. This white paper outlines the market relevance of TPMs and their applicability for various embedded systems markets. However, including a TPM into embedded systems is not always an option. The additional hardware surely increases security and trustworthiness but also adds cost to the bill-of-materials. In contrast, these systems cost only a small fraction of enterprise-level equipment, making the impact of additional materials more severe. Moreover, TPMs are incapable of mitigating physical attacks, which are an emerging threat especially for cyber-physical systems (see Section 4.4) and the unprotected interfaces are prone to well-known attacks (cf. Section 4.6).

The measures incorporated into the TPM specification are not directly applicable to reconfigurable cyber-physical systems. As previously outlined, cyber-physical systems have to fulfill tight resource constraints opposing to the generic approach advocated by the TCG. A huge amount of supported commands and resource consuming cryptographic algorithms are examples violating these constraints. Moreover, using less of the available resources within a reconfigurable device leaves more space for the actual implementation.

Although, existing trust-anchors, such as the TPM, are infeasible to protect reconfigurable devices, similar functions are required for building trustworthy reconfigurable systems. The trustworthiness of a system has to be anchored at some mechanism or function comparable to the trust anchor provided by the authentication and integrity measurement facilities specified by the TCG. These services are currently nonexistent in commercially available reconfigurable systems.

The commercially available protection mechanisms for configuration data of reconfigurable platforms are constantly improving. However, a platform integrity measurement attesting the current system configuration, which is reflecting hardware and software in this case, is not available. This circumstance is gaining more and more importance, as designers tend to include highly specialized IP-cores from third party sources. The current protection mechanisms are solely taking the design time protection of IP-cores into account. The exploitation of the partial reconfiguration technology to extend a product's lifetime is still in its infancy.

Partial reconfiguration is currently mainly targeting hardware consolidation, which allows for time slicing of hardware resources to exploit more resources then there are actually available. Neither the effective configurations on the FPGA are measured, nor the history of previously active configurations is tracked.

Several approaches aiming at these requirements have been presented in literature. Glas et al. advocate an approach including an external TPM in [GKS+08b, GKS+08a]. A crucial precondition of their approach resides in the fact that their initial configuration data is provided by an external trust block. It is composed of an configuration memory, a Joint Test Action Group (JTAG) controller for configuration, and the actual TPM residing within a logical security boundary. A solution for the proposed trust block has not been included in this work. More related literature is addressed in Section 2.5.

Since one of the most restrictive constraints for cyber-physical systems is the resource utilization, an efficient approach thwarting the aforementioned issues is envisioned. Moreover, the implementation shall be included within the FPGA fabric mitigating simple physical attacks, such as bus probing (cf. Section 4.4.2).

1.3 Summary of Contributions

A comprehensive approach mitigating the hereinbefore outlined deficiencies is presented within this thesis. Reconfigurable platforms shall benefit from the generic architecture providing trustworthy reconfiguration services.

With the enabling technology of trustworthy reconfiguration in place, more complex applications may be envisioned. Thus a proof-of-concept for a dynamic context management architecture providing access to multiple TPMs is detailed in Section 5.5. Although the improved performance is mostly useful for cloud computing applications, a simplified version of this architecture may also be exploited in mobile application scenarios.

The major contributions of this thesis are listed in the following:

- A generic architecture for building trustworthy reconfigurable systems
- A novel hardware architecture unveiling royalty-free authenticated encryption on a single-pass performance level
- Inclusion resistive measures against physical attacks in a variant of the generic architecture
- Dynamic management system reflecting the requirements of mobile and cloud computing applications
- Survey of existing measures, protocols, and product life-cycle definitions
- Various applications of the generic architecture, such as IP protection, hard disk encryption, and media content protection

This also includes the fact that these systems can be physically accessed by an attacker and therefore are prone to any kind of physical attack (cf. Section 4.4.2).

The majority of the contributions detailed in this thesis are not limited to FPGAs-based applications. However, the main focus of this thesis lays mainly on the specific requirements of FPGA-based systems.

1.4 Limitations

In this thesis several architectures for trustworthy systems are presented. The focus of this thesis is on the features necessary for building trustworthy cyber-physical systems. Further, it lays on hardware realizations of trust anchors for a broad range of applications. Software based attacks are not covered within the scope of this thesis.

In general, there is no holistic approach to the design of trustworthy and perfectly secure systems. The main goal of security research is to raise the level of protection until it becomes unfeasible for an adversary to perform an attack. Moreover, security measures may be circumvented by social engineering, which is often much easier than breaking the actual security mechanism. Layer by layer, the protection mechanisms are added to the system design thwarting the adversary's attack.

Attacks on the surrounding infrastructure, such as the network itself or server systems are not addressed in this thesis. It is further assumed that device specific keys are used, such that the successful extraction of key material from one device does not support attacking others.

In this thesis security flaws resulting from algorithmic, protocol or implementation errors are not considered. If an implementation may be considered trustworthy, but in the end it turns out that there had been implementation errors, this can in principle not be prevented by any measure used herein or elsewhere.

The focus of this thesis is on architectures supporting trustworthy operation, therefore it is assumed that servers, users and providers are honest and trustworthy. More specifically, the case in which users collaborate with the adversary, intentionally or by force, are not taken into account.

The effects of untrustworthy modification during manufacture, which includes the threat of *Hardware Trojans* (cf. [PNNM09, FD10]) are not taken into account. Further, modifications carried out while the device being in the supply chain are also out of the scope of this thesis.

1.5 Remainder of this Thesis

Throughout this thesis the term trustworthy computing is favored over Trusted Computing and a reasoning for this choice is given at the beginning of Chapter 2. An overview of the existing TPM specification content is detailed to present the basic principles for subsequent definitions. Several concepts realizing measures for the resource sharing between multiple entities are outlined. Further, an overview of similar solutions providing sealed execution environments to ensure the protection of security-sensitive applications is given. Existing approaches realizing trustworthy reconfigurable architectures are additionally reported.

Chapter 3 reviews the requirements for trustworthy systems. The issues present in storing security-sensitive key material are detailed with respect to trustworthy systems. Identification and authentication measures for reconfigurable architectures are elaborated consecutively. The chapter concludes by presenting various approaches towards measuring security.

Objectives towards achieving design security and the typical threats are denoted in Chapter 4. The generic design security goals applicable to all reconfigurable systems are outlined. This is followed by the presentation of vendor specific solutions to design security and IP protection. A definition of the typical threats a particular device has to face is given in Section 4.4. Finally, some TPM specific attack scenarios are highlighted, as they may impact the measures presented hereinafter.

The architectures supporting trustworthy cyber-physical systems are highlighted in Chapter 5. The security challenges of volatile FPGAs are illustrated by the complexity of security-sensitive data storage. The original generic architecture realizing trustworthy reconfiguration is analyzed subsequently. A life-cycle definition, bootstrap procedure, and communication protocol specifications of this architecture are amongst others discussed in detail. Moreover, a comprehensive evaluation on the resource utilization and the overall architecture performance is presented. Further details on the utilized implementations have been shifted to Appendix A. Several optimizations of the original scheme are in turn presented. These optimizations include the design of a novel hardware architecture for the well-known authenticated encryption scheme Cipher Block Chaining (CBC) Message Authentication Code (MAC) with Counter Mode (CCM). As a sequel, a specialized architecture supporting multiple stakeholder applications is presented. This architecture is targeting mobile and cloud computing applications.

Chapter 6 sheds some light on potential applications exploiting trustworthy reconfigurable systems. The IP protection scenario is inherently present, as the generic architecture has been designed for this task. Two other case studies are presented in the following, namely a hard disk encryption service and a pay TV content protection scheme.

Chapter 7 concludes this thesis with an outlook on future work and a summary of the contribution.

2 Trustworthy Computing

The decision, if a utilized platform may be considered trustworthy, is not a trivial one. Even if the complete software configuration of a computing platform is known, there is still the uncertainty of inadvertent modification. A paramount example of such modifications are computer viruses and Trojan Horses, which may be detected by the sophisticated heuristic methods embodied in current virus scanners, but their detection is not guaranteed.

Trustworthiness itself is a rather vague expression and therefore the meaning of this term within the scope of this thesis is clarified in the following.

> **Definition: Trustworthiness**
>
> Notion of the dependability of a specific entity to comply to a given policy within the scope of a relationship. A trustworthy entity is expected to behave honestly. For the application to computing systems, trustworthiness shall be a verifiable property of the system.

The plain definition of trustworthiness does not cover the semantic difference between *trustworthy* and *trusted*. To *trust* sth. is an action that defines relationships between entities and it does neither have to be complete nor mutual. If an entity is *trusted*, the decision whether the entity will act honestly within the scope of this particular relationship, has already been made. In contrast, the term *trustworthy* denotes to the estimation of the *worthiness* of an entity to be *trusted*. An entity is referred to be *trustworthy* if it behaves honestly according to a given policy. If an entity is *trustworthy* it may be also *trusted*, but if it is *trusted* it is required to be *trustworthy*. Within this thesis, the term *trustworthy* is favored, which is oppositional to the term Trusted Computing advocated by the TCG.

The *trustworthiness* of a device relies on the continuous monitoring of the *system integrity* and the devices' capability to proof its *authenticity*. Establishing trustworthiness in a device is only possible if the system state is known and if it can be verified. The determination, if a system is trustworthy or not, can be made by a comparison to previously recorded known-good system states. Moreover, *trustworthiness* is a dynamic decision which in principle needs to be evaluated continuously.

During the *trustworthiness* evaluation of a given platform, the *system integrity* and the *authenticity* are assessed. Both fundamental properties of a *trustworthy* system may be regarded as binary (0/1, true/false) decisions. A signature is authentic or not and the integrity of a system is within the defined constraints or not. The decision on the *trustworthiness* fails with at least with one of these properties. For simplification, often only a subset of the systems properties are assessed for trustworthiness.

A failing *system integrity* check, for example, is indicating a malicious modification or a yet unrecorded update of the platform had taken place. *Authenticity* is provided by cryptographically signed messages that unveil modifications of the platform upon signature verification. In special cases, a finer granularity is favored to record the system integrity, allowing the user to trust the device only for certain tasks. An example for this is the usage specification of the Platform Configuration Registers (PCRs) in a TPM. Including a subset of the available PCRs within an assessment allows the user to select which components are crucial for a trustworthy system (cf. Section 2.2.3). This assessment may be recorded by utilizing a bit-vector representation of *system integrity* measurements. If and only if all of the selected values are matching the expectation, the application shall be able to access confidential data.

All components being critical to the systems security, namely hardware, software, and firmware, are often referred to as Trusted Computing Base (TCB). Due to the complexity, these components are not included in the TCB as a whole, but only relevant parts affecting the security policy. For the remainder it is assumed that vulnerabilities shall not provide the attacker with elevated privileges higher than the ones already given outside of the TCB.

Exhaustive security assessments by means of compliance to security policies or by program verification are only feasible for reduced complexity problems. Consequently, developers as well as research are striving to minimize the TCB [MPP+08, Par10]. Moreover, Heiser et al. are advocating solutions supporting formal verification in [HMK12]. Their verification of a microkernel forms the basis for building trustworthy systems.

A judgment on whether a device is considered to be trustworthy or not, can only be made if certain conditions are fulfilled. Current systems face different threats, which have to be taken into account while compiling the list of requirements.

The basic component to realize Trusted Computing for commodity computers is the TPM. It is a hardware-based security module providing the functions to measure and attest the system state of the underlying platform. Although the TPM provides mechanisms to facilitate the decision about the trustworthiness of the platform, it is not able to deduct any notion of trustworthiness by itself. This kind of service may be provided, if the software part of the TCB is supporting the comparison to known-good values. A TPM is mainly providing a secure storage on the one hand and access to certain cryptographic primitives on the other. The cryptographic primitives include components providing signature generation, encryption, and protocol operations. The secure storage is utilized to protect cryptographic keys and to record a representation of the system state. Digital signatures are generated by applying the RSA. Cryptographic protocols always require random numbers to guarantee the freshness of every query or reply in order to prevent replay attacks. Therefore, the TPM is additionally providing a random number generator.

The remainder of this chapter will shed some light on Trusted Computing, especially on its capabilities and its limitations. A reasoning on the practical implications of trustworthiness will be given. Then, the measures provided by the TCG will be detailed, followed by a presentation of specific concepts for mobile application and virtualization scenarios. Additional commercial products providing similar or extended protection mechanisms are outlined afterwards. This chapter finally concludes with a compilation of existing approaches utilizing TPM(-like) technology for reconfigurable cyber-physical systems.

2.1 The Meaning of Trustworthiness

Trustworthiness cannot be derived from the knowledge of the current system configuration alone. An initial assessment is required to enable the decision which components need to be included in the configuration. The consideration if a system is trustworthy, is carried out based on these values. The comparison of the known-good values to reported measurements of current configurations enables the final decision on the trustworthiness of a given device.

In general, there are multiple entities involved in a Trusted Computing architecture, at least the system under assessment and a remote requester questioning the trustworthiness of a given platform. The system is able to present its configuration to a remote requester exploiting the remote attestation protocol (cf. Section 2.2.7). With the knowledge of the system configuration, the remote requester decides if the system is operating within a certain set of valid configurations. The identity of the system is additionally revealed, as cryptographic digital signatures are used. The identities may be matched to different valid system configuration according to a given policy. Therefore, a given system state may represent a trustworthy configuration for one identity, but an untrustworthy for the other.

A practical premise for trustworthiness is the certification of utilized components. Meaningful certifications are carried out according to certain standards, such as Common Criteria for Information Technology Security Evaluation (CC) (cf. Section 3.4.2) or the National Institute of Standards and Technology (NIST) FIPS 140-2. The Federal Office for Information Security (BSI) identified this as a key requirement for trustworthy systems in [BSI07] and required a minimum certification of Evaluation Assurance Level (EAL)4+ for governmental use. Certified systems may be built exploiting a common security architecture, such as the TPM. Together with a TCB and its higher level services, effective measures for representing the system configuration are provided.

According to Parno, the TCB may be realized following two approaches, namely solutions providing the identity of code, such as Trusted Computing and solutions monitoring the behavior, such as information flow control [Par10]. The identity of code may be verified utilizing a TPM and to additionally certify the integrity of software. The other approach advocated by Parno, is to include certain functions during the development of the TCB, such as static code analysis or the use of hypervisors/security kernels for the separation of privileges. As already mentioned, the security-relevant code shall be assessed and therefore needs to be reduced to enable formal verification (cf. [HMK12]). A smaller TCB further simplifies the effort for assessing a systems configuration.

A trustworthy system shall fulfill the aforementioned requirements to support the assessment of the system configuration. Complying to this requirements, such systems may be considered trustworthy to process confidential information as they guarantee high security standards.

2.2 Trusted Computing Group

The Trusted Computing Group (TCG) is an non-profit organization developing and promoting industry standards of building blocks used for Trusted Computing. Members of the TCG are divided into three groups consisting of 11 promoters, 59 contributors, and 38 adopters[1]. Trusted Computing solutions are based on *data protection* mechanisms, *strong authentication* schemes, and measures to provide *network security*. The paramount contribution of the TCG is the specification on how to use a Root-of-Trust when building trustworthy systems. This Root-of-Trust is mostly implemented as a dedicated HSM separating the security-sensitive cryptographic key material and the security sensitive functions from the rest of the system.

Further, the TCG is organized in working groups, which focus on certain topics, ranging from PC-clients and servers to mobile systems and cloud solutions. These working groups define specifications reflecting the needs of the particular applications they focus on. The PC Client Work Group, the Storage Work Group, and the Mobile Platform Work Group are some examples.

A recent outcome of the Mobile Platform Work Group is an article relating to the growing threat of compromised SmartPhones [TCG11a]. The updated mobile platform specification includes use cases of trustworthy mobile phones for strong authentication of enterprise employees and privacy sensitive e-Health applications.

2.2.1 Trusted Computing Limitations

Trusted Computing only includes static program analysis and does not prevent against runtime attacks which may occur after a program has been loaded. Moreover, it is not mandatory to do statical program analysis to assess programs before they are included. Runtime vulnerabilities, such as buffer overflows, exploited by return oriented programming [CFK+09, CDD+10] and similar attacks, are not covered.

TPMs being used in cyber-physical systems have to face various threats, which have not been considered in the specification, e.g. physical attacks. These attacks range from reverse engineering attacks on TPMs, as presented by Tarnovsky in [Tar10], to other sophisticated techniques (e.g. side-channel analysis), as outlined in Section 4.4. Although, physical attacks have been explicitly excluded from the protection profile of the TPM, they may have practical relevance. The often required CC certification of EAL4+ (cf.

---

[1]http://trustedcomputinggroup.org/about_tcg/tcg_members (2012-08-16)

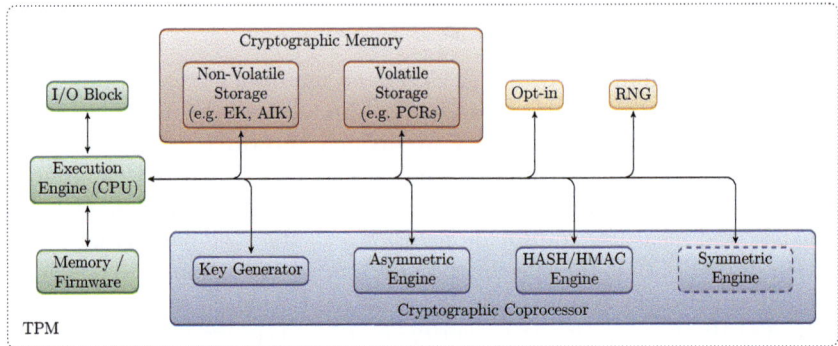

Figure 2.1: Conventional TPM Architecture [TCG11c, p. 17]

Section 3.4.2) only provides protection against moderate attack potential, which does not include any of the aforementioned physical attacks.

2.2.2 Trusted Platform Module Specification

The TPM specification [TCG11c] is an extensive compilation of schemes to provide a variety of different features. These features range from data protection to anonymous authentication, to name a few. Each of these features is realized by successively executing a well-defined sequence of commands. The specification contains the descriptions for each of the more than one hundred commands available on current TPMs.

The TCG defines the minimum set of required features for a trusted platform as: *protected capabilities*, *integrity measurement*, and *integrity reporting*. *Protected capabilities* refers to the shielded execution environment and a protected cryptographic key storage. *Integrity measurement* refers to the process of cryptographically hashing the executed programs before execution. Whereas system *integrity reporting* is referring to the process of attesting the system state to an external requester.

The TPM is in principle a coprocessor realizing cryptographic services, similar to the services provided by SmartCards. Some manufacturers even share the security controller architecture between SmartCards and TPMs. The main difference between a TPM and a *SmartCard* is the ownership concept [Tom08]. A SmartCard is usually owned by the issuer, especially the keys and data on the card. In contrast, the user of a TPM is able to reset all cryptographic keys, destroying the identity of the TPM, while still being able to make use of it after reinitialization.

2.2 Trusted Computing Group

An overview of the conventional TPM architecture is given in Figure 2.1. A TPM is conceived as System-on-a-Chip, hence all security-sensitive services are executed within a closed system. This, together with a cryptographic key storage, allows for the realization of the *protected capabilities*, as documented in the TCG specification [TCG07]. The execution engine is a microcontroller which forms the basis of the TPM realization. This execution engine processes incoming commands and controls the cryptographic engines accordingly. It is also intended for the realization of cryptographic communication protocols.

Integrity measurement is accomplished using the hash engine to obtain a digest of the characteristics representing the platform state. The hash engine facilitates the *integrity measurement* of the platform configuration and additionally supports the generation of Hash-based Message Authentication Codes (HMACs), which are essential for certain steps in the cryptographic protocols. Hash values at the beginning of a measured boot procedure (cf. Section 2.2.4) are generated by applying the Secure Hash Algorithm (SHA) engine.

Authentication is a fundamental component of *integrity reporting* and it is provided by an asymmetric engine. The *Key Generator* and the *Asymmetric Engine* are performing the RSA-based encryption / decryption and signature generation / verification schemes. The most important cryptographic engines of the cryptographic coprocessor are, RSA and SHA supplying means for authenticity verification and integrity reporting. The TPM additionally provides a secure storage for cryptographic key material and may include hardware-based accelerators for cryptographic services.

A common warrant for the freshness in cryptographic protocols is supplied by means of NONCEs (Number used ONCE). An Random Number Generator (RNG) is provided with every TPM as the utilized protocols require a NONCE for the execution of commands. The RNG, supplied with a TPM, may be implemented in hardware or in software, as the TPM specification does not distinguish between those two variants. Additional external sources of entropy may be included to guarantee unpredictable behavior of the RNG, but the inclusion of these measures is decided by the manufacturer.

The operation modes of the TPM and further permanent configuration flags are stored in the Opt-In configuration, reflecting the state of the TPM. The mode of operation defines the subset of the commands available to the user. These modes may be set to disable certain commands, in particular handling the deletion of owner specific data.

The specification does not require any of the above mentioned algorithms to be implemented in hardware. However, it is practical to implement some as hard-wired modules to improve performance. A *Symmetric Engine* may

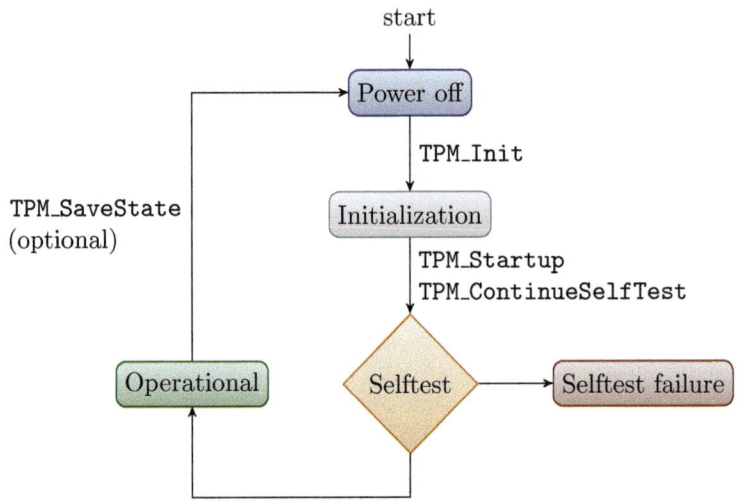

Figure 2.2: Initialization Procedure of a TPM

be provided as an optional component to accelerate symmetric encryption schemes.

The TCG differentiates between three Root-of-Trusts assembling the Trusted Building Block (TBB), namely the Core Root of Trust for Measurement (CRTM), the Root-of-Trust for Storage (RTS), and the Root-of-Trust for Reporting (RTR). In commodity computer systems the CRTM is realized as the initially executed part of the Basic Input Output System (BIOS). The CRTM represents the fundamental component for integrity measurements. The RTS and RTR are both implemented in the TPM itself and guarded by the Storage Root Key (SRK) and the Endorsment Key (EK), respectively. Securely storing the data being processed by the TPM is the purpose of the RTS. Reporting the system integrity information to an external requester is provided by the RTR (cf. Section 2.2.7).

The initialization procedure of current TPMs is visualized in Figure 2.2. It additionally details series of necessary commands for initialization to reach the operational state after a reboot.

Trusted Platform Module Lifecycle

The Protection Profile (PP) for PC client specific TPMs [TCG11b] documents the activities related to a certain phase in the TPM life cycle. A simplified definition of the TPM life cycle is depicted in Figure 2.3. This life cycle covers all necessary steps to exploit the TPM functions. The first several phases of the life cycle concentrate on the generation of the EK key pair. There are in general three specific possibilities within the life cycle by whom the EK may be generated or downloaded, namely the manufacturer, the Original Equipment Manufacturer (OEM), or the enduser. The different impacts of these approaches are outlined in the following.

During manufacture, the EK key pair may be either downloaded to the TPM or generated by the TPM internally. This has the major advantage that the manufacturer is able to issue a EK credential certificate. A genuine TPM is then guaranteed by verification of this certificate. Additional conformance testing ensures the functional correctness of the device.

During the platform delivery phase, the OEM may also start the EK key pair generation process. Furthermore, the certification of this key pair supports authenticity checks in relation to the OEM. These first two possibilities of issuing an EK certificate are optional in the specification. However, these options provide the only measure to cryptographically protect the supply chain and effectively protect against substitution with malicious devices.

The EK and its corresponding certificate may also be generated at a later stage during the *take ownership* procedure. In the platform deployment phase, the owner of the platform initializes the TPM. In corporate environments, this initial phase is utilized to collect reference measurements of integrity values and adjust the TPM to comply with the company specific policies. Subsequently, the identity utilizing the TPM is initialized to support anonymous authentication during the platform identity registration phase.

During the platform operation phase most of the services of the TPM are enabled. The main purpose of platform authentication and data protection is carried out in this phase of the life cycle.

At the end-of-life of a TPM, issued certificates need to be revoked, data needs to be archived, and the ownership of the platform shall be cleared.

Monotonic Counters

A monotonic counter is a useful primitive to prevent replay of data, without the requirement for a secure system clock. This type of counter is required

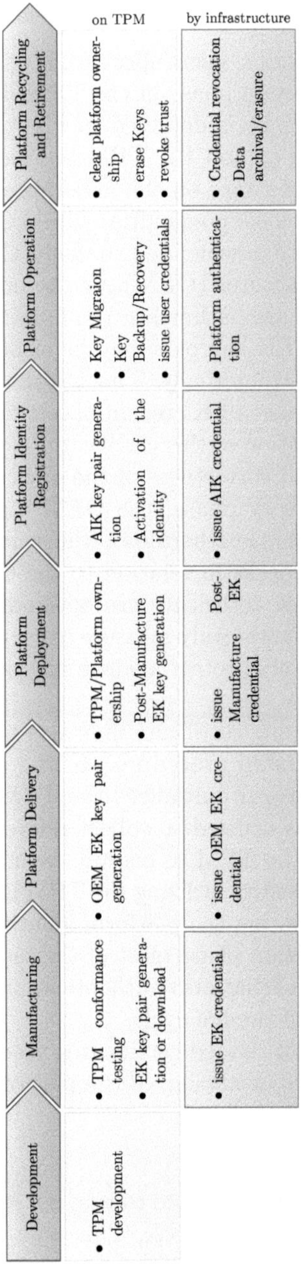

Development	Manufacturing	Platform Delivery	Platform Deployment	Platform Identity Registration	Platform Operation	Platform Recycling and Retirement
						on TPM
• TPM development	• TPM conformance testing • EK key pair generation or download	• OEM EK key pair generation	• TPM/Platform ownership • Post-Manufacture EK key generation	• AIK key pair generation • Activation of the identity	• Key Migraion • Key Backup/Recovery • issue user credentials	• clear platform ownership • erase Keys • revoke trust
						by infrastructure
	• issue EK credential	• issue OEM EK credential	• issue Manufacture credential • Post-EK	• issue AIK credential	• Platform authentication	• Credential revocation • Data archival/erasure

Figure 2.3: Simplified TPM Life Cycle [TCG11b]

to count unidirectional and to be non-resettable. According to the TPM specification, a TPM must support one of these counters, which may be utilized by at least 4 concurrent counters. Additionally, the counter must be designed not to wear out within 7 years of operation if incremented once every 5 seconds. The output of the counter value is required to be 32-bit, although 18-bit would have been sufficient in supporting this requirement.

The counter may be used for generating serial numbers to get some assurance of uniqueness. Additionally, information may be tagged with a monotonic counter value. The information is only accepted if the counter value matches, which is exploited to realize the revocation of certificates. Whenever a certificate is revoked, the counter is incremented and the new certificate is tagged with the incremented value. The signature of the old certificate is still valid, but the counter value is lower than the current value, indicating the revocation of the certificate.

2.2.3 Platform Integrity Measurements

The *platform integrity measurement* denotes to the process of generating cryptographic hashes of the actual platform configuration. In case of a TCG specification compliant TPM, these hashes result in integrity measurements of 160 bit SHA-1. The results of this measurement process are stored within the TPM to guard their integrity. An actual measurement of the current system state extends the previously stored value in a PCR by using the TPM_Extend command by means of

$$\text{TPM\_Extend}(PCR_N, value) = H(PCR_N | value). \tag{2.1}$$

Where PCR_N denotes the content of the Nth PCR and *value* is representing the SHA-1 hash of the next executable. Former measurements, in form of the current PCR values, are taken into account during this procedure and by doing so, a history of all previous states is implicitly included. Along with the measurement there is always a Stored Measurement Log (SML) available, containing the list of measurements, which have been performed since last reset. Although there exists an example for a collision search attack on a hash function, such as SHA-1 [WYY05], it is still not easy to forge entries stored in the PCRs. The construction of the TPM_Extend function, as given by (2.1), hinders the collision search. Additionally, the SML needs to be forged accordingly without revealing the true state of the system.

Table 2.1: The Designated Purpose of Platform Configuration Registers (PCRs) [TCG12b]

PCR	PCR Purpose	Resettable
0	CRTM, BIOS and Host Platform Extensions	no
1	Host Platform Configuration	no
2	Option ROM Code	no
3	Option ROM Configuration and Data	no
4	IPL Code (usually the MBR)	no
5	IPL Configuration and Data (Initial Program Loader)	no
6	State Transition and Wake Events	no
7	Host Platform Manufacturer Control	no
8–15	for use by the Static Operating System (OS)	no
16	Debug	yes
17	Locality 4 – Trusted Hardware	yes
18	Locality 3 – Auxiliary Components	yes
19	Locality 2 – for use by the OS	yes
20	Locality 1 – Environment set up by the OS	yes
21	Locality 0 – legacy support for TPM 1.1 compatibility	yes
22	for use by the Dynamic OS	yes
23	Application Specific – reserved	yes

Platform Configuration Register

The TCG requires every TPM to feature at least 24 PCRs to conform with the 1.2 specification. A PCR is a 160 bit wide volatile register to store the platform measurements. The purpose of each of these registers is denoted in Table 2.1. Whenever a PCR is updated, a new entry to the SML is created to reflect the inputs and their temporal sequence.

The five localities in PCR17 to PCR21 define special usage for PCRs to allow various trusted processes to communicate with the TPM. Using these localities, the TPM is aware of which process is sending commands. The locality 4 is usually utilized to authenticate the processor and to enable the dynamic Root-of-Trust execution (cf. Section 2.4.1). Hence, the representation of a particular process may remain unchanged, even if other parts of the configuration have been modified. Additional information about the distinct purpose of certain localities is provided by Grawrock in [Gra06].

2.2 Trusted Computing Group

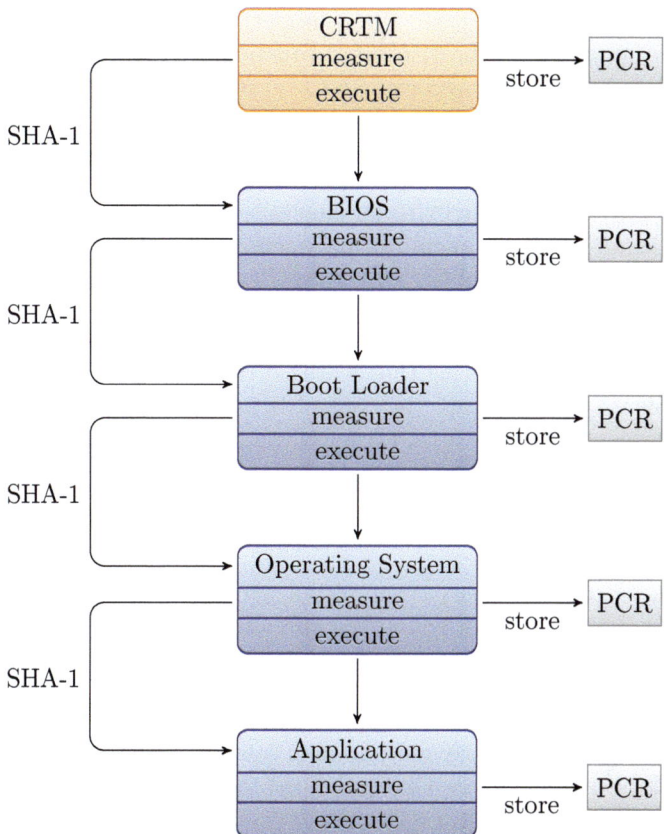

Figure 2.4: Measured Boot Procedure [TCG07, GKMB09]

2.2.4 Measured Boot

The *measured boot* keeps track of all applications executed on a commodity computing platform since the last reset. Whenever a process calls another, the *measured boot* takes care to prior measure the called application and transfer the control afterwards, as depicted in Figure 2.4. The CRTM, a fraction of the BIOS, represents the initially executed program after a commodity computer turned on. Since the BIOS is responsible to setup the memory management unit, the CRTM is partitioned to reflect the availability of this unit. The first operations performed by the CRTM is to measure itself and the static part of the BIOS using the TPM_SHA-1 commands to generate a cryptographic hash. Please note that, only during the execution of the initial partition, the TPM_SHA-1 functions of the TPM are used. As soon as the memory management unit is available, the hash computations are executed on the CPU for performance reasons. A positive side-effect is that the integrity of the CRTM is guarded by the TPM itself.

The results of the hash computations, regardless where they have been obtained, are then stored in PCRs for later reference. During the initialization of the second section a memory management driver becomes available, supporting the execution of the SHA-1 [NIS12a] function in the main memory of the commodity computer.

The main difference of the measured boot to a normal boot procedure is the additional step of storing the measured representation of the following executable. After this step, the control is passed to the next executable. The relationship of consecutive measurements is often referred to as Chain-of-Trust.

2.2.5 Secure Boot

The term *secure boot* is very often mistakenly used synonymously for measured boot, but it actually refers to a special variant of the *measured boot* procedure. Within this procedure every integrity measurement is compared to reference values. In case of a mismatch between the measured and the known-good value, the boot procedure is aborted. Exploiting the *secure boot* enables a system to directly react to malicious modifications.

The Mobile Phone Work Group defined the Reference Integrity Metric (RIM) certificates to offer a reference that can be applied by the Trusted Software Stack (TSS) for comparison with actual measurements. The RIM certificates have been introduced as a part of the Mobile Trusted Module (MTM) specification [TCG10] (cf. Section 2.3.1).

Exploiting this procedure allows for an early abort of the boot process in case of an integrity mismatch. However, the TPM itself is not aware which boot procedure is carried out at system startup. This selection is only a matter of the TSS.

2.2.6 Authentication Protocols

In contrast to the mere function of algorithms providing authenticity (see Section A.1.2), authentication protocols generally ensure the unique identification of an entity. The entity proofs the knowledge of a (common) secret and thereby identifies itself. Of course these algorithms are exploited to

2.2 Trusted Computing Group

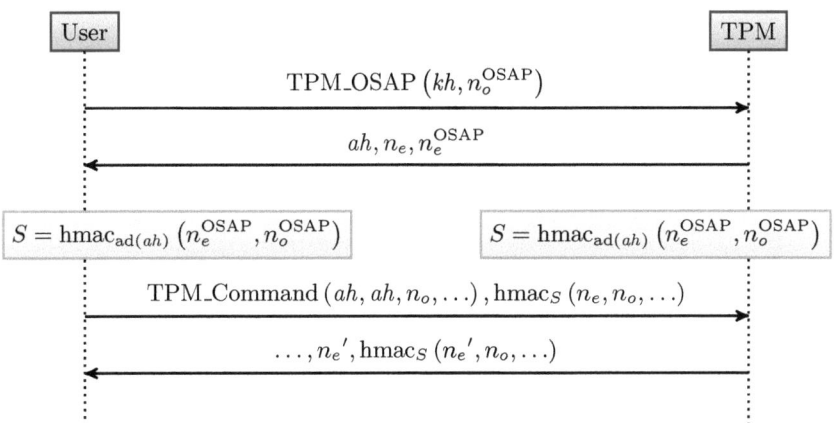

Figure 2.5: Object-Specific Authorization Protocol (OSAP) [TCG11c]

guarantee the authenticity of the communication. Authentication protocols, such as PEAP, Kerberos, CHAP, and simple password authentication protocols are commonly used for entity identification. For user identification mostly challenge-response based identification is exploited (see [vT05]).

For trusted computing the Object-Specific Authorization Protocol (OSAP) and Object Independent Authorization Protocol (OIAP) protocols are most important and therefore the OSAP is outlined in the following. The OSAP protocol, as depicted in Figure 2.5, employs a rolling nonce scheme. The first two nonces n_o^{OSAP} and n_e^{OSAP} are used for session key generation. To support multiple identities for a fine grain access control an authentication handle ah is supplied with the first transmission. Subsequently only n_e and n_o are used to guarantee the freshness of the communication session. After both entities agreed on a session secret, commands may be issued.

2.2.7 System Integrity Reporting

Reporting the system integrity is one of the fundamental requirements for a trustworthy platform. A platform should present means to proof its current system status and the integrity of its data. The integrity and authenticity of this warrant is mandatory. Hence, this report, as gathered by the TPM, is finally signed protecting its integrity and authenticity.

The term *remote attestation* refers to the process of reporting system integrity information to a remote entity. Therefore, the current system state,

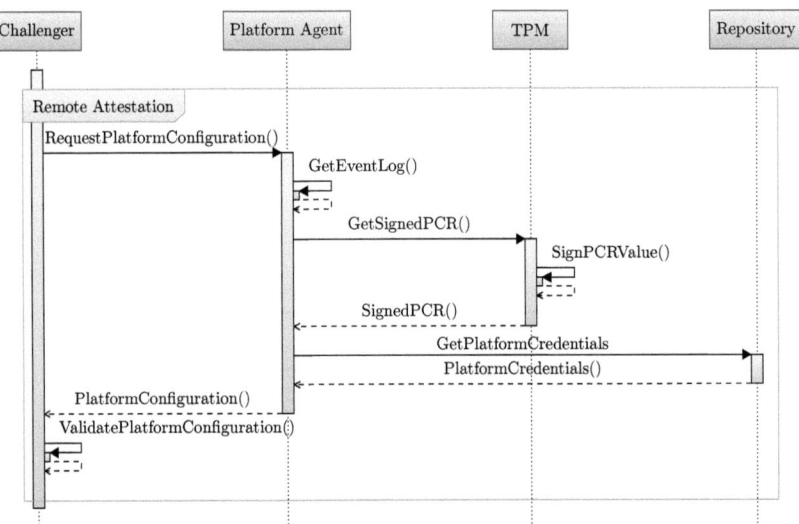

Figure 2.6: TPM Remote Attestation Protocol [TCG07]

being represented by the content of the PCRs, is reported to the requester. The `TPM_Quote` command is issued to request a signed set of PCR values from the TPM.

The process of *system integrity reporting*, often referred as remote attestation, is visualized in Figure 2.6. The challenger is requesting the integrity measurements of the platform configuration from the TSS (Platform Agent). The TSS in turn collects the measurement log and the signed PCR values together with the platform credentials and supplies this to the remote requester. The challenger is then validating the supplied configuration against known-good configurations.

In a corporate environment, Trusted Computing may be utilized to protect company assets. This is accomplished by exploiting the system integrity reporting capabilities of a TPM before access to company resources is granted. Any device trying to access resources shall provide an attestation of its current system configuration. Changes in the system configuration are continuously recorded by TPM in its cryptographic memory. Hence, it is able to provide an authenticated system integrity report to any remote requesting entity.

2.3 Supporting Multiple Stakeholders

Sharing resources of a platform amongst multiple entities is a common task in mobile and cloud computing applications. Particularly in mobile scenarios where cellular service providers, cellular operators, phone manufacturers, and users need to execute programs mutually exclusive to protect their individual assets. In cloud computing scenarios, providers and an arbitrary number of users share resources to maximize utilization of a computing platform, also known as hardware consolidation.

The inability of current trust anchors in providing mutually exclusive access for multiple stakeholders hinders their application in these cases. A common requirement of existing concepts is the establishment of trust relations between the involved entities, which in general is not the case. Moreover, a typical TPM is designed to leverage the requirements of a single platform with only one or a strictly limited amount of users, i.e. the administrator and the designated user. Therefore, a TPM is incapable in providing its services to multiple stakeholders, as needed in the above mentioned scenarios. To mitigate this issue, each stakeholder configuration is represented by an individual context. By decoupling the context information from a specific TPM it is possible to support a virtually unlimited number of stakeholders.

The virtual TPM (vTPM) by Berger et al. at IBM [BCG+06, BGPS10] is an approach to tackle multiple stakeholder support, suitable for virtualized environments. The basic vTPM variant exploits a commercially available TPM to protect a dedicated virtualization domain hosting the vTPM-manager. Within this domain the requests of other domains are processed by the vTPM-manager utilizing multiple software instances realizing TPM functions. They further propose a variant utilizing a specialized security subsystem, such as the IBM-4758 or its follow-up model IBM-CEX3C/4765 [IBM12]. Mechanisms integrated into this security subsystem provide maximum protection for security-sensitive data. These security subsystems, mainly targeting server and data center applications, are more expensive because they are being optimized for performance.

Another approach is the MTM specification, which was initiated by Ekberg et al. in [EK07] to cope with the requirements in multiple stakeholder applications. The MTM has been included in the TCG ecosystem as an additional specification [TCG10]. As of June 2012 the MTM is referred to TPM MOBILE [TCG12c]. This follow-up specification mitigates the fact that TPMs are not included in current mobile phone devices. However, similar techniques may be applied to realize the TPM MOBILE. Trusted

Execution Environments (TEEs), such as M-Shield [AF08] (cf. Section 2.4.3) and TrustZone [ARM09] (cf. Section 2.4.2) are exploited for the implementation of the TPM MOBILE specification. Broadening the applicability by allowing to utilize TEEs, is an acknowledgment of the requirements in the mobile phone and SmartPhone market. The MTM specification has been implemented in selected high-end Nokia mobile phones, such as N95 [EAK+08]. These devices feature an M-Shield enabled processor providing the TEE. It is very likely that these features are used for Digital Rights Management (DRM) and/or configuration management in current Nokia mobile phones.

Several patents cover methodologies and systems for multi-context TPMs, especially for virtualization environments. Bade et al. utilized an off-the-shelf TPM to enable the creation of logical TPMs used by Virtual Machines (VMs) in [BBK+08]. Their hypervisor-based approach is intended to manage access to the logical TPMs. These logical TPMs and their corresponding virtual EK are created under the supervision of a physical TPM. In contrast to the system introduced by Berger et al. in [BCG+06, BGPS10], the additional functions are implemented within the hypervisor itself, whereas the vTPM approach resides either in a virtual machine or within a specialized security subsystem. Further, the concept of virtualized multi-context TPMs has been applied to the Intel TXT technology by Smith in [Smi11].

Stumpf et al. envisaged a concept enhancing TPMs in order to support hardware-based virtualization [SE08]. Their multi-context TPM approach introduces the usage of so called control structure representing the platform specific data of a generic TPM. The control structures for each VM are loaded into the TPM each time they are accessed. In addition to the components present in generic TPMs, the approach by Stumpf et al. requires additional storage for the active control structure. The process of loading and unloading control structures is protected by a root data structure, present in the multi-context enabled TPM. Moreover, they introduced a context migration procedure in order to move a VM from one platform to another without comprising the trustworthiness of the VM.

2.3.1 Reference Integrity Metric Certificates

Within the concept of the MTM, the so called RIM certificates have been introduced. Known-good reference measurements of configurations are included in these certificates. Hence, it is possible to compare the actual measurement with a certified known-good measurement before passing control to the measured program. The characteristics of the *secure boot* process, exploiting RIM certificates, is detailed in the following.

A typical RIM certificate contains an authenticated and integrity protected reference measurement. The additional `MTM_Verify_RIMCertAndExtend` command, introduced in the MTM specification makes use of these reference values. The extend operation is only executed iff the reference values in the RIM certificate match the real measurements. These certificates from the basis of the *secure boot* process. Whenever the verification of the RIM certificate fails, the *secure boot* process is aborted.

In general, there exist two types of RIM certificates, namely internal and external. External certificates may apply to various MTM instances, whereas internal certificates are specific to one particular instance. Both types are authenticated by either digital signatures (e.g. RSA) or MACs. The evaluation of RSA-based signatures is relatively slow in comparison to authentication codes. Hence, internal RIM certificates exploit an HMAC utilizing a key which is only known to the MTM itself and thereby are efficiently ensuring authenticity. It is not explicitly required to authenticate internal certificates by a MAC, but it is assumed to be common as this leverages performance.

Any external RIM certificates may be transformed to internal certificates to speed-up the boot process. The digital signature verification of the RIM certificate is only evaluated once and the authenticity of the certificate is further protected by a MAC. This allows for the efficient use of transformed RIMs during the *secure boot*.

The temporal validity of the RIM certificates is provided by a reference counter value. Since a TPM does not have a notion of time, the monotonic counters (cf. Section 2.2.2) are exploited to support the expiration of a certificate. Otherwise it would not be possible to invalidate a certificate's signature.

2.4 Beyond TCG Specifications and Related Products

Some more examples for trustworthy computing systems beyond the specifications provided by the TCG are outlined in the following. In general, Trusted Computing approaches may be categorized into three classes according to their realization. First, there are modules such as the TPM or SmartCards, which can be considered as HSMs. Traditional SmartCards fall into the the same category. The second class refers either to additional hardware functions, added to processors (i.e. Intel Trusted Execution Technology (TXT), ARM TrustZone, and Texas Instruments M-Shield), or to further processing capabilities included in systems on a chip, such as modular arithmetic processors in SmartCards. This is often referred to as Secure Hardware Extension (SHE) or TEE. Software realizations of TPMs (cf. [SS08]) or special virtualization enabled realizations are defining the third class.

Research strives on supplying solutions for secure architectures in vehicular applications (cf. EVITA[2], OVERSEE[3]). These solutions foresee the implementation of the HSM as an extension to automotive controllers realizing the hardware-based Root-of-Trust. Moreover, the vehicle manufacturers in Germany bundled their activities in protecting electronic control units from attacks as a part of the HIS[4] program. They proposed the usage of SHEs (a subset of the EVITA HSM) for implementing authenticated software update procedures mitigating software attacks. Target applications for the automotive industry are: theft protection, car immobilizer, component protection, and after sales feature activation.

Apart from commodity computers and automotive security, the security in energy grids requires the use of HSMs. Several vendors, such as SafeNet[5], supply solutions, aiming at the creation of a network between customers and utility companies, for better understanding on the energy consumption and the workload across the energy grid. Essentially three tasks need to be performed by HSMs: authentication, system integrity measurements, and validation for network access. Guidelines for SmartGrid deployments have been stated by NIST in [NIS10]. In Germany, additional regulations, acts, and technical directives have been released to ensure privacy and security in SmartGrid environments [Els11]. The Federal Office for Information Security (BSI) has established a Protection Profile (PP) for specific components [BSI11] as the energy grid is conceived as critical infrastructure. These specifications propose the usage of HSMs in SmartGrids.

Apart from the solutions for cyber-physical systems, HSMs are also applicable for data center solutions, as outlined in Section 2.3. Advantages of these solutions are among others: validation (cf. Chapter 3.4), strong RNGs, tamper resistance, and the support for widely accepted cryptographic algorithms. Major drawbacks of these high performance solutions, as provided by IBM [IBM12], are the inflexibility in upgrading and there immense cost. This inflexibility in upgrading is a consequence of the validation requirement by the HSM users.

---

[2] http://www.evita-project.org
[3] http://www.oversee-project.com
[4] http://www.automotive-his.de
[5] http://www.safenet-inc.com

2.4 Beyond TCG Specifications and Related Products

2.4.1 Intel Trusted Execution Technology

The Intel TXT [Int11b] and AMDs Secure Virtual Machine (SVM) [AMD12], are extensions of the processor architecture and the corresponding chipset. Current generations of Intel processors supporting the vPro architecture [Int11a] are including all TXT capabilities.

The major contribution originates from enhancements by means of providing separated execution environments for security-sensitive programs. In addition to this modification, certain TXT chipsets include a TCG compliant TPM v.1.2 as part of the chipset itself. Similar to generic TPM environments, all security-sensitive services, such as cryptographic key storage, data storage, and integrity reporting are located in the chipset's internal TPM implementation. To exploit the full potential of the TXT technology, a generic TPM is added if the chipset is lacking TPM support.

The key capability of TXT is the establishment of a dynamic Root-of-Trust providing security properties being similar to an OS after a measured boot. Authenticated code execution establishes a dynamic Root-of-Trust for measurement and ensures its integrity and authenticity. To execute the dynamic Root-of-Trust a cryptographically signed software is executed within a special CPU operation mode. Within this mode, all programs are suspended by means of providing an isolated execution environment to the Root-of-Trust. TXT utilizes launch control policies to facilitate the verification of TXT components, similar to RIM certificates. The generic term for the establishment of a dynamic Root-of-Trust is *late launch*, combining the approaches advocated by Intel and AMD.

x86 processors supporting the *late launch* technology, additionally include virtualization support (VT). This feature may be exploited in virtualization scenarios to support the execution of a measured Virtual Machine Manager (VMM). Executing a *late launch* of security-sensitive code resets the CPU's state and enables memory protection for this piece of software. The typical TPM-based *measure then load* approach is followed before executing the code in this memory area. In a nutshell, the *late launch* technology provides properties similar to a measured boot without the need for rebooting the system. Furthermore, the measured boot is still supported, as the *late launch* is the more generic approach. It supports secure boot of a trusted hypervisor, which mitigates the susceptibility to attacks on virtualization techniques required in cloud computing scenarios.

An advanced protection scheme called Flicker, providing a secure execution environment on demand, has been presented by McCune et al. in [MPP+08]. Flicker is isolating the security-sensitive code from other parts of the system, by exploiting the *late launch* capabilities of current processors. Whenever security-sensitive code is executed, a Flicker session is started. The *late launch* capability is exploited to securely load the Flicker code, while all other system functions are paused during this session. The necessary security-sensitive operations are then carried out. Afterwards the session is closed and the execution of the system is resumed.

2.4.2 ARM TrustZone

The ARM TrustZone hardware architecture defines a security framework by partitioning the system into two separated environments, namely trusted and untrusted. Only in the trusted environment certain assets may be accessed. The TrustZone architecture supports the selection of components, which are included in the secure environment. This architecture aims at providing protection against specific attacks on the integrity of the platform and the confidentiality of data.

Wilson et al. give an overview on the implementation of embedded security on TrustZone enabled hardware, in their article [WFM+07]. A TrustZone enabled CPU mimics two virtual processors to support the separation of trusted and untrusted subsystems. Secured and unsecured environments are accessed through a monitor mode software, allowing only the time-sliced execution of trusted and untrusted code. The isolation between the virtual processors is facilitated by a memory management unit, holding two states for both implementations. The TrustZone architecture provides two separate environments, namely the normal zone and the trust zone. Security-sensitive software running in the trust zone is able to access the normal zone's memory, but the reverse is impossible.

Winter conceived an approach to facilitate Trusted Computing functions with the ARM TrustZone extensions of current ARM microprocessors in [Win08]. Relying on the security boundary created by the TrustZone hardware features, a monitor mode software was implemented to control an unsecured guest VM. This approach is facilitating a secure boot loader to instantiate a CRTM for the platform that is utilizing RIM certificates. Winter presented a prototype of a mobile trusted platform taking advantage of the TrustZone features to realize the MTM functions.

Wave Inc.[6] in collaboration with Trusted Logic[7] held a mobile security demonstration at the Mobile World Congress (MWC) [Wav12]. Based on the TCG Mobile Phone Specification (TPM.MOBILE / MTM) they were

---
[6] http://www.wave.com/
[7] http://www.trusted-logic.com/

able to unlock a Self-Encrypting Drive (SED) using a mobile phone. This demonstration utilized an ARM TrustZone based implementation to show how a phone can be used as authentication token. This is a good example of cyber-physical systems utilized for data protection and authentication, as their capabilities are exploited to support stronger cryptography.

2.4.3 Texas Instruments M-Shield

The M-Shield security technology [AF08] is presenting similar features, as provided the ARM TrustZone architecture. It includes means for hardware-based acceleration of symmetric and asymmetric encryption schemes. Furthermore, hardware support for hash generation, such as SHA and MD5 is provided and a unique device specific hardware key is supplied. Some variants of M-Shield enabled devices even support TrustZone extensions, although this is not mandatory. Moreover, hardware-based tamper protection mechanisms are included.

TEEs enable the realization of mechanisms to efficiently handle security services. Kostiainen et al. have presented a credential management system in [KAE12] exploiting the M-Shield architecture. They present a twofold approach for credential management. It provides a mechanism to quickly disable stored credentials by removing a personal security element, such as a SIM-card in mobile phones on the one hand; and on the other, they present a second approach using a "semi-trusted" server that substitutes the SIM-card as personal security element.

The security services provided by the M-Shield architecture are exploited for multimedia streaming applications on mobile devices. Texas instruments announced in [TI11] the successful certification by a premium quality streaming content provider. Thus, the M-Shield security system is providing means for a silicon reference implementation for mobile devices.

2.5 Trustworthy Systems using FPGAs

In general, increased flexibility is provided by utilizing reconfigurable devices for the implementation of digital systems hardware. Reconfigurable devices, such as FPGAs realize the desired hardware functions of digital systems using programmable components, namely logic functions, interconnection, and the external interfaces. Most FPGA provide additional functions for common purposes, to ease the implementation or to reduce the utilization of resources. Dependent on the application, the processing capabilities and thereby the behavior of the digital system may be modified to suit the specific needs. Moreover, current FPGAs feature methods to partially reconfigure the fabric during runtime. This is referred to as *dynamic partial reconfiguration* (see Appendix B.2). Hence, not only the software configuration of the cyber-physical system, but its underlying hardware architecture may be modified during runtime. Given this flexibility, changes in the environment may be reflected by the architecture very quickly. Additionally, highly efficient hardware modules can be utilized to save both, power and/or execution time. The flexibility gained by updating the system's architecture is currently lacking effective protection mechanisms, as outlined in the following.

A paramount issue in FPGA security is the protection of its configuration data. The commercial FPGA vendors tackle the IP protection problem to a certain extent in their products (cf. Chapter 4). Most of the approaches do not provide integrity and authenticity verification of IPs but merely support static encryption of configuration data. A static measurement of the system configuration, similar to the integrity measurements provided by TPMs, is not commercially available.

Several approaches to include attestation mechanisms, both hardware-based and software-based, have been presented in literature. The properties of the available solutions are outlined in the following.

2.5.1 Software-based Attestation

In general, software-based attestation is possible with every microprocessor but requires a fully trustworthy CPU. To achieve this goal without the necessity of additional secure hardware components, Seshandri et al. have presented an approach purely relying on software-based measurements in [SPvDK04]. Their technique provides measures to externally attest memory contents of cyber-physical systems using several techniques for checksum computation. By exploiting a pseudo-random addressing scheme together with sophisticated methods to make memory access dependent on the current checksum values enables an external verifier to attest the device configuration.

These features make the checksum computation itself serial by nature and force an attacker to insert an **if** statement into the verification procedure. Keeping the verification code size as small as possible allows for an external verifier to notice the runtime delays and thus discover modifications. Although this approach is not explicitly designed for FPGA-based systems, it may be utilized as common yardstick for the implementation on soft-core processors.

2.5.2 Hardware-based Attestation

The integration of complete TPM capabilities within the FPGA fabric was advocated by Eisenbarth et al. in [EGP+07]. Their goals are, among others, to support updatable TPM functions and design a manufacturer independent TPM. Instead of utilizing existing features available in current FPGAs, they demand modifications on the existing encryption cores protecting configuration data. In short they require support for integrity verification, authentication, and configuration measurement within the FPGA fabric. The estimations, however, as detailed by theses authors, are providing evidence that a reconfigurable TPM may be implemented using FPGAs.

Glas et al. proceed a step beyond this state, as they propose measurement of configuration data to implement trustworthy reconfigurable systems in [GKS+08a, GKS+08b]. They achieve their goal by adding a generic TPM to the platform, providing the measurement and reporting facilities required. Moreover, they require the TPM, together with a non-volatile memory and some control logic, to be included in a tamper resistant package. This hardware component exceeds the capabilities of a commercially available TPM and thus the logic security boundary they require is not given by this solution. Additional hardware may not always be a feasible option for reconfigurable cyber-physical systems as this increases the related power consumption and costs.

Schellekens et al. elaborate on the protection of the persistent state of FPGA-based implementations for trusted computing in [STP08]. The general issue of current protection mechanisms shipped with FPGAs do not remedy the demand for external storage. In case of reconfigurable trusted computing the key material, uniquely identifying a particular device, need to be stored. Moreover, this data should be only accessible by this device. The authors propose the usage of an intrinsic Physically Uncloneable Function (PUF) to derive the authentication keys. Those keys are further used to authenticate the device to an external non-volatile memory, accommodating storage space for the persistent state of the system.

3 Requirements for Trustworthiness

Trustworthiness is the expectation that a given entity behaves according to an established policy. When looking at digital systems this expectation boils down to the fact that a system shall be able to proof its known-good configuration. This unmodified configuration has been previously assessed to ensure that it is complying to the given policy.

Essentially, there exist two major requirements, which need to be addressed to enable an assessment of whether to trust a particular system or not; the ability to uniquely identify systems on the one hand, and presenting an evidence that the system has not been tampered with, on the other. Authentication and identification provide measures for the former and system integrity reporting for the latter. In order to guarantee the authenticity of messages, the system needs to be equipped with a secret, known only to a tightly constraint set of entities. Regardless of the particular implementation of the authentication scheme, the identifying secrets need to be protected. In the case of asymmetric cryptography it is preferable that this secret will never leave the device after initialization and the set of entities knowing the secret is reduced to the system itself. If symmetric schemes are utilized, the key distribution scheme plays a major role on the overall security of the system. It is necessary to supply every system with a unique key, to prevent a device from cloning (cf. Section 4.4.1).

Heiser et al. state in their article [HMK12] that the advances achieved over the last few decades in machine-checked formal proofs and formal analysis enable to sufficiently cover the entire TCB. They outline that using formal verification of a micro kernel enables the isolation of trustworthy program code. Moreover, their approach enables the separation of the TCB from the OS. The corresponding proof of functional-correctness aims at providing both, security and safety in software implementations. The authors expect to see full proofs within the next one to two years. Even if the compliance to an abstract functional specification has been assessed, it in turn does not proof the correctness of the functional specification. In addition, a complete formal verification may not be possible for all system components as complexity is constantly increasing. Nonetheless, formal proofs are useful tools in building trustworthy systems, however their capabilities and features are not covered within this thesis.

The software is only one aspect in system security, it has to be further guaranteed that the underlying hardware is operating as expected. Especially FPGA-based systems are prone to hardware attacks even after manufacture. A fundamental property of FPGA-based systems by means of building trustworthy systems is the protection of the configuration data.

The importance of security for computing platforms has been tackled by different vendors, such as Intel by including more security functions into their commodity computer products [Int11a]. This particular example is providing measures for identity protection, data protection, security monitoring, and threat management, to name a few. Additionally, it includes special instruction to accelerate symmetric encryption using Advanced Encryption Standard (AES). Seen from the fact that a major vendor includes sophisticated protection mechanisms in mainstream products, together with technologies to support the trustworthy execution of programs, further emphasizes their importance.

Of course the quality of the cryptographic algorithms also determines to which extent a particular system can be trusted. The focus of this work is set on the general architectures, not on the cryptographic strength of certain algorithms. Although, the selection of signature schemes, encryption algorithms, and hash functions follows best practices. Additionally, recommendations as stated by NIST in [BREK11] have been taken into account.

The non-trivial question of which components are required to trust a device are detailed in this chapter. The common methods, as advocated by the TCG have been outlined in the previous chapter. In the following the requirements to build similar systems will be given.

3.1 Key Storage and Certificate Management

A major issue of any (cyber-physical) computer system in general is the storage of cryptographic key material. The protection of this data is of paramount importance to the overall level of security provided by a system. Software-based approaches usually use passwords for protection. This either requires the user to input this password whenever a key has to be used or the cryptographic key is stored in a protected area. This area is often protected

3.1 Key Storage and Certificate Management

by software measures only, leading to the fact that encrypted data and the corresponding key or password are stored on the same physical media.

HSMs usually provide hardware mechanisms to protect security-sensitive data. For maximum protection, the cryptographic keys are generated within the HSM itself and no direct external access to these keys is provided. Ideally, whenever data has to be encrypted, decrypted or signed, the data is sent to the HSM for processing. Hence, direct access to the keys is only provided to HSM-internal methods. The computational capabilities of HSMs are often limited, leading to the fact that only a subset of the cryptographic key material is handled within the HSM. Further cryptographic key material may only be revealed if the system is in a certain state, often referred to as sealing.

Additionally, cyber-physical systems generally need to operate without user interaction. Therefore, the cryptographic key material needs to be stored securely inside the device. The solutions are ranging from simple storage of cryptographic key material hard-coded into the program itself, to storage in shielded volatile or non-volatile memory locations. Depending on the area of application an the desired security level, additional features for tamper protection are included. One generic measure to protect cryptographic keys is to use device specific secrets, as this is providing the highest level of protection. In contrast to device family specific secrets, the successful extraction of a single cryptographic key only affects one particular device. The TPM specification requires the usage of device specific secrets to ensure that such attacks reveal only a single key. Device specific keys create a management overhead that is considered to be negligible in comparison to the level of protection gained by this approach.

Often there is more than one cryptographic key present in a system, i.e. one key pair for RSA signature generation and another key pair used for encryption. Hence, a key hierarchy is built to manage different keys within one system or device. This is organized in a chain or a tree starting from a commonly accepted Root-of-Trust as outlined in the following.

The certificate management or the Public Key Infrastructure (PKI) management refers to the process of handling cryptographic certificates for asymmetric cryptography. This involves Certification Authorities (CAs) as the issuer of these digital certificates. Certification refers to the process to proof the ownership of a private key by the entity or subject named within this certificate. The public key together with the name of the subject is combined to a certificate, that is signed by the CA. Commercial CAs undergo audits and externally reviewed assessments of their certification process to proof the trustworthiness of their process.

One major drawback of symmetric cryptography is the key management. Every entity taking part in a communication must be in possession of the symmetric key in order to decipher the messages on the communication channel. If an entity needs to communicate with many others, an individual key is needed for each of the communication partners. Each of these keys has to be kept secret.

For asymmetric encryption schemes, only the private key has to be kept secret, simplifying the key storage requirements. Public keys, utilized for encryption or signature verification may be retrieved on request or they are supplied with the ciphertext. The International Telecommunication Union (ITU) has supplied the X.509 standard to establish a hierarchical PKI which enables the verification of certificates [ITU08].

The root certificates of a CA are signed by the CA itself. Such *self-signed* certificates are in turn representing a single point, which needs to be trusted. In practice this trust relation is enforced by legislative regulations, such as contracts or assessment certificates of accredited authorities. The trust anchor or Root-of-Trust of a specific system may contain externally signed or *self-signed* certificates. This selection is mainly depending on the given security policy.

3.1.1 Cryptographic Memories

The storage of cryptographic secrets is one of the paramount requirements in building trustworthy systems. In the FIPS 140-2 standard [NIS02] published by the NIST, cryptographic secrets are referred to as *"critical security parameters"*. These secrets are providing the authenticity of devices and the confidentiality of communication. Supposing that one of these secrets is compromised, the trustworthiness of the system is at risk. For most applications at least two cryptographic keys have to be provided, one for encryption of data and the other for signature generation. Since the implementation of a secure storage is costly, most systems restrict this to facilitate only a small amount of cryptographic keys. Hence, to support a virtually unlimited number of keys, a key hierarchy may be introduced, as outlined in the following.

A common recommendation is to store security-sensitive data in dedicated memories on the same chip *(on-chip)*. If this data is stored in a dedicated memory *(off-chip)* it shall feature tamper protection mechanisms, such as shielding against direct physical access. Furthermore, this shielding may provide two categories of protective measures: (i) *tamper evidence*, utilizing protective seals that must be broken to gain access or (ii) *tamper protection*,

3.1 Key Storage and Certificate Management

Table 3.1: Comparison of Volatile and Non-Volatile Key Storage Properties

Key Storage	Power Supply	Memory Type	Programmability
non-volatile	not required	FLASH, EPROM	multiple times (Flash, EPROM)
		antifuse (e.g. eFuse)	one time
volatile	battery required	SRAM	multiple times, erasable

which triggers a response circuit to erase memory contents as soon as tampering is detected. Tamper evidence is only effective if the device under consideration is returned in regular maintenance intervals for inspection. Tamper protection may also be exploited to mount a denial-of-service attack on the device.

An orthogonal approach to tamper protection is the cryptographic protection of the memory contents. Every externally attached memory may be copied, as this is an inherent property of memories. In order to undermine unauthorized cloning, measures to authenticate and protect data need to be supported (cf. [HT09]). Hence, at least some of the security-sensitive secrets have to be stored in a protected area on-chip, if tamper protection is not applicable. Depending on the level of security that is desired by the end user, the implementation ranges from device specific secrets, laser programmed during manufacturing, to one-time programmable anti-fuse technology. Memories are generally discriminated by the underlying technology – if applied to the storage of cryptographic secrets, a discrimination between volatile and non-volatile realizations is more feasible (cf. Table 3.1).

An excellent overview of different realizations of flash memories, their operation, and their endurance is given by Bez et al. in [BCMV03]. These authors elaborate on the reliability of different implementations, being a vital property when considering cryptographic key storage. De Vries et al. outline the trade-offs of currently available memory technologies in [dVM07]. In addition, they provide a comparison of non-volatile memory implementations in terms of program/read/erase performance and field programmability.

According to [Coo06], NAND type flash memory features fast write and erase operations, whereas NOR type flash is providing better random access performance. To provide fast random access for NAND type memory, the content may be shadowed in faster volatile memory.

If such a memory is used to store cryptographic keys, then having a shadowed copy is an undesired property, as attacks for both memory types would become feasible.

In conclusion, these technologies may be exploited to provide a small on-chip memory, as larger storage capacities would require additional steps in the manufacturing process. These surveys mainly focus on the technological aspects of non-volatile memories and do not focus on the requirements usually present when storing security-sensitive data. Depending on the actual requirements for the resulting products different properties have to be considered. For instance, the fast erase operations may be exploited for the efficient implementation of key erasure in case of device tampering, as required by NIST in [NIS02] to comply to security level 3 (cf. Section 3.4.3).

3.1.2 Storing Cryptographic Secrets

Handschuh and Trichina conducted a survey [HT09] elaborating on the basic protection mechanisms of current memories, which in summary boils down to the authenticated access to stored data in memory. These authors present a summary of methodologies usable with existing flash memory products, in order to prevent against both accidental and malicious memory operations. Furthermore, they detail standard protection features of current flash memory products as outlined in the following. Unique device identification is provided by means of an one-time programmable out-of-memory area, that is externally inaccessible and can only be addressed from the internal identification logic. Regarding the physical level, common measures include a protection against write commands on power-on, disabling write cycles if the supply voltage is out of certain conditions, and the rejection of very short pulses on write-enable pins.

One-time programmable sectors using a special write-protect pin, represent commercially available solutions, supporting the permanent lock-out of write operations for specific sectors [Atm12a]. This lock-out of write operations is performed for all sectors at once, resulting in sectors having their sector protection registers set to be write protected afterwards. In contrast, a more flexible approach is supported by software/firmware-based one-time programmable sector protection registers, as this supports the lock-out of individual sectors, one at a time. The sector protection registers may be configured to be resettable by software-based approaches, however permanent lock-out of certain sectors is still supported, preventing access by malicious software. Moreover, the conditional access to locked sectors by means of password protection is shielding the reset of these registers. Using the

3.1 Key Storage and Certificate Management

precedingly outlined mechanisms, combined with the ARM TrustZone (cf. Section 2.4.2) features of current processors, represent a feasible approach also addressed in literature [AR07, EA10]

Generic memory authentication protocols commonly used for non-volatile memory access are depicted in Figure 3.1. The authentication protocols outlined in [STP08, HT09, Ber07] follow a similar structure. Sending an authenticated command to the memory is performed by first requesting access, as visualized in Figure 3.1(a). The memory then replies with a nonce and an optional session identifier (session$_{id}$). The actual command is issued by sending the command data including an HMAC digest of the session$_{id}$, the nonce, the command, and the corresponding data. To further protect the confidentiality of the data included in these transactions, it may be encrypted before sending and decrypted after retrieving from memory. As this encryption in general requires an additional key, an authenticated encryption (e.g. AES-CCM) may be utilized realizing the same functionality, as depicted in Figure 3.1(b). In this case, Enc(Data) refers to the encrypted part of the AES-CCM scheme, whereas the rest of the command is associated data (cf. Appendix A.5). Alternative memory encryption schemes may be exploited. One such example is the optimized memory encryption scheme presented by Suh et al. in [SCG+03]. Note that the key K in Figure 3.1 must not be the same for message authentication (HMAC) and authenticated encryption (AES-CCM). If a generic composition of algorithms is used to implement the authenticated encryption, two different keys are required for authentication and encryption.

Commercially available non-volatile memory products provide means for storing security sensitive data. In general, these devices (e.g. ATSHA204 [Atm12b], DS2432 [Max12]) feature laser-programmed device identifiers (IDs). An ID may be utilized to realize mutual authentication of host and memories alike.

Elbaz et al. outline further hardware mechanisms for memory authentication in [ECG+09]. The main idea of their approach is to include additional storage capabilities to the system, in order to facilitate the integrity verification of memory contents. They require this additional storage to reside inside the security boundary of the trustworthy device. The simplest form of memory authentication stores the hash values of the external memory contents within the device. In contrast to the previously outlined solutions, the approach by Elbaz facilitates simple non-volatile storage without cryptographic capabilities.

With reference to Table 3.1, the volatile SRAM approach is mostly feasible for FPGAs, as the majority of FPGAs are SRAM-based. The inexpensive

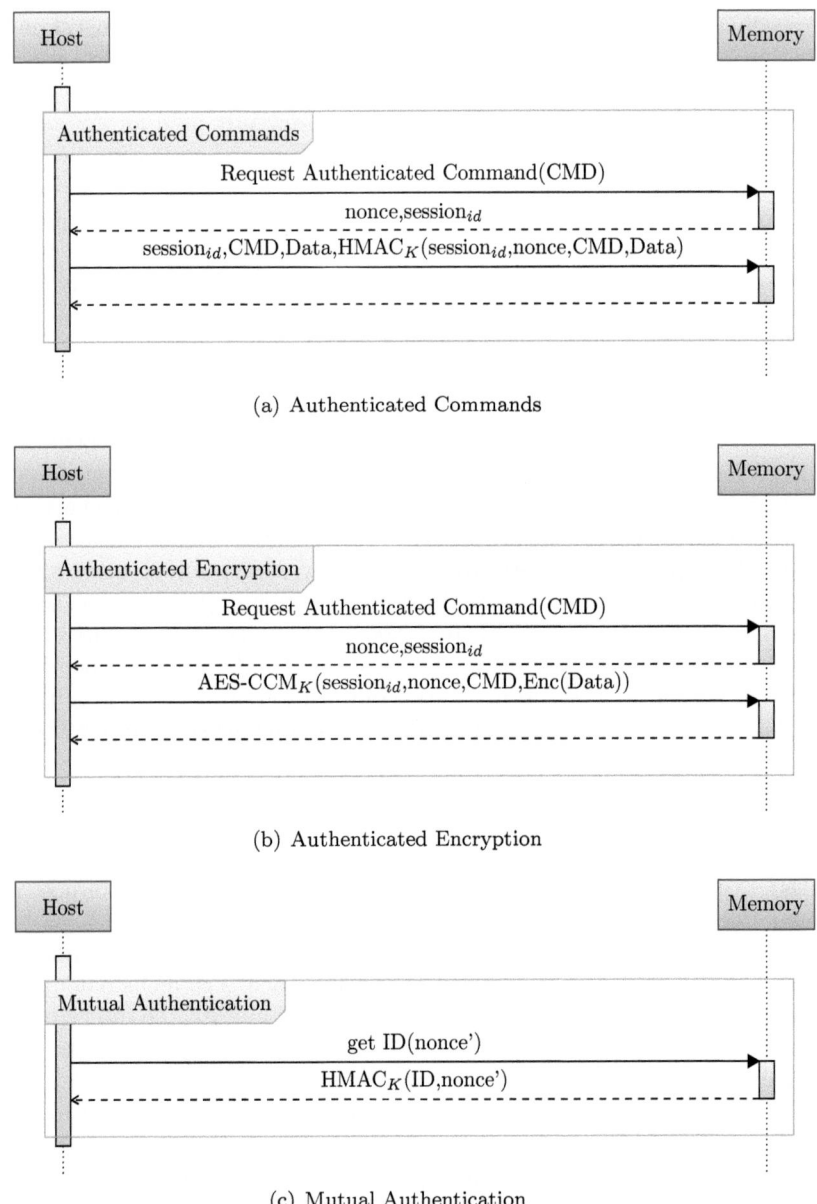

Figure 3.1: Generic Memory Authentication Protocols

3.1 Key Storage and Certificate Management

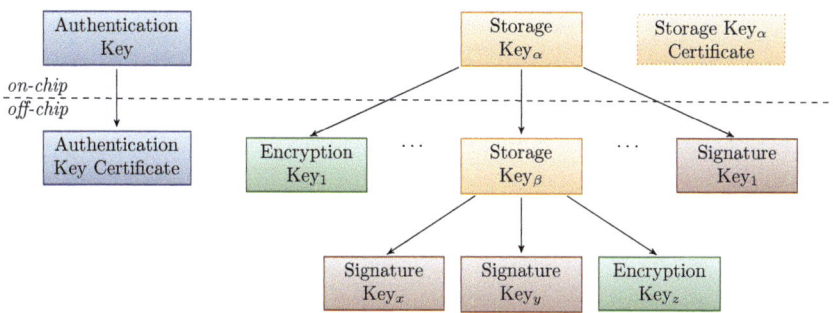

Figure 3.2: Generic Key Hierarchy for Hardware Security Modules

realization utilizing a volatile memory together with a battery, to back-up the memory contents while the device is not powered, is often preferred. Again, this approach may also be exploited for fast key erasure by disconnecting the battery back-up in case of a detected device tampering attempt. From a certification point of view, the battery is contributing to the tamper protection of devices (cf. [NIS02]), but consequently adding costs to the Bill of Materials (BOM) and the Printed Circuit Board (PCB). User accessible cryptographic secrets are mainly included in the configuration data and hence rely on the reverse-engineering complexity of the FPGA configuration. One of the major FPGA vendors, Xilinx has presented a solution to access commercially available authenticated memories [Xil10] (cf. Section 4.2) to provide measures for the authentication of the configuration data. The paramount interest of FPGA vendors is to protect against cloning and overbuilding of devices. The reconfiguration is an intrinsic property of FPGAs making them prone to this kind of threats.

For maximum protection of security-sensitive data, all the aforementioned solutions require a key storage and the cryptographic processing unit to reside within the same chip fabric. FPGAs may additionally benefit from a user accessible cryptographic service that can be facilitated for encryption and authentication with external entities. Providing access to a key storage is not enough, since an adversary is able to load a rouge configuration, which then dumps the content of this key storage. In addition, multiple layers of metal together and bus obfuscation techniques can be utilized to further protect this secure storage area.

Key Hierarchy

As aforementioned, *on-chip* non-volatile memories are usually very small, due to economic aspects of the realization. Notwithstanding this limits, applications may require multiple cryptographic keys of arbitrary sizes. These limitations can be mitigated by introducing a key hierarchy, supporting a virtually unlimited amount of memory for key storage. An example of a generic key hierarchy for HSM is depicted in Figure 3.2. It mainly consists of an authentication key and a storage key being stored within the chip fabric. The corresponding certificates may be also stored within the chip and can be externally accessed to simplify roll-out. To enable virtually unlimited key storage, the lower parts of the hierarchy are encrypted using the storage key and may be stored *off-chip*. The introduction of multiple intermediate storage keys enables the partition of the hierarchy to reduce the computational overhead when accessing particular keys in the leaf nodes of the hierarchy.

Two symmetric keys, one utilized for message authentication and the other for data encryption, represent the simplest form of a key hierarchy. In this case, no certificates or other keys are required to be present within the cyber-physical system. Only the respective communication partners are in possession of these authentication and encryption keys.

The TCG specification [TCG11c] denotes the *Storage Key$_\alpha$* in Figure 3.2 as Storage Root Key (SRK). The term Endorsment Key (EK) is utilized to refer to the *Authentication Key*.

3.1.3 Certificate Management

A major advantage of asymmetric cryptography is the almost effortless key management for multiple communication partners. The keys used for signature verification and the keys for encryption are publicly available. Standards, such as the X.509 [ITU08] provide measures for certificate verification using a so called PKI. This standard also handles the certification and revocation of certificates.

Symmetric schemes require every pair of communication partners to agree on or exchange a key to be used during protocol execution. If the communication between numerous entities has to be implemented, the quadratic effort of key distribution makes this approach quickly unfeasible. However, for the applications considered within this thesis, only a few communication partners are involved, which does not hinder the use of symmetric cryptography.

3.1 Key Storage and Certificate Management

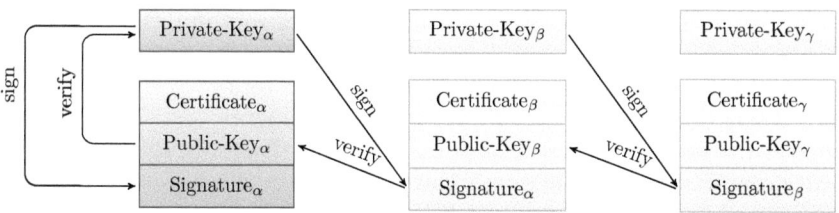

Figure 3.3: Certificate Chain-of-Trust

Root-of-Trust

The Root-of-Trust is the core component upon which trustworthy environments may be built. Trust and security policies are forming the basis on the Root-of-Trust. A Root-of-Trust is existing at different levels of abstraction, such as a particular certificate being used as the starting point of an X.509 [ITU08, CSF+08] certificate verification chain. At higher levels of abstraction it represents the concept of a component which behaves honestly and can be utilized to monitor other parts of the system. Depending on the point of view, a Root-of-Trust is sometimes used synonymously to the trust anchor itself. This results from the fact that the trust anchor contains the necessary measures and certificates providing information about the system state. Moreover, the trust anchor has to be trusted in the first place in order to establish trust in the platform, which is also true for any Root-of-Trust.

In order to do this, these subsystems or software modules are usually evaluated by a standardized process for information security compliance, such as outlined in Chapter 3.4. A HSM is often considered to act as the Root-of-Trust from which all relations regarding the trustworthiness of a platform are originated. Hardware-based approaches are favorable for realizing a Root-of-Trust, as in general, the systematic manipulation of hardware in comparison to software is more complex.

Chain-of-Trust

In a Chain-of-Trust all certificates on a particular path are verified starting form the topmost certificate down to the Root-of-Trust. By chaining the certificates as visualized in Figure 3.3, a trusted path is transitively established. This certificate verification path is an integral component of the X.509 standard [ITU08, CSF+08]. From an implementation point of view the Chain-of-Trust is a series of certificates, which root in a certificate of a trustworthy entity.

The most abstract case of a Chain-of-Trust is a series of certificates that have been subsequently signed, as depicted in Figure 3.3. The leftmost depicts the self-signed certificate of the Root-of-Trust often being a certification authority. Starting with this certificate, the following signatures are created by using the previous private key. Verification is done by using the public key in the previous certificate, as specified in the X.509 standard [ITU08]. In particular, the Signature$_\beta$ of Certificate$_\beta$ has be generated using Private-Key$_\alpha$.

In the Trusted Computing community however, the Chain-of-Trust is often related to the secure boot procedure ensuring the integrity of a platform through the standardized process of program execution. It specifies the transitive trust provided by the *measure-then-load* approach advocated by the TCG. Transitive trust is provided by subsequently loaded programs as sub-programs are only trustworthy iff there exists a trusted path from the parent program to the Root-of-Trust. This corresponds to correct measurements stored in the trust anchor and a corresponding SML.

Verbauwhede and Schaumont specify a tree-of-trust to support systematic design of a Root-of-Trust in [VS07]. This can be seen as a more general version of a Chain-of-Trust to specify the individual components of a Root-of-Trust. It may seem that this will create a cyclic dependencies but it can be seen as an extension of the Chain-of-Trust down to the building blocks of any Root-of-Trust.

For instance, the certificate Chain-of-Trust for Infineon TPMs looks as follows. The Endorsment Key (EK) is signed during manufacturing by the Infineon CA. Infineon and the well-established Verisign corporation have agreed on cross-signing their certificates, in particular the Verisign Trusted Computing Root Certificate and the Infineon CA [Inf05]. Hence, every owner of an Infineon TPM is able to verify that this device is genuine by following the Chain-of-Trust from the EK to the root CA. Of course this verification is only possible for TPMs which have been shipped with certified EKs. Nevertheless, TPMs from other vendors may have their certificates signed by the Information Technology (IT) departments providing also a Chain-of-Trust. In a company IT infrastructure utilizing TPMs the certificates are organized hierarchically. All EK certificates are additionally signed by the CA of the IT department to enable the enforcement of access control policies guarding the company's internal resources.

3.2 Identification and Authentication

Trustworthy relationships can only be established if the entities taking part can be identified correctly. To distinctively identify an entity, authentication schemes, such as passwords and digital signatures are used. The authentication is by far the most important function of Trusted Computing, as something or someone can only be trusted if unique identification of this entity is possible.

Passwords are a common authentication method to identify users, but especially in corporate environments multi-factor authentication schemes become more and more popular. This type of authentication takes a couple of basic authentication mechanisms and combines them. In general, there are three categories of authentication mechanisms, which can be utilized to identify an entity. These are: "something you have", "something you know" and "something you are". The first category, "something you have", refers to all kinds of tokens providing an One-Time Pad (OTP) or similar cryptographic measure for authentication. All kinds of secrets, most often passwords belong to the second category, "something you know". Biometric properties are belonging to a user itself and therefore are categorized in "something you are".

In general, user authentication utilizes authentication strings which can be remembered easily and hence are usually short. Typical user authentication mechanisms for this include:

- Personal Identification Number (PIN)

- Password (string, one-time pad, challenge-response, ...)

- Token (SmartCard, USB-stick, OTP-generator)

- Biometric data (Fingerprint, Face, Iris, Voice, and more recently vein patterns)

These kinds of authentication mechanisms are used to grant user access to a cyber-physical system or parts of it. The entropy provided by these kinds of authentication strings is quite limited. To further protect systems against the limited entropy of the authentication strings, multiple of the following authentication measures are used. If more than one of this factors are used, it is referred to as multi-factor authentication. The combination of multiple authentication mechanisms increases the complexity of forging the authentication procedure. The more mechanisms are utilized, the harder it is for an attacker to successfully conduct an impersonation or a substitution attack.

To authenticate devices or software other measures are typically used as they provide a higher level of security. A MAC is a keyed hash function providing authenticity and integrity verification mechanisms of a message.

Different realizations of identification and authentication tokens, as utilized in FPGA-based systems, are outlined in the following sections. In particular, the usage of PUFs to implement key storage has several advantages in mitigating the threats of current SRAM-based FPGAs.

Cryptographic keys (see Section 3.2.1) and device identifiers (see Section 3.2.2), as outlined in the following provide feasible security measures. However, when it comes to identification and authentication, it should always be kept in mind what Schneier and Shostack said about SmartCards:

> [...] digital signatures on the software are not effective here since a rogue card can always lie about its signature, and there is no way for the terminal to peer inside [...]
> BRUCE SCHNEIER AND ADAM SHOSTACK [SS99]

Hence, physical properties, as exploited by PUFs, enable the effective identification and authentication of devices. The physical nature of PUFs makes it hard for an adversary to forge signatures (cf. Section 3.2.3).

3.2.1 Requirements for Cryptographic Keys

All of the approaches outlined in the following are based on the storage of cryptographic key material. This security-sensitive data is forming the basis for most identification and authentication schemes. Depending on the utilized algorithms the requirements for cryptographic keys differ.

Symmetric schemes, such as AES, rely on a relatively small number of bits (128, 192, 256) representing the key. Often, no requirements are stated regarding the cryptographic key generation procedure (cf. [NIS01]). Any possible cryptographic key shall be used with same probability, therefore, random numbers are used as key material.

Taking a closer look at asymmetric cryptography, the situation is different. Keys for asymmetric cryptography have to fulfill certain properties and cannot be selected naïvely. Furthermore, the large prime numbers used in RSA need to be selected in a way that the factoring of the RSA modulus is hard, which is not trivial. Current research has further shown, that the key generation itself is crucial for the security of RSA. Lenstra et al. outlined that one of every thousand RSA moduli is providing no security at all [LHA+12].

3.2 Identification and Authentication   49

3.2.2 Device Identifiers

Using cryptographic keys is one method to identify an entity, but when considering FPGAs the key storage is a major issue. In this case, device specific identifiers, which reside inside the FPGA fabric, are often used. These device identifiers realize the identification and the authorization following the schemes presented in [Alt07, Xil08, Xil07a].

Some generations of Xilinx FPGAs provide a so called Device-DNA to identify a particular device, which is embodied inside the FPGA fabric [Xil06]. The basic idea behind this scheme is to utilize the 57-bit device dependent read-only identifier to generate a key being used for identification.

A major issue of this solution is the fact that access to the device dependent identifier is not protected. An attacker is able to load a malicious design onto the FPGA, which enables the extraction of this device identifier. This data may be exploited to reduce the computational complexity of a *brutforce* attack. However, the attacker will only get knowledge of a single device identifier at a time. This ID shall not be applicable to other devices. Unauthorized devices fail during the evaluation of the identifier and cloned devices may then be excluded from further communications.

3.2.3 Physically Unclonable Functions

The class of Physically Uncloneable Functions (PUFs) represents a versatile new type of cryptographic primitive [RSS09]. In contrast to other primitives, the development of PUFs is driven more from the practicality of the solutions then from the mathematical properties. The physical properties of PUFs are exploited by measuring the *response* to a given *challenge*. These characteristics originate from small differences during the complex chemical, optical and physical production process of Integrated Circuits (ICs), leading to a variation of resistance or capacitance in the circuit. A *response* can be considered as the result of a (parametrized) mathematical function of the *challenge* [KST07]. In digital electronics and also for FPGAs mostly memory-based or delay-based approaches are applied to implement PUFs, although there exist non-electric and analog PUFs (cf. [MV10]).

The construction of a typical delay-based PUF is depicted in Figure 3.4. The challenge is applied to the arbiter PUF selecting the actual path of the signal. Since the propagation delay of each path is different, either the clock signal or the data signal arrives first at the arbiter latch, resulting in a zero or one response, respectively.

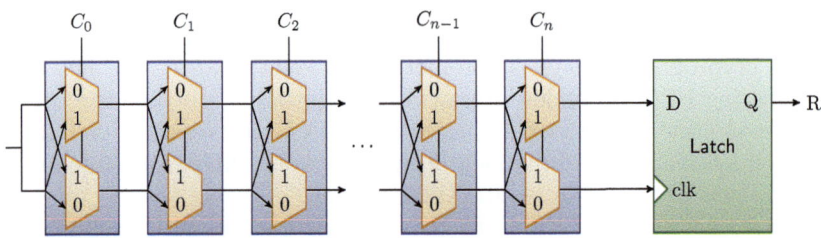

Figure 3.4: Arbiter PUF Construction [SD07]

This simple delay construction is effective for Application Specific Integrated Circuit (ASIC) implementations. According to Morozov et al., the variation in routing delays between the functional elements in FPGAs is an order of magnitude higher than the expected process variations [MMS10]. Hence, simple delay based approaches are not applicable for FPGA-based systems, but rather a ring oscillator-based approach shall be considered.

The intrinsic benefit of PUFs is that they are unclonable by design and hence for each device an individual key is provided. They further mitigate the need to store cryptographic key material, as this security-sensitive data may be regenerated by using approaches, as presented by Maes et al. in [MVHV12]. Since the physical realization of the PUF itself defines its responses, modifications of the circuit, e.g. by using a Focused Ion Beam (FIB), is expected to lead to the destruction of (at least some) the physical properties defining the PUF.

Although, PUFs do not provide services directly related to trusted computing, PUFs are perfectly feasible in providing means for authentication and may further be used for cryptographic key storage. The authors of [LSS[+]12] detailed on a PUF-based TRNG. This in turn makes a PUF an universal cryptographic primitive which can be used for authentication, random number generation, and secure key storage.

Integrated Circuits (ICs), as many other physical objects, may be characterized by unique and hard to clone features usable for identification. In the area of biometrics, concepts are provided to discriminate between individuals based on their physiological properties. These recognition methods require characteristics or so called *modalities* of the individual objects.

3.2 Identification and Authentication

The measurements of *modalities* have to show a sufficiently large variation between individual objects to enable discrimination between them (μ_{inter}). Additionally, different *modality* measurements of one object, shall feature only small variations (μ_{intra}) as outlined in [MV10]:

Inter-distance (μ_{inter}): This metric measures the distance of two responses to the same challenge by two different devices (between-entity variation).

Intra-distance (μ_{intra}): The distance of two consecutive responses to the same challenge by one device (within-person variation).

An IC undergoes several successive deposition, implantation, and etching steps during manufacture. These chemical, optical and physical processes used in IC fabrication, are only accurate to a certain level. The etching process as example, may dissolve a slightly larger area within one gate on the chip, resulting in differing resistance values. Even two neighboring gates of the same type on the same wafer, differ in their exact physical properties. A difference in the resistance of gates is directly related to a variation in the propagation delays. If a PUF is challenged with some value, the variation between these propagation delays lead to different responses.

Utilizing PUFs requires a characterization of the implementation to determine the parts of the function, that tend to remain constant and the parts which more or less behave randomly. As this behavior is device specific, several constant bits may be present in a particular PUF realization, but these response bits may generate different outputs on other devices. This is especially the desired behavior, if the PUF is utilized to generate cryptographic key material. Utilizing the PUF as an entropy source for a RNG requires the elimination of constant bits in order to maximize the provided entropy.

A PUF is a function that replies to a challenge with a certain response based on the physical properties. Usual PUF protocols for authentication exploit this feature and record the response to various challenges before the roll-out of the device in so called Challenge Response Pairs (CRPs). Afterwards the reply to the challenge is verified against the previously recorded values. These responses are usually noisy by nature, as for instance the delay of two disjoint paths is measured, which heavily depends on the operating conditions, such as temperature and supply voltage. Therefore, the response may be still accepted even though it does not perfectly match the recorded response.

The margin for accepting and rejecting responses is delimited by the False Accept Rate (FAR) and False Reject Rate (FRR) which may be tolerated.

In general, these two properties, as well as the μ_{inter}, and μ_{intra} parameters define the amount of tolerated errors in the response.

Although, PUFs do not feature a biometric property, as they lack the biological features, they somehow fall into the same category of authentication methods. The "biometric" features of a PUF are defined by the physical variations between the devices, whereas for true biometrics the physical representation of e.g. a fingerprint is influenced biologically. "Something you are" is indeed an appropriate description of a PUF, as the physical features of every device differ to a certain extent.

An authentication system based on PUFs requires the following features [Sim91, Rav01, GCvDD02]. It shall be

- easy to fabricate,
- easy to probe,
- hard to clone,
- structurally stable.

Especially the hard to clone property is questioned in literature very often (cf. [RSS09, RSS$^+$10], as there may exist measures to model the behavior of the function. The structural stability of certain PUF implementations has been shown by Katzenbeisser et al. in [KKR$^+$12], but a similar study regarding FPGAs is currently not (publicly) available.

3.3 A Notion of Time

In addition to a secure key storage to protect the identity of a cyber-physical system, a notion of time is required to prevent against replay attacks. Simple measures, such as monotonic counters (cf. Section 2.2.2) are a feasible approach to mitigate this kind of attacks. Most cryptographic protocols require timestamps, e.g. certificates featuring validity information tags (not before/not after) (cf. [ITU08, CSF$^+$08]. Moreover, the ability to invalidate older versions of configuration data shall be provided. Otherwise an accurate and tamper protected system clock is required to realize the same functionality at a higher cost.

3.4 Measurements for Security

Security is not a continuous property, nor it is plain binary. This makes it difficult to decide on the level of security provided by a system. Hence, relative measures to compare different algorithms regarding their cryptographic strength are often used. There is no absolute security measure available for cryptographic algorithms, as even a thorough cryptanalysis may miss some properties. If a system can be considered to be secure is not just determined by looking at the length of the key. Neither it is just the selection of one algorithm to guard encrypted data. Various measures have to be considered simultaneously to enable an evaluation of the overall system security.

The hardness of measuring security, as it is fundamentally different from other measurements, is denoted in a list of reasons compiled by Pfleeger and Cunningham in [PC10]. They state that, amongst other things, not all security requirements can be tested. Moreover, no system stands for itself, environmental and contextual changes as well as the adversary himself are affecting security. Security is a multidimensional composition of attributes telling about the resistance against adversaries. These findings give evidence for security measurement being hard as there is no accurate scale to reflect the level of security. The adversary himself has a major influence on the environment. Whenever the adversary gains new capabilities the security of the system has to be assessed. The concluded measurement result is not static, it has to be (re-)evaluated on a regular basis to cope with upcoming threats. Newly discovered capabilities may exploited by attackers, as well as the system modifications to accommodate new requirements.

In general, the specific economic value of the protected data has to be considered. It does not make much sense to protect invaluable data with high grade encryption schemes. The selection of algorithms has to be guided by a threat analysis, that acknowledges the value of the protected data. An estimation of the economical cost of one attack shall be made to enable a comparison of the economic value of the protected data against the cost of a countermeasure and the estimated cost of an attack. Even if the cost to thwart different classes of attacks is known, there is still uncertainty to be embraced (cf. [PC10]).

Stolfo et al. argue that for measuring security, a metametric – measuring the risks under all assumptions – is required [SBE11]. These authors additionally outline certain security metrics, ranging from computational complexity to empirical metrics. Indeed, it is hard to quantify the security of two systems, which only show subtle differences. One such difference may lead to new capabilities gained by the adversary.

Table 3.2: Trusted Computer System Evaluation Criteria Classification [DoD85]

Class	Description
D	minimal protection
C	discretionary protection
B	mandatory protection
A	formal verification

It is clear that the simple composition of security properties, as presented by [DFG+11], does not necessarily lead to a secure system. These authors state the composition of the measured boot with the late launch capabilities, which are both sound security properties, may introduce weaknesses. In this example an adversary exploits the late launch capability to measure the same programs as done by a measured boot. Hence, the state of the system is not effectively represented by the system integrity measurements stored in the TPM.

Analysis and testing of a cyber-physical system design commonly concentrates on the functional requirements of the system. The security requirements are often neglected or employed at a later stage in the development cycle. In [Moc09] the authors detail on common best practices for security testing.

Another approach measuring the security of real-world systems is to employ security proofs. The importance of provable security to be used as a tool to design systems using cryptography has been outlined by Degabriele et al. in [DPW11]. The design of secure systems has to follow best practices as well as formal approaches to proof the security of the resulting systems.

A number of security measurements and evaluation criteria which are commonly used today are outlined in the following. In particular for Trusted Computing the so called *Orange Book* [DoD85] can be considered as the basis for evaluation criteria specifications. It is additionally considering the trustworthiness of a given platform. The rest of the chapter outlines a selection of the most accepted specifications used for security evaluations.

3.4.1 The Orange Book

The Department of Defense (DoD) issued the *Trusted Computer System Evaluation Criteria* specification [DoD85], also known as the *Orange Book*.

3.4 Measurements for Security

It is the first of a series of books published by the DoD, named by the color of their cover and often referred to as the *Rainbow Series*. The *Orange Book* provides security and the evaluation guidelines for manufacturers to comply to the DoD directive and a metric for the evaluation of security. A first trusted computer system has been specified in the *Orange Book* and the requirements stated therein have heavily influenced the standards issued by the TCG. It further includes the first formal definition of the Trusted Computing Base (TCB).

The book defines the fundamental requirements for any system processing security-sensitive data. Every computer system shall feature a well-defined security policy containing a marking of all data with labels defining the permitted access control. Identification and accountability are also included in the list of fundamental requirements. The above mentioned properties have to be evaluated to gain assurance of the systems functionality. Furthermore, these fundamental properties shall be provided continuously.

A general overview of the criteria for Trusted Computing systems is given in Table 3.2. The classifications denoted in the *Orange Book* range from minimal protection to verified protection of trusted computer systems. Minimal requirements only comply to the above mentioned fundamental requirements. Discretionary protection defines the a baseline for protection, namely access control lists should enable users to enforce data access restrictions. The *Orange Book* provides a higher granularity description of the classes presented in Table 3.2.

The requirements stated in the *Orange Book* have been combined with additional security specifications for security evaluation to form the CC in 2005.

3.4.2 Common Criteria for IT Security Evaluation

The Common Criteria for Information Technology Security Evaluation (CC) is a well-respected standard for the evaluation IT products. CC is the commonly used short name for *Common Criteria for Information Technology Security Evaluation*. Certification and evaluation using the CC has been introduced in many countries, such as Canada, France, Germany, UK, and the US. Any cyber-physical system that undergoes CC evaluation has a high potential to be accepted in the member countries. The CC specification is divided into three parts [CC09a, CC09b, CC09c]. The first part covers an introduction of the general concepts and principles of IT security evaluation alongside a general model of evaluation. In the second part the standard

Table 3.3: Common Criteria Evaluation Assurance Levels [CC09c, CC07]

Level	Description	Attack Potential
EAL1	Functionally tested	basic
EAL2	Structurally tested	basic
EAL3	Methodically tested and checked	basic
EAL4	Methodically designed, tested and reviewed	enhanced-basic
EAL5	Semiformally designed and tested	moderate
EAL6	Semiformally verified design and tested	high
EAL7	Formally verified design and tested	high

templates defining security functional requirements are presented. Finally, the third part details on assuring these security requirements.

The CC specification superseded the aforementioned Orange Book and has been improved continually. It has additionally been standardized as the ISO/IEC 15408 international standard. For product certification a set of rules apply which require certain steps to be performed during implementation. Depending on the desired Evaluation Assurance Levels (EALs) different standards have to be met. The EALs range from *functionally tested* (EAL1) to a *formally verified and tested* design (EAL7). An overview of the requirements hierarchy and the associated potential of an attacker (cf. [CC07]) is given in Table 3.3.

The EAL is the most respected part of the CC approach and constitutes several concepts of assurance for a Target of Evaluation (TOE). Despite the strict hierarchy given in Table 3.3, there exist intermediate levels, which conform to some parts of the upper level specification. For instance, the Infineon TPM is certified at EAL4+, exceeding the requirements of the TCG Protection Profile (PP). An overview of the different levels is given in the following.

EAL1 is the simplest assurance level with in the Common Criteria and is only applicable if threats are not considered to be of serious outcome. The main purpose of this evaluation is to provide evidence that the TOE functions conform to the documentation. The evaluation involves an independent third party, supporting the argument that care has been taken to protect personal or private information. An assurance level of EAL1 not only provides an assessment of the TOE but also the functional and

3.4 Measurements for Security

interface specifications as well as the documentation. Furthermore, the EAL1 rating requires a survey for potential vulnerabilities and penetration testing against adversaries with a basic attack potential.

EAL2 aims at securing legacy systems, where a low to moderate level of independently assured security is required. Although, the EAL2 demands a co-operation of the developer to supply information, it should not substantially increase the developers effort. Based on the functional specification, a vulnerability analysis against adversaries with basic attack potential shall be provided. Additionally, evidence for a secure supply chain and the use of a configuration management system is required.

EAL3 provides in comparison to EAL2 a test coverage analysis and stricter rules in the configuration management to thwart tampering during development. The TOE, its development process, and the development tools are assessed by extensive tests. It supplies a moderate level of independently assured security. The re-engineering effort for EAL3 compliance should be kept at a minimum.

EAL4 is reached by relying on best-practices in security engineering, without the requirement of substantial specialist knowledge. It represents the highest level, allowing to retrofit existing products. Independent assurance from moderate to high levels are maintained by EAL4 assured systems. The EAL4 includes an analysis of the implementation representation (i.e. source code) and thereby representing a substantial increase in assurance in comparison to EAL3. A focused vulnerability analysis is conducted to determine the attack resistance of an adversary with enhanced-basic attack potential.

EAL5 requires semi-formal design descriptions and a structured analyzable architecture. In order to achieve EAL5 assurance the development should be started with the intent of reaching EAL5 conformance. A security engineering specialist supporting the development, by taking care of a semi-formal specification, is required. Moreover, a modular design of the security functions, as well as a semi-formal description thereof is needed. In summary, the EAL5 permits a high level of independently assured security without substantially increasing the development costs. An independent testing of a sample of test vectors provided with the test documentation is executed by the evaluator. The methodical vulnerability analysis assumes a moderate attack potential of the adversary.

EAL6 is applicable for applications facing high risk situations. The protected assets justify the additional costs for the rigorous application of security engineering techniques. Additional assurance is gained by a formal TOE security policy model and a semi-formal modular design. In addition to the modular design of the security functions required by the EAL5, a (layered) formal specification of all security subsystems is needed. The advanced methodical vulnerability analysis assumes a high attack potential, which is assured by the evaluator using penetration testing. The configuration management support utilized during development and the development environment have to comply to stricter requirements. Configuration changes shall only be accepted by persons not involved in the development of this particular configuration.

EAL7 provides assurance even for extremely high risk applications and/or the protection of high value assets. A comprehensive analysis on the formal representations and an in-depth testing of the security functions provide the highest assurance level. Moreover, a proof the consistency between the formal specifications and the functional specifications has to be given. The evaluator executes the complete test suite provided by the test documentation and runs further tests to confirm that the entire security functions operate according to the specification.

The CC also includes a metric to calculate the attack potential of an adversary. For instance the time required and the expertise of the adversary are rated to sum up to an overall value for the attack potential. Then these values are rated in vulnerability/resistance classes (see [CC07, Section B.4.2.3]) used in Table 3.3.

3.4.3 NIST-FIPS 140-2

The NIST releases a specification on the "security requirements for cryptographic modules" [NIS02]. The hierarchy of the security levels correspond to the classes provided by the Orange Book (see Table 3.2). The security levels range from level 1 to level 4 whereas the security level 1 represents basic security requirements and the security level 4 constitutes the highest level provided by this standard. These four security levels are defined for the different areas of the development process ranging from physical security, operating system requirements, development environment and the supply-chain management. In [NIS02] three realizations of cryptographic modules are considered, namely single-chip modules, multiple-chip embedded modules, and multiple-chip standalone modules. Table 3.4 denotes the individual

Table 3.4: Cryptographic Module Requirement for Compliance to NIST-FIPS140-2 Security Levels [NIS02]

Security Level	General Requirements	Single-Chip Module	Multiple-Chip Embedded Module	Multiple-Chip Standalone Module
1	production-grade components	–	production-grade enclosure, if applicable	production-grade enclosure
2	tamper evidence	opaque tamper-evident coating	opaque tamper-evident encapsulation	tamper-evident seals or pick-resistant locks
3	automatic zeroization	hard opaque tamper-evident coating	hard opaque encapsulation of multi-chip embodiment	strong enclosure with removal attempts causing serious damage
4	fault attack protection and testing for temperature and voltage deviations	hard opaque removal-resistant coating	tamper detection and response envelope with zeroization	active tamper detection and response

requirements for the specific level of security for each type of cryptographic module.

The cryptographic module shall include tamper detection mechanisms even from the lower security levels. The probability of detecting a tampering attempt shall be very high. At the highest levels, the fast erasure of cryptographic keys and security-sensitive parameters are required as countermeasures against tampering attempts.

4 Design Security and Cyber-Physical Threats

The trustworthiness of reconfigurable hardware, such as FPGAs is defined by the mechanisms protecting the configuration data. The field programmability of an FPGA is a distinct feature enabling various possibilities, but it is also introducing new vulnerabilities. Therefore, the protection of the overall platform and all configured Intellectual Property (IP) is of utmost importance. As aforementioned, authentication and system integrity reporting are the most important measures required. However, for the protection of IP, confidentiality is an additional issue. The Overall level of design security determines the general conditions for the trustworthiness of a device.

The enforcement of protection mechanisms always implies that cryptographic key material has to be stored somewhere in the reconfigurable device. For the general case, where ICs as a whole are considered, there are two possible approaches to store cryptographic keys. Either a battery backed-up volatile memory or an NVM, such as anti-fuses or flash-based memories are included. A feature overview of these approaches has been noted in Section 3.1.

For FPGA-based approaches there exists a third possibility of cryptographic key storage; the key may be included as a part of the configuration data, which in turn means that the protection relies on the reverse-engineering complexity of the configuration data. As the configuration data is a proprietary structure, the reliance on the reverse-engineering complexity is generally considered as a bad design practice. The simplest case is represented by storing the key inside one of the memory blocks. The extraction of key material from these sources is directly supported by the design tools, as the same mechanism is used to exchange the instruction memory of soft-core processors. In particular, the tools provided by the FPGA vendors support the extraction and substitution of memory contents directly [Xil11a]. Extraction of Look-Up Tables (LUTs) content has been shown in literature by Ziener et al. [ZAT06] for IP identification purposes, but it may also be applied to the extraction of security-sensitive information. In contrast to the mere extraction of data, the creation of an automated process for analyzing and converting configuration data is considered to be much harder [Dri08]. However, even if the key is hidden within the configuration data itself, it often features a high entropy which may make it easy to distinguish within the configuration data.

Currently, most utilized FPGAs are SRAM-based and are hence volatile by nature. Their configuration data including the designers IP, have to be protected from theft and counterfeiting. SRAM-based FPGAs require an external configuration memory residing on the PCB, thus being easily accessible by an adversary. Hence, most FPGA vendors provide measures to protect the configuration data of their products. These protection mechanisms, especially for older devices, are no longer effective. Most importantly, the authentication of the configuration data is not protected at all, except for very recent devices.

In [Tri07], Trimberger states that vendor specific tools for FPGA development support the "Trusted Design in FPGAs". Since the realization of the functionality of an FPGA design resides in its configuration data, it has an inherent advantage over traditional ICs. ASIC designs are exposed to malicious modifications within the foundry, violating the confidentiality of the IP. If FPGAs are considered, the configuration remains in the hands of the designer. The FPGA fabric itself is of course subject to malicious modifications. However, these modifications then have to follow a generic approach, which disregards the specific properties of a particular implementation. The latter issues are present in all technical products and may only be overcome, if the whole supply-chain, namely suppliers and manufacturers themself, are trustworthy. To mitigate this issue, a rather large number of devices may be (destructively) tested to rule out malicious modifications of the FPGA itself [Tri07].

The configuration data of FPGAs has to be verified regarding their authenticity. Moreover, if Partial Reconfiguration (PR) is exploited, the subsequent configurations need to be authentic as well. Trimberger additionally proposes the verification of the design of fielded devices, however the presented approach does only include the most recent data and disregards the history of the configurations. An adversary may tamper with the device and afterwards load legitimate configuration data without detection.

FPGAs feature mechanisms to update the configuration during runtime. This speciality is referred to as Partial Reconfiguration (PR) (cf. Section B.2). Most available devices today, disable protection mechanisms of configuration memories with the condition that PR is exploited. Only the most recent devices support PR together with the encryption of the configuration data.

The term IP, if used in conjunction with reconfigurable technologies, often refers to third party IP-cores included in the design. FPGA vendors provide tools to integrate these IP-cores. These tools support the customization of these cores to a certain extent. The licensing of these building blocks and the protection of the corresponding assets may in turn be referred to as IP-protection. Within the scope of this thesis, the term IP and IP-protection refers to the intellectual property without any restriction. In particular, any design may include the IP of at least one entity. The configuration data of an FPGA is often representing the IP of multiple entities.

4.1 Design Security Goals

The most important security goals in the context of design security are authenticity, integrity, and confidentiality. Authenticity ensures that no modified configuration data is loaded, which may elevate the capabilities of an adversary. The integrity of the data is often protected by Cyclic Redundancy Checks (CRCs), but this is not sufficient to protect against malicious modification of the configuration data. Encryption of configuration data is used to ensure confidentiality of the designer's IP. In the following the particular measures are outlined with respect to reconfigurable devices.

Protecting Authenticity Apart from the fact that authentication is a general requirement for HSMs as outlined in Section 3.2; the importance of authentic configuration data is outlined in the following. Drimer advocates that the versatility of FPGAs gained by in-field updates comes with the exposure to various attacks [Dri07]. The authentication of configuration data is included in recent products of the major FPGA vendors (cf. [Xil11e, Xil11c, Xil12a, Mic11a, Mic12c]). Until now, only the confidentiality of configuration data is protected on almost every commercially available FPGA. The encryption schemes are ranging from Data Encryption Standard (DES) [NIS99, withdrawn May 19, 2005] (or Triple-DES) to AES [NIS01] on more recent devices.

Tampering of configuration data may permanently damage a device due to short circuits in the pass gates of the FPGA [HUS99]. If only encryption is utilized to protect configuration data, it is fairly simple to construct tampered configuration data. Randomized bit manipulation of encrypted configuration data may lead to a congestion in routing resources, which in turn is destroying the device.

Integrity protection, such as CRCs, within the configuration data do not effectively prevent this kind of attacks. In this case the attacker has to test the randomization of the configuration data in order to find a collision in the CRC. According to the birthday paradox the number of bitstrings required to generate a collision in the widely used CRC-32 function is 77163 (cf. [Buc04, Equation 5.2]). Without authentication, the randomization introduced in the encrypted data translate to configuration data itself. However, the number of modifications, which need to be tested is still limited by the birthday paradox. Hence, it can be seen that CRCs provide only measures protecting against errors during the transmission of configuration data.

Drimer and Kuhn proposed in [Dri07] that authentication is required to protect from malicious modification and to resolve the aforementioned issues. Their update protocol, utilizes monotonic counters to protect against replay of previously valid configurations. The underlying technology has been taken into account by the authors in [Dri07], as multiple approaches depending on the capabilities of the FPGAs have been presented. In this work, mainly SRAM-based FPGAs are considered and the authors require the non-volatile storage to reside within a security boundary. Hence, the adversary is not allowed to access the off-chip NVM. This may be realized by securely packing the device in a housing supporting intrusion detection, as specified by NIST FIPS 140-2. However, the same authors present a successful attack on certified payment terminals, actively subverting this requirement.

Authentication is perceived to be more important than encryption [FS03]. Encryption prevents against eavesdropping of information, whereas authentication identifies trustworthy entities. Moreover, the authentication of configuration data ensures the intended behavior of a device.

A crucial property of authentication mechanisms is the ability to proof the authenticity of configurations even if the device is offline. This implies, if a configuration is invalidated, the device has to be synchronized to determine actual valid configurations. Simpson and Schaumont presented a mechanism to authenticate configuration data of IP providers for reconfigurable devices in [SS06]. Their approach includes an online phase, in which the externally included IPs are authenticated using a Trusted Third Party (TTP), and an offline phase which allows their usage within the system.

Protecting Integrity Rudimentary measures for integrity protection are included with every commercially available device. Misconfiguration may potentially lead to the physical destruction of an FPGA. This is effectively

4.1 Design Security Goals

thwarted by using CRC to verify the integrity of the transmitted configuration data. Not only transmission errors in the configuration data have to be considered, but also the intentional malicious modification. Hence, using a CRC to protect against adversaries is not sufficient.

Hadžić et al. have presented the hardware equivalent to software viruses in [HUS99]. They outline how conflicting interconnections in the FPGA logic can be exploited to create high currents inside the device. In short, they propose to use the following measures to protect against these modifications: (i) Verification of the internal structure of the configuration data to avoid multi-source routing; (ii) or by including additional circuitry monitoring the current levels within the FPGA. However it is generally possible to analyze these conditions, but the FPGA has to implement these features in the first place. The routing verification of a device requires an examination of all nets in the design, which is computationally infeasible to be performed on the FPGA.

An effective measure to protect configuration data against modification is to use cryptographic protection schemes, such as hash functions. Using a cryptographic hash function instead of a CRC compensates the issue (i), without adding to much computational overhead. The circuit monitoring feature proposed in (ii) will not only help to disclose the current consumed by FPGA-Viruses but it can also be used to detect tampering attempts. Recent FPGA devices already provide simple implementations of this feature, which allow to monitor voltages and the core temperature.

Subverting the integrity of configuration data enables the adversary to insert so called Hardware Trojan Horses (HTH). Tehranipoor and Koushanfar survey the existing methods to prevent against modifications in silicon [TK10]. However, these methods are considering the "verification of the physical trustworthiness of ICs and systems", the underlying problem is present for reconfigurable devices. A malicious modification in the Internal Configuration Access Port (ICAP) may enable an adversary to subvert security mechanisms. As aforementioned, the evaluation of FPGAs for security applications may include an examination of the gate-level implementation of the chip.

Protecting Confidentiality Most protection mechanisms supplied by the FPGA vendors solely focus on the confidentiality of the configuration data. Only the most recent devices support further measures to protect configuration data. Apart from these commercial approaches supported even for low-cost devices, research strives to present vendor independent solutions protecting the confidentiality of the configuration data.

The mere encryption of the data is already supported by the FPGA vendors. An additional approach, which aims to increase the reverse-engineering costs is presented by Yip and Ng. Their partial encryption approach selectively encrypts few sequences within the FPGA configuration data. This enables cloned devices to perform the intended functionality up to a certain level until they have to use some of the partially encrypted functions [YN00].

A well-known approach in order to protect software implementations against reverse-engineering, is the obfuscation of the implementation binaries. This has been adapted by Chakraborty to protect hardware implementations by the obfuscation of the design (cf. [Cha10]). He proposes, a transformation procedure of hardware implementations (i.e. netlists) to represent a functionally equivalent design, which is harder to reverse engineer. This approach only protects against attacks during the design flow, before the design has been mapped to the vendor specific format for the configuration data. With this step, all the different labels existent in the netlist are replaced by the actual nets of the resulting design. Additionally, it is not clear how these netlist modifications interact with the optimization algorithms of the vendor specific tools.

4.2 Vendor Specific Design Security

The various FPGA vendors are providing measures to thwart cloning and overbuilding when using their devices. Depending on the underlying technology of a given device, a diversity of approaches is feasible to realize countermeasures against IP-theft. Antifuse-based devices are one time programmable and cannot be altered or reprogrammed afterwards. In this case, the protection of configuration data relies on the physical measures to prevent attackers from reverse engineering. Due to the homogeneous structure of antifuse technology it is hard to distinguish the programmed value of a given cell [Kil10b, Kil10a]. The high level of security provided by antifuse technology qualifies for excellent secure key and ID storage.

In 1997, one of the major FPGA vendors distinguished between two situations to be considered for the design security of their SRAM-based FPGAs [Xil97]. At that time, neither encryption nor authentication where available to protect the configuration data. According to [Tri07], the encryption of configuration data has been introduced in 2001 by Xilinx in their Virtex-II family.

IP protection for FPGAs directly corresponds to the protection of the configuration data. The authors of [Xil97] differentiate between two scenarios

4.2 Vendor Specific Design Security

on how the configuration data is provided to the FPGA. The first situation is that configuration data resides in an NVM on the PCB. NVMs may be accessed by probing their specified interfaces and hence the configuration data is simply copied to clone a device (cf. Section 4.4.1). Moreover, the same document states that it is almost impossible to get an understanding of the functionality from configuration data. Thus, intelligent modification of configuration data has been rendered impossible by FPGA vendors in [Xil97] . Note and Rannaud have in contrast revealed in recent developments [NR08] that the reverse mapping of configuration data to the netlist representation is possible (cf. Section 4.4.2).

In the second situation the configuration memory is removed after the FPGA has been configured and the configuration data is retained using a battery-backup. This is a special case, in which the extraction of configuration data is possible iff the configuration readback capability of the FPGA is available. Depackaging and microprobing (cf. Section 4.4.2) of the homogeneous structure of an FPGA seems at this time impossible. Moreover, a microprobing attempt may lead with high probability to a data corruption in the configuration data.

The encryption of FPGA configuration data provides means to protect against theft and reverse engineering. Encryption is an effective measure to prevent unauthorized copying of devices, as the configuration data can only be decrypted if and only if the correct decryption key is present inside the FPGA. Nevertheless, tampering with the configuration data is still possible, as encryption may not prevent an FPGA from loading unauthorized data. As aforementioned, the authentication of data is even more important than the encryption itself.

A list of security measures by Vendor is compiled in Table 4.1. Although, most FPGA vendors provide measures to encrypt configuration data, authentication is included only in a fraction of the available devices. Especially volatile SRAM-based FPGAs face the threat of modified configuration data and therefore enable an attacker to perform a Chosen Ciphertext Attack (CCA). Further, authentication is required for FPGAs having remote update capabilities in place, as the injection of a maliciously formed configuration may also result in a denial of service on the FPGA. As Drimer pointed out in [Dri07], encryption of data prevents from threats such as cloning and overbuilding, but authentication safeguards the intended behavior. Hence, for the application in building trustworthy systems, authenticity plays a major role.

Microsemi FPGAs additionally provide access to the Cryptographic Research (CRI) Differential Power Analysis (DPA) patent portfolio in order

Table 4.1: Available Protection Mechanisms for FPGA Configuration Data

Manufacturer	Device	Bitstream Encryption	Authentication	Technology	Key Storage
Achronix	Speedster22i HD [Ach12]	AES-256 (CBC)	–	SRAM	eFuse
Altera	Stratix II/II GX [Alt11b]	AES-128	–	SRAM	NVM
	Stratix III/IV/V [Alt11c, Alt11d, Alt12]	AES-256	–	SRAM	volatile/NVM
	Cyclone III LS [Alt11a]	AES-256	–	SRAM	volatile
Lattice	ECP2/M SS-Series" [Lat12a]	AES-128	–	SRAM	eFuse
	ECP3 [Lat12b]	AES-128	–	SRAM	eFuse
	ECP4 [Lat12c]	AES-128	–	SRAM	eFuse
	XP2 [Lat12d]	AES-128	–	Flash	eFuse
Microsemi	IGLOO [Mic12a, Mic11a]	AES-128	128-bit FlashLock® [a]	Flash	NVM
	ProASIC3 [Mic11c]	AES-128	128-bit FlashLock®	Flash	NVM
	SmartFusion [Mic12b]	AES-128	128-bit FlashLock®	Flash	NVM
	SmartFusion2 [Mic12c]	AES-256	SHA-256	Flash	PUF
Xilinx	Spartan3-AN [Xil06, Xil08, Xil07a]	–	–	Flash	NVM
	Virtex-II [Xil07b]	DES / triple-DES	–	SRAM	volatile
	Virtex-4 [Xil09]	AES-256	–	SRAM	volatile
	Virtex-5 [Xil11d]	AES-256	–	SRAM	volatile
	Spartan-6 [Xil11e]	AES-256	Device-DNA	SRAM	eFuse/volatile
	Virtex-6 [Xil11c]	AES-256	SHA-256 HMAC	SRAM	eFuse/volatile
	7 Series FPGAs [Xil12a]	AES-256	SHA-256	SRAM	eFuse/volatile
	Zynq-7000 [Xil12e][b]	AES-256	SHA-256	SRAM	eFuse/volatile

[a] The FlashLock® technology prevents unauthorized access to internal flash memory content.
[b] Zynq devices support a secure boot protection using TrustZone

4.2 Vendor Specific Design Security

to include countermeasures against side-channel analysis. This makes Microsemi the only FPGA vendor including this kind of countermeasures. In addition, PUF-based approaches have been recently made available for these FPGAs using IP-Cores by Intrinsic-ID, providing true random number generators [Mic11b] and secure key storage [Mic11d]. These implementations are available as an IP-core implementation for most Microsemi FPGAs. The newest generation of SmartFusion FPGAs is equipped with similar technology as additional hardware. The SmartFusion2 FPGA includes a PUF-based key storage and side-channel resistant encryption cores to protect configuration data. Moreover, all these functions are accessible from within an FPGA implementation.

In order to protect multiple IPs within one system, each of the IP providers need to be in possession of a unique key, protecting the IP providers assets. Moreover, the creation, handling, and disablement of these keys has to be in full control of the IP provider. An architecture supporting these features is outlined in Section 5.5.1.

The use of battery backed key storage is a relentlessly debated in the security community. On one hand it makes it more difficult to tamper a given device as a disconnect from the battery results in the loss of the security-sensitive data. On the other hand this adds also a risk of denial of service by removal of the battery or in case of a failing battery. For this reason, vendors providing devices with battery backed key storage are currently switching to non-volatile decryption key storage based on anti-fuse technology to mitigate these risks [Xil11b].

Cloning and overbuilding of FPGA-based implementations may be effectively thwarted by disabling the readback and configuration capabilities of the devices. For Spartan-3 devices certain levels of protection exist, ranging form the mere disablement of the readback capabilities, to disarming most of the JTAG access features (cf. [Xil06, Xil08, Xil07a]). Other vendors, such as Microsemi are additionally protecting the device from unauthorized access. These devices only enable the configuration interface, if and only if a 256-bit passcode is supplied prior to the programming of the device.

An effective measure to protect against overbuilding is to include an authenticated NVM. This scheme exploits the ability of authenticated NVMs to proof the presence of an unique external element. Figure 4.1 depicts the generic architecture of this scheme, often referred to as "Identification Friend or Foe (IFF)" (cf. [Alt07, Xil10]). This scheme utilizes a randomized HMAC uniquely identifying the external element. The secret keys, stored in the authenticated NVM, cannot be cloned. This scheme uses a hash based authentication mechanism to proof the knowledge of a shared secret key.

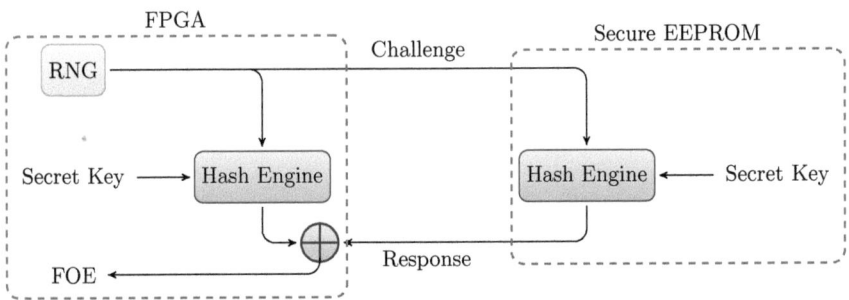

Figure 4.1: Authenticated Non-Volatile Memory [Alt07, Xil10]

The responses to the random challenges are compared on the FPGA side to enable or disable user logic.

Flash-based FPGAs, such as Microsemi IGLOO [Mic11a] or ProASIC [Mic11c], store configuration data in on-chip flash memories thereby including the configuration into the FPGA fabric. In contrast to SRAM-based FPGAs no external configuration memory is required to provide the configuration during system power-up. Single chip solutions may provide further measures to protect flash cells, which use device design and layout techniques to protect even against invasive attacks. Moreover, using the FlashLock® technology, the access to the device can be disabled. After authentication with the correct key, the device is unlocked and it can be accessed again. The Microsemi devices may be permanently locked to provide further measures against cloning [Mic03].

Skorobogatov and Woods have presented an attack [SW12] on the disregarded debugging features of Microsemi FPGAs and have been able to extract a key to reactivate the debug and test mode. The major drawback of preprogrammed keys is, that the user of the system is not able to verify the key distribution scheme of the manufacturer. In the end it cannot be verified if the keys of one system are also valid for another. Especially if the same keys are shared between various devices, adversaries are able to subvert the security mechanisms of many devices as soon as one key has been disclosed.

4.2.1 Tamper Protection

More and more FPGAs are being used in security-sensitive applications leading to the requirement of extended protection mechanisms. A plethora of protection mechanisms for tampering attempts exist, ranging from supply voltage monitoring to active shielding of security-sensitive areas with additional layers of metal. In genereal, a distinction between tamper evidence and tamper resistance is made. Tamper evidence may be provided by sealing the enclosure and tamper resistance refers to active monitoring techniques mitigating the impact of attacks.

Guidelines for building tamper resistant designs are provided by the vendors [Xil11b, Alt08]. IP-cores to increase the tamper resistance of FPGA-based systems, are available for several FPGA devices (e.g. [Xil12d]). These IP-cores include tampering penalties ranging from a global reset, to the zeroization of configuration data and cryptographic keys. Automated monitoring functions are used to trigger penalties, signal alarms, and provide status outputs. Current devices include measures to monitor temperature and voltage levels within the FPGA fabric [Xil11b]. Battery backed-up cryptographic memory is additionally providing protection against tampering of the device, as the adversary has to make sure that the power is not disrupted during the attack. Moreover, cryptographic memories may additionally support a high speed erase to protect the device secrets [BDWJ08].

4.3 Generic IP-Protection

The protection of IP has been tackled in the context of ASIC realizations. In the following an example of the existing IP-protection mechanisms is given. Similar approaches are applicable for FPGA-based systems.

During manufacture in the foundry an overproduction of the supplied design may happen without the knowledge of the designer. Alkabani et al. presented an approach [AK07] which renders all manufactured devices non-functional at the beginning. After a measurement on the device, the respectful owner of the IP is able to unlock and activate the device. Hence, the device cannot be used without the approval of the designer and overbuilt devices will stay non-functional. Later, Alkabani et al. enhanced this concept by adding a remote activation and deactivation mechanism in [AKP07]. Moreover, a tampering detection mechanism on this unlocking procedure may be included with negligible overhead. In the case of too many unsuccessful activation attempts, occurring during a brute-force attack, the device may be locked down to prevent further damage.

4.4 Cyber-Physical Threats

The most critical threats of current reconfigurable cyber-physical systems are *reverse engineering, overbuilding, cloning*, and *tampering*. In general, most physical attacks fall into the category of reverse engineering, as they make use of the internal structure of the system to gain knowledge of the system. Side-Channel attacks, as presented by Kocher et al. utilize the non-functional physical characteristics of a device to gain insights of the internally processed data [KJJ99]. Most of these attacks require sophisticated equipment, such as high resolution microscopes and wafer probing equipment to directly probe busses on the die. FPGA-based systems are especially prone to *overbuilding* and *cloning*, due to the ease in copying their configuration data.

The threats outlined in this section mainly target the security of volatile FPGAs. Non-volatile or one-time programmable logic devices are not explicitly covered. However, most of the threats detailed hereinafter, are also present to any other integrated circuit. The outlined issues should be considered separately, if applied in cases other then volatile FPGAs.

Based on the hierarchy of attacks given Verbauwhede and Schaumont in [VS07], an extended hierarchy of various threats and the corresponding attacks are given in Table 4.2. If FPGA-based systems are considered, an additional level of abstraction has to be added. The configuration data represents the overall functionality of the system and may be analyzed independently from the physical implementation. Consequently, the configuration abstraction level has been added to the hierarchy.

Attacks at the implementation level are of minor importance for FPGA-based systems, due to the homogeneous structure of the physical implementation. For an FPGA-based implementation the configuration data has to be linked to the physical implementation to identify the probing positions. It is a well-known fact, that the meaningful extraction of implementation details from configuration data is a cumbersome task. To additionally annotate these results with the placement and routing of the physical representation, i.e. identifying the exact probing positions, may be harder then directly tracing the configuration data. Mapping the placement and routing results to exact positions is not too complex, since FPGAs are open market devices with a high regular structure. Simple configurations may be exploited to sweep through the configuration memory and thereby find matching physical positions. In contrast, if the configuration data is protected and unknown to the adversary, an implementation level attack is almost rendered useless. The generic approach of such an attack requires the visual inspection of

4.4 Cyber-Physical Threats

Table 4.2: Extended Hierarchy of Cyber-Physical Attacks (based on [VS07])

Abstraction Level	Attacker Proximity	Countermeasure	Example Attack
Cryptographic	Off-line	Algorithm	Cryptanalysis
Interpreter	Connected	Protected Partition	Software Tampering, Scan-Chain readout [YWK04], Fault Attack [BDL97]
Configuration	Connected	Authentication, Encryption	Cloning, Overbuilding
Time	Connected	Constant-Time	Software timing, Cache Misses, Branch predictions
Power	Close-range	Constant-Power	Differential and Higher-order Differential Power Analysis [KJJ99]
Radiation	Close-range	Electromagnetic Shield	Remote Power Analysis
Implementation	Physical	Physical Shielding	Circuit Tampering, Semi-Invasive attacks

promising position for bus probing, which is indistinguishable in physical realization of FPGAs.

The abstraction levels on interpreter and configuration level are considered to be most important for the architectures presented in Chapter 5. However, side-channel attacks, in particular power attacks have been addressed in [SFH11] for the concept of trustworthy reconfiguration, as detailed in Section 5.4.

Other implementation level attacks have been presented by Kucera and Vetter in [KV07]. These authors advocate that hardware rootkits may bypass or replace existing code blocks to subvert encryption mechanisms. Furthermore, an FPGA-rootkit may lead to the destruction of the device as outlined in [HUS99].

Braeken et al. outline the existing protection technologies of current FPGA based systems in [BKT+09]. This survey presents an overview of mechanisms to protect FPGA-based implementations and additionally details the properties of different FPGA realizations in terms of invasive attacks. According to their metric, most of the measures provided hereinafter, focus on mitigating frauds on the architectural and micro-architectural level.

Not only the threats and attacks have to be considered but also the adversary plays a major role to classify the severity of an attack. In [AK96], Anderson and Kuhn use a reasonable distinction from Abraham et al. [ADDS91]. Abraham et al. distinguish between clever outsiders, knowledgeable insiders, and funded organizations as the three classes of adversaries, referred to as class I, II, and III respectively. Clever outsiders have access to moderately sophisticated equipment and are considered to be very talented, but generally lack a deeper understanding of the system. Knowledgeable insiders have access to highly sophisticated equipment and have the potential to access most of it. Funded organizations develop special attack tools and work in groups of specialists on a specific attack (e.g. Cryptography Research[1], Flylogic[2]). The complexity of the attack and the capabilities of the attacker can be used to estimate the cost of an attack and in turn provide the level of protection provided by certain measures.

4.4.1 Cloning, Overbuilding and Counterfeiting

The increased reconfiguration speed and flexibility of FPGAs comes at the cost of protecting the IP residing in the configuration data. Most FPGAs used today are SRAM-based devices, which need to be programmed on power-up utilizing an external non-volatile Memory. Widely deployed memory access mechanisms, such as Serial Parallel Interface (SPI), Byte Peripheral Interface (BPI) or SelectMAP interfaces (cf. [Xil11d]) are used in FPGA-based systems. These standardized interfaces not only allow for straightforward configuration of FPGAs, but also enable simple cloning of the configuration data.

The design and manufacture of FPGA-based devices is in general carried out by two distinct companies, whereby the control over the number of actually produced units is no longer under the control of the designer. If the design is not protected against overbuilding, additional units can be sold by applying the given configuration data to the overbuilt devices.

To mitigate the fact that SRAM-based FPGAs utilize external non-volatile memory, several commercial FPGA vendors support configuration data encryption in some of their products, cf. [Xil11d, Xil11e, Alt09]. Currently only static encryption is provided for most commercially available solutions and only a few support authentication of configuration data. A detailed compilation of the utilized technologies has been compiled in Table 4.1.

---

[1] http://www.cryptography.com/
[2] http://www.flylogic.net/

4.4 Cyber-Physical Threats

Table 4.3: Top-5 Semiconductor Counterfeits in 2011 (Percentage of Overall Reported Counterfeit Parts) [IHS12]

Part	Reported Counterfeits
Analog IC	25.2%
Microprocessor IC	13.4%
Memory	13.1%
Programmable Logic	8.3%
Transistor	7.6%

Counterfeit and fraudulent components are a big issue in the semiconductor industry. In general there are two major varieties of counterfeiting resulting from refurbishing old parts on the one hand and cloning or overbuilding on the other. Electronic waste is used to make refurbished parts by removing part numbers and other markings indicating manufacturing date. False markings are placed on the parts afterwards, identifying them as new.

The functional safety of a device is at a great risk if counterfeit parts come into use, especially in automotive and aerospace applications. Counterfeit ICs may have different impacts ranging from a false reading of a temperature sensor to a catastrophe in aviation applications. IHS Inc. noted in a press release [IHS12] that mostly counterfeited semiconductor types are analog ICs, microprocessors, memory, programmable logic and transistors. The percentage of the top-5 reported incidents is denoted in Table 4.3.

Although, this only underlines the impact of counterfeits on the semiconductor industry as a whole, the estimation is that cyber-physical systems are facing the same threats. Especially the counterfeits affecting analog components are alarming, as these may be utilized for manufacturing new systems, including all aforementioned risks. Further, the US Senate confirms the existence of counterfeit electronics in the DoD supply chain to exceed one million parts in 1800 individual cases [Com12].

4.4.2 Physical Attacks

The class of physical attacks represent measures, which require physical access to the device. These can be further classified into two subclasses, namely non-invasive and invasive attacks, sometimes also called non-destructive and destructive, respectively. This common taxonomy for the classification of attacks is detailed in the following.

Non-invasive attacks may be carried out if a device is in the possession of the adversary only for a short period of time. The attack itself leaves no visible traces on the device and it is still functional after the attack. An invasive attack is visible at the chip or package level, but it might also not be visible if the outer package or housing is carefully treated by the adversary. Invasive attacks often need to destroy a number of devices to gather all information required to carry out the attack. Once the procedure to carry out the attack is determined, the target device is modified using the gathered knowledge.

Not only the cryptographic processing elements have to be considered, but also the memories holding security-sensitive data. SRAM memory leaves traces of the data it contained over a longer period of time. Gutmann raises the issue that specialized processors are using the same data for a long period of time (e.g. a private key). Having SRAM cells configured continuously with the same data causes long-term retention (cf. [Gut01]). The SRAM in generic processors does not show this property very often, as the memory is used for different purposes during lifetime.

Skorobogatov has compiled a comprehensive list of different physical attacks in [Sko05]. Additionally he divided the class off invasive attacks, by introducing a third class named "semi-invasive attacks". Within this class he places all attacks, which leave the devices functional during or at least after the attack. This distinction is not made hereinafter, as such attacks will most likely lead to markings or other visible traces on the device under attack.

Considering FPGA-based architectures, *reverse engineering* is twofold, invasive and non-invasive. This is due to the fact that the reverse engineering can be performed at two different levels. On the one hand, the configuration data of the FPGA may be reverse engineered to gain knowledge about the function and discover possibilities to circumvent security mechanisms. On the other, the adversary may try to attack the protection technologies provided by the FPGA vendors. If the design is exploiting both security mechanisms, the adversary has to carry out an attack on both protection mechanisms.

Non-Invasive Attacks

The term non-invasive attack represents a class of attacks that do not harm or destroy the device under attack. Additionally, it is not visible from the outside of a device, that it has been tampered with. A prominent example of this class of physical attacks are side-channel attacks.

4.4 Cyber-Physical Threats

When looking at reconfigurable systems several types of non-invasive attacks are important, which will be outlined in the following. In general, side-channel analysis is applicable for all hardware modules processing security-sensitive data. Furthermore, the reverse engineering of configuration data is considered to be non-invasive, as the access to external configuration memory is unprotected in most cases. The upgrade of configuration data is a desired feature of reconfigurable systems and it shall be performed in a non-invasive manner; hence, the downgrade of configuration data is also non-invasive. Some of the approaches presented hereinafter rely on PUFs. Recently, there have been some non-invasive attacks on PUFs, that are outlined subsequently. A threat being generally present for all current ICs is the fact of disregarded debug features used during silicon validation and product testing.

Side-Channel Analysis Side-channel analysis attacks utilize information leaked by non-functional properties of the cryptographic system. These analysis methods range from the power consumption and electromagnetic emission to the timing analysis of an cryptographic algorithms.

Even if the algorithmic properties of a cryptographic system are perfectly secure, a naïve implementation of the system shall disclose some information on the key-dependent data. Kocher et al. have demonstrated the extraction of cryptographic key material from a cryptographic system, by only monitoring the physical properties of the implementation (i.e. power consumption) [KJJ99]. The side-channel analysis is more then the power analysis alone. Every information flow through an unintended communication channel may be considered a side-channel attack.

Reverse Engineering of Configuration Data Apart from the fact that reverse engineering at the chip-level usually destroys the IC, reverse engineering of an FPGA configuration data does not damage the device. If the FPGA configuration resides unprotected in an off-chip flash memory it can be easily copied (cf. Section 4.4.1) and analyzed independent from the system.

Even if the whole configuration data cannot be reverse engineered, security-sensitive material may be extracted. In particular if well-known cryptographic algorithms are used, the substitution functions (SBoxes) may be easily identified in the configuration. This enables the backtracking to the keyschedule and therefore the key data. Hence, the security-sensitive material shall not be stored within the configuration data itself. Another also well-known practice to mitigate this issue is to supply a device dependent key, such that the impact of a successful leakage of a single key is only affecting a single device.

Note and Rannaud reveal in recent developments [NR08] that the reverse mapping of configuration data to netlists is possible. Using the XDLRC files present for Xilinx devices, the structure of the FPGA is known and the configuration data may be analyzed using recent tools [BSH12].

For instance, the intermediate representation of the configuration data (ie. Xilinx Design Language (XDL)) often contains all information of the placed and routed design. An adversary may exploit this information and directly manipulate the routed design. The entire software tool flow may be bypassed to create XDL representations from scratch. The open source tool TORC, as presented in [SWS+11], provides measures for manipulation of configuration data even after synthesis. Tavaragiri et al. have exploited this tool to generate an antenna using the remaining interconnection resources on the FPGA itself [TCA11, CA11].

Additionally, the CAD tools themself have to be reviewed as they are subject to modifications. Roy et al. raised the issue of tampering design tools in [RKM08]. These authors state that even if the development of FPGAs is done at secure facilities, the design tools may cause unintended side-effects.

System Downgrade Apart from counterfeiting a feasible attack on configuration data is performing a system downgrade. Without the knowledge of any key material or any secret present in the system, a replay attack of older configuration data may be performed. However, the mitigation of this threat has been intensively tackled in the literature (cf. [DK09, BET08]). For instance, Badrignas et al. proposed an architecture providing configuration data confidentiality and integrity between the IP provider and system developer and additionally avoid replay attacks [BET08]. These authors propose the extension to the existing vendor specific protection mechanisms (cf. Section 4.2) to support their approach. In particular they require additional registers to store versioning information of valid configurations.

The actual threat is well-known from software implementations. A known vulnerability exists in an older version of a configuration, allowing the adversary to access security-sensitive data. Although the configuration has been updated in all instances of the system, the attacker may still be able to make use of this exploit by foisting an older configuration. Therefore, the configuration data must be invalidated by some time information, such as a monotonic counter.

4.4 Cyber-Physical Threats

Disregarded Debugging Features Developers often include special features to simplify the silicon validation and debugging of ICs. Most often these features are neither documented, nor they are turned off after production. Developers have to take care that no single bit modification can be exploited to turn on these features again. A single fuse, may be activated using wafer probing workstation, or a FIB workstation.

The recommendation for these features is to document them and disable them properly for series production. According to Skorobogatov in [SW12], an FPGA vendor sold some of its products featuring military grade protection, but disregarded functions enabled a backdoor access to the device. Ignoring to disable these debugging features, inevitably results in an uncontrollable weakness of the product.

Configuration methods, such as JTAG are utilized for debugging during product development but also during product testing. Often these scan-chains or scan outputs reveal inside information of the implemented functionality and thereby they may be used to reduce the computational complexity of brute-force attacks. Thus, scan-chain interfaces have to be disabled for series production preventing readback access.

Invasive Attacks

In contrast to the non-invasive attack, an invasive attack requires physical modification of the device. Such an attack may also destroy some devices to gain deeper knowledge on the implementation. Consequently, these physical modifications can be detected by visual inspection. Invasive attacks usually study the design internals of devices to reverse engineer the functionality. With a general understanding of the device functions, the attacker is then able to extract security-sensitive information, e.g. by measuring the communication on the system bus.

Chip manufacturers also try to harden to devices against invasive attacks. Additional metal layers are placed upon the top of the device. These maze-like structures are intended to make it more difficult for the adversary to mount invasive attacks. The active shielding mechanisms may trigger a penalty as denoted in Section 4.2.1.

Chip Reverse Engineering In the classical sense, *reverse engineering* is considered an *invasive attack*, as the device may be (partly) destroyed. At least the package of the IC will be damaged during the process to get access to the silicon substrate of the IC. The structure of the chip is analyzed in layers to gain knowledge of the circuit function. Usual methods to gather this type of information on the circuit structure include etching, polishing, and even the modification of small structures on the die.

The package of a chip may be removed using chemicals, such as fuming nitric acid. After this step, the wafer is directly accessible for inspection and may be processed further. Similar procedures are also used during chip manufacture and during testing and debugging. Hence, wafer probing stations, electron microscopes, x-rays, and FIBs are present in many companies to analyze faults and for quality control.

An inexpensive variant of a chip reverse engineering attack is represented by polishing the wafer to disclose one layer of the hardware implementation at a time. Nohl et al. have demonstrated how they were able to reconstruct the different metal and transistor layers of a standard Radio-Frequency IDentification (RFID) chip in [NESP08]. They have taken pictures of the polishing results and used measures from panorama photography to stitch the resulting images together, to get a full view of each layer. The most expensive type of equipment they have used, has been a standard microscope for less then 1000$.

A very promising approach to mitigate the effectiveness of invasive attacks has been presented by Matthias Wagner in his COSADE keynote [Wag12]. An optical PUF at the bottom layer of the chip protects it form *flip-side* attacks. Polishing and even depackaging of the chip will lead to a failure in the PUF responses, rendering the device unusable.

Moreover, polishing and similar modifications of the chip are expected to influence the responses of an intrinsic PUF. Using the delay lines of certain PUF implementations, such as arbiter PUFs, to shield the security sensitive areas can be a feasible countermeasure against chip reverse engineering. Any modification or even measurements on such a shielding metal layer will most likely lead to failing PUF responses.

Bus Probing Bus probing refers to the process of recording or injecting messages on the system bus. This kind of attack can be carried out at PCB-level but is also possible at chip-level. Once the bus lines are identified, an adversary may use fine needles to connect to the wires on the PCB. A well-known communication bus may then be analyzed and messages can be eavesdropped or inserted by an adversary. The only difference between the chip-level and the PCB-level are the tools required to mount the attack.

An attack at the chip-level requires the device to be depacked first, before the adversary gains direct access to the bus lines. As already mentioned, the chip manufacturers try to hinder these attacks by additional layers of metal, covering the security-sensitive parts. At the chip-level the attack is more complicated. The width of the structure being much smaller on the one hand and the probing needle is adding additional capacitance to the signal on the other, leading to potentially incomplete signal transitions.

Especially the unencrypted data transfer from external memories is prone to *bus probing* attacks. This threat is especially present, if SRAM-based FPGAs are used. In this case, security-sensitive data shall neither be stored unencrypted in an external memory, nor it shall be included in the unencrypted configuration data of the FPGA.

Focused Ion Beam A Focused Ion Beam (FIB) workstation is a very powerful tool and also a very expensive type of equipment. During manufacture of a chip it is used to repair any defects or bugs in the masks used in chip lithography. It is possible to remove existing structures and deposit new layers of metal on the wafer level.

In general, the development of software for embedded systems requires a readback function of configuration data. During roll-out this function needs to be turned off for protection against adversaries. The easiest solution to accomplish this protection is to burn a fuse to disable access. Using a FIB workstation, the adversary is able to *repair* the fuse and thus get access to the protected information.

Christopher Tarnovsky at Flylogic was able to extract the key material from an off-the-shelf TPM chip, as presented in [Tar10]. Although this chip had active protection features on the top metal layer with active protection circuitry, Tarnovsky was still able to circumvent this protection and extract the security-sensitive key material. After he was able to expose the bus lines on the chip, the unencrypted parts of the data bus and the executed instructions have been monitored.

Fault Injection Fault injection attacks try to circumvent protection mechanisms by exploiting the unconditional behavior of integrated circuits on the edges of valid operating conditions. As an example, a device functions flawlessly at the specified core voltage, but if the voltage is dropping below a certain level, not all parts are functioning correctly. The same is true with the operating frequency. An adversary will try to abuse this property to his benefit.

An fault injection, using high energy pulsed light, been presented by Skorobogatov and Anderson in [SA03]. They were able to change to contents of SRAM cells using a photo flash on a depackaged chip. For a more effective and controllable solution they propose using laser flash pulses instead.

4.5 Common Security Scenarios

A common requirement in cryptanalysis, for systems processing security-sensitive data, is the Kerckhoff assumption. Kerckhoff stated that the it shall not matter if all details of the cryptographic system except the cryptographic secret fall into the adversaries hands. Given this knowledge, the adversary shall be unable to break the cryptographic function. In reverse, security-by-obscurity shall be avoided at any cost.

A security scenario includes all considerations that have been taken into account while designing the cryptographic system. Hence, it is crucial to know the considerations of system providers to deduct their provided level of security. In the following, the security scenarios by the TCG and the FPGA vendors are outlined. Common measures of security (cf. Section 3.4) are often taken into account.

4.5.1 Trusted Computing Group

According to [TCG11c], the TCG considers attacks threatening the integrity of protected capabilities or data in shielded locations. Undesirable side effects of protected capabilities and backdoor access to all protected data shall not be provided. The TCG requires the ability and preparation of each compliant module to be certified using the NIST FIPS 140-2 certification (cf. Section 3.4.3). However, the level of certification is not stated as a requirement within the TPM MAIN Specification [TCG11c].

A TPM shall also be resistant to any software attack from the underlying computing platform. Protected capabilities shall only be modified by authenticated commands. Non privileged modification of these capabilities is strictly forbidden. Moreover, shielded data may only be accessed or modified through authenticated commands.

4.5.2 FPGA Vendor

Most FPGA vendors do not explicitly state the *security scenario* they consider. The vendors are mostly interested in the protection of the IP in the FPGA rather then the overall system security. Hence, the major concern of FPGA vendors is counterfeiting and overbuilding of designs. Therefore, most of the vendors provide protection mechanisms for the configuration data in their products. Table 4.1 summarizes the solutions provided by FPGA vendors. Since authentication and encryption are included in current devices, the more and more security features are provided with recent devices.

4.6 TPM Specific Attacks

A security chip, such as a Trusted Platform Modules (TPMs), is always scrutinized by adversaries. Since the introduction of the first TPM-enabled systems in 2003 various weaknesses have been discovered. The most popular ones are outlined in the following.

The TPM is in general implemented as an additional chip attached to the computers motherboard. The connection to the platform is realized using the Low Pin Count (LPC) bus. The simplest attack performed on an TPM has been presented by Kauer [Kau07]. All security mechanisms provided by the TPM may be disengaged by simply connecting the reset signal on the LPC bus to ground using a paper clip. Thus, the adversary is able to fake a system reset and reinitialize the TPM after the modifications of the system are in place. The TPM is resetting its contents and the adversary is able to inject any measurement in the PCRs. Depending on the system configuration, this special attack may be characterized as invasive, i.e. the TPM is enclosed in a sealed area.

The *evil maid* is an adversary who has a (repeated) short term access to a computer using hard disk encryption, such as the cleaning personel in a hotel. This adversary is able to install a fake bootloader onto the device, which is logging keyboard inputs to password challenges. In a second step, either the maid has access to the same device again, or the malicious software sends the password via an established network connection. The TPM static root of trust should prevent this type of attack, but an adversary is still able to carry out this attack. After the user has entered the password the malicious software has to remove itself and trigger a reboot to enable the genuine boot process. The adversary then needs to access the device under attack a second time to extract the password.

A similar type of attack has been recently presented at the Chaos Communication Congress in Hamburg [MLF12]. During system standby the Full Disk Encryption (FDE) is still in the authenticated state, which allows the reconnection of the hard disk to another computer. As the protection of the encrypted device is disabled, an adversary may access all data on the device. In this setting, most hard disks do not require the authentication of the host platform after reconnection of the signal cable.

The name *cuckoo attack* reflects the fact that a user is not able to determine if the software is using a local TPM or if the commands are forwarded to a rouge TPM elsewhere. Parno detailed the problems of this attack in [Par08]. One of the solutions advocated by Parno is to put a hash value of the TPM keys on a tag on the computers case. The user may then use a QR-Code recognition software to scan this tag as a part of a usable authentication mechanism.

A successful chip reverse engineering attack has been presented by Tarnovsky in [Tar10]. Although the chip attacked by Tarnovsky featured numerous tamper protection mechanisms (on-chip light sensors, active metal protection mesh, etc.), he was able to circumvent all these. The development of the attack procedure took almost six months, showing that a highly motivated attacker, having exclusive physical access to a device, is able to break numerous anti-tampering measures. The impact of the attack is fairly small, since all TPMs use device specific keys and an attack to a particular TPM has to be carried out individually. For the implementation of trustworthy systems, as detailed in the following, the threats presented hereinbefore are considered wherever feasible.

5 Towards Trustworthy Cyber-Physical Systems

Cyber-physical systems are almost omnipresent in our daily life and are increasingly used to process security-sensitive data. Their complexity requires effective mechanisms to assess the trustworthiness of devices for this use-case. Users of these systems tend to imply the correctness and trustworthiness of utilized devices due to the lacking capabilities in providing information about the authenticity of devices. Moreover, service providers need to protect their own assets before access to security-sensitive data is granted. Consequently, solutions leading towards trustworthy cyber-physical systems are required.

A special case in this regard are reconfigurable systems based on FPGAs. These devices are getting more and more popular as building blocks for cyber-physical systems, to realize specialized components. Reconfiguration of hardware resources is beneficial for the realization of optimized components, but it may also be seen as a threat. The hardware configuration is also subject to malicious modifications and thus has to be protected.

The additional flexibility further enables shifting from resource efficient implementations to more throughput oriented ones, almost on the fly. In comparison to ASICs, the product cycle times are much shorter. The updates may be as short as software updates on commodity computers. Moreover, during development the designer benefits from this flexibility as it provides the ability for rapid prototyping.

An FPGA implementation may only be considered trustworthy if the configuration data is well protected throughout the product life-cycle. The commercial protection mechanisms available in current FPGAs completely lack capabilities to verify the configuration status of a system. A security architecture aiming at trustworthy reconfigurable systems is presented in the following. This architecture can be applied to various commercial solutions and it may be extended to support multiple trust anchors within a single system. A reference architecture for the latter is presented in sequel.

Commodity computers utilize specifications provided by the TCG together with a Hardware Security Module (HSM), namely the TPM, to establish trustworthy relationships. In contrast to commodity computers, cyber-physical systems have to fulfill much tighter constraints, which often leads to the inapplicability of generic approaches. The same is true for utilizing a TPM to realize this functionality. However similar techniques are required, the implementations valid for commodity computers may not be applied to cyber-physical systems directly. Provided that protection mechanisms are required to improve the overall security of cyber-physical systems, they may ideally be included within a single device. The application of an off-the-shelf TPM to serve as security anchor for cyber-physical systems is not always the best choice. Cyber-physical system need to thwart at least simple physical attacks, such as the TPM reset attack [Kau07] (cf. Section 4.6), which can be exploited to attest modified system states.

Since the currently valid TPM specification has been initially presented a decade ago in 2003, various other application areas emerged. The following list summarizes the major drawbacks of commercially available trust anchors with regard to cyber-physical systems:

- Unsuitability for resource constrained systems
- Deficiency in considering physical attacks
- Insufficiency in supporting multiple stakeholders

In particular, the concepts provided for trusted computing are merely applicable for resource constraint systems. TPMs support more than a hundred different commands realizing complex protocols. The utilized algorithms often operate on large keys, and consequently this require a lot of resources. Moreover, resource efficient symmetric cryptography is only an optional feature in the TCG specification [TCG11c].

The deficiencies of commercially available TPMs can be mitigated by the implementation of flexible reconfigurable trust anchors. The authors of [WP03] and [WGP04] already elaborated on the security of reconfigurable devices. They detail issues of commercially available FPGA-based systems and their use for cryptographic applications. One of the major advantages of FPGAs is their agility and flexibility to be customized for special use cases. Even the algorithms in fielded systems may be exchanged while still maintaining similar performance levels. Another important aspect they outlined is the implementation efficiency gained by throughput oriented parallel implementations. Of course, the use of reconfigurable devices may introduce certain weaknesses to the resulting system. These deficiencies by means of security, have been discussed in Section 4.4.

In sequel, novel trust anchor architectures are presented with reference to the aforementioned requirements on trustworthiness. Each of the architectures aims at mitigating one of the drawbacks presented above. A solution to all of these drawbacks at once is not presented, as the resource footprint is of the resulting architecture is to large in still being generally applicable to cyber-physical systems. Hence, the selection of the appropriate approach has to take environmental constraints into account.

5.1 Reconfigurable System Challenges

Apart from the fact that current TPMs are infeasible for the utilization in most cyber-physical systems, FPGA based systems lack measures to trustworthily report their configuration state. Only a fraction of the available devices fulfill the basic requirement of authenticated and encrypted configuration data. Moreover, by enabling the encryption of configuration data, the PR technology (cf. Section B.2) is unavailable for many devices.

For the given implementation platform utilizing FPGAs, it is a paramount requirement that trustworthy configuration and reconfiguration is provided. Without this support, the implementation of flexible trust anchors is virtually impossible. The FPGA vendors provide measures to protect the configuration data, but the trustworthiness of a reconfigurable platform can not be evaluated using the commercially available protection mechanisms.

Looking at commodity computer systems, it is only required to protect the software configuration of a system to determine its state. For reconfigurable architectures, for instance FPGA-based systems, the underlying hardware has to be taken into account. The configuration data of these systems represents the hardware and the software configuration alike. Thus, it is necessary to guard and protect this data in order to guarantee a trustworthy overall behavior of the platform. This can be achieved by constantly measuring incoming configurations and presenting a representation of the system state to a remote requester, to fulfill remote attestation. Not only the IP protection but additionally the correct system behavior metering is addressed by the approach presented in [FMMH11].

5.1.1 Storage of Security-Sensitive Data

The secure storage of cryptographic key material is of paramount importance as all data being protected relies on the secrecy of cryptographic keys. Additionally, the authentication and identification of devices and entities is provided by this keys. If any of these keys gets compromised all data and/or the system state protected by this particular key is at risk. In case of a compromised key it is save to assume that all data, under protection of this key, is considered to be unprotected.

The protection mechanisms of current FPGAs have been detailed in Section 4.2. According to user data storage, the provided measures by the hardware vendors are limited. Mostly the focus is on the protection of the configuration data, not on the processed user data. Consequently, the key storage, if present, does only feature a single slot for configuration data protection.

The protocol for secure remote updates of FPGA configurations as defined by Drimer et al. [DK09], mainly concentrates on the integrity and authenticity verification of an update. Additionally, this protocol requires the configuration memory to reside in a security boundary together with the FPGA. This corresponds to the security level 4 requirements stated in the multi-chip standalone scenario in [NIS02] (cf. Section 3.4.3). The security boundary may be realized using a hard epoxy material as suggested in [NIS02].

5.2 Trustworthy Reconfigurable Systems

Reconfigurable systems provide an additional degree of freedom to the designer but additionally require a reasonable amount of care when it comes to security. The following approach forms the basis for building trustworthy reconfigurable systems. This approach mimics the behavior of commercially available TPMs and applies a subset of their functionality to FPGA platforms. By doing so, the hardware configuration of the FPGA is monitored and the device status may be externally verified.

Although the hereinafter advocated concepts focus mainly on the implementation using FPGAs, they are not limited to these platforms. In particular, the security functions may be offloaded to an ARM TrustZone implementation and thus are usable in many microcontroller applications.

As aforementioned, the configuration data of FPGA-based devices requires maximum protection as it represents the intellectual property of the respective product. A naïve approach to achieve this kind of protection has been proposed by Eisenbarth [EGP+07] or Glas [GKS+08a]. These authors advocate to include a commercially available TPM to provide this functionality. However, a fraction of the features provided by a TPM is sufficient for the protection of the configuration data and hence the majority of the features will stay unused. Following this approach consumes too many

5.2 Trustworthy Reconfigurable Systems

resources, usually not available in resource constraint systems. Consequently, this creates an unacceptable overhead in cyber-physical system applications.

To ensure the trustworthiness of a reconfigurable platform, the protection features provided by TPMs are desirable. Nevertheless, the implementation should be additionally optimized to feature a reasonable resource/performance ratio. Due to the fact that reconfigurable systems can be applied in various scenarios, the presented approach shall also be efficient, to accommodate higher performance requirements. Even a step further is a concept providing multiple trust anchors, which enables the trust anchor architecture to be modified during their life-cycle.

The paramount requirement in implementing such flexible trust anchors, is however to ensure the trustworthy reconfiguration. For this, novel methods to partially reconfigure FPGA functionality while still monitoring the system state, have been developed. Utilizing an approach similar to common trust anchors, the hardware configuration is measured/hashed prior to loading. The measured state is then stored within the configuration registers of this architecture. To attest (i.e. trustworthy report) the current system state to an external entity, the entries of selected configuration registers are cryptographically authenticated and sent to the requester. This enables a remote requester to perform a simple verification of the system state by comparing the obtained values with previously recorded known-good values.

In addition to the trustworthy reconfiguration, mechanisms to protect the confidentiality of the configuration data are as well required. But confidentiality alone is not enough. The authenticity of the data is even more important than confidentiality. One might argue that an encrypted configuration bitstream may not be effectively modified, as the outcome of any modification is unclear. This is only partly true, as the adversary may not be interested in a specific modification but rather the tampering of the device to force unintended or unspecified behavior.

Imagine a malicious configuration, that may be able to physically destroy the FPGA (cf. [KV07]). An authentication mechanism effectively thwarts this kind of threats and protects against malicious modifications of the configuration data. The configuration data is protected by an authenticated encryption scheme, which is verified prior to the actual configuration of the device.

The *TinyTPM* architecture providing these features has been initially presented in [FMMH11]. This concept is more generic than the approaches provided by the FPGA vendors. Even if encryption and authentication schemes included in the most recent devices are available, the herein advocated solution is still providing additional benefit. The protection mechanisms by the vendors mainly focus on cloning and overbuilding of FPGA devices. Thus, authentication and encryption are limited to a single entity providing configuration data. The *TinyTPM* can be used to provide reconfigurable regions for multiple entities, which may be shared amongst these entities. The configuration data of the reconfigurable regions is protected by individual cryptographic keys. Moreover, the configuration history, as well as the current configuration, can be assessed for correctness.

Designing trustworthy, partially reconfigurable cyber-physical systems, demands at least for one dedicated cryptographic module for authentication and encryption. Additionally a cryptographic key storage is mandatory. The architecture presented hereinafter exploits a symmetric cipher and a generic PUF (cf. Section 3.2.3) for this purpose. Although AES has been used in most of the cases, the architecture is not limited to a specific block cipher. The authentication and encryption schemes may be replaced by others according to the requirements for the specific application.

5.2.1 The Use of Partial Reconfiguration

The *TinyTPM* concept presented hereinafter exploits the PR technology available in various FPGAs. Regardless of the availability of encryption and authentication mechanisms provided by the FPGA vendors, the *TinyTPM* is applicable for the implementation of a trustworthy system. Note that, the partial reconfiguration feature is disabled in various FPGAs if the encryption of the configuration data is activated. Hence, an effective mechanism providing cryptographic features is mandatory for these systems.

Systems that do not feature PR may not be monitored by the *TinyTPM*. The users of such systems have to rely on the protection mechanisms provided by the vendor. Although, the encryption and authentication schemes for static configuration data may seem sufficient, the measurement of configuration data and the provided encryption and authentication keys allow the implementation of trustworthy systems, even in these cases. Vendors may include similar features in their configuration controllers, allowing the users to exploit the full potential of trustworthy systems. The overhead to include these features may be derived from the resource requirements of the *TinyTPM*. Most FPGAs already feature a block cipher to encrypt configuration data, which may be exploited to implement trustworthy reconfiguration.

To guarantee a correct and trustworthy overall behavior of the platform, it is necessary to guard and protect the configuration data, as it contains both, hardware and software implementations. The concept of the *TinyTPM* further allows for partitioning the system in trusted and untrusted sections.

Trusted partitions are fully measured prior to (re-)configuration, whereas for untrusted partitions only the integrity and authenticity of the configuration data is verified. Thus, security-sensitive tasks may be separated from the others and may be monitored more closely, ensuring their integrity.

The trustworthy reconfiguration further enables IP providers to protect their assets. Each module is protected by individual authentication and encryption keys. Moreover, the system may be partitioned such that certain IP-cores reside in their own reconfigurable area. For this purpose, the reconfiguration architecture provided by the *TinyTPM* is additionally supporting the IP protection measures provided by current design tools.

5.2.2 System State Reporting

A digital system may only be evaluated as being trustworthy if the configuration can be reliably reported to an entity. The knowledge of installed software and utilized components is not sufficient to describe the configuration of any computer system. The decision if a system is trustworthy or not cannot solely rely on this static knowledge. Software/firmware and in the case of FPGAs also hardware can be modified. The current active configuration of the system has to be taken into account to determine the trustworthiness of the system.

As detailed in Chapter 4 most FPGA vendors provide measures enabling design security. However, there exists no generic solution to assess the integrity of the FPGA after configuration or (partial) reconfiguration. To support debugging during the design and development phase of an FPGA-based system, the external read back of the configuration data is often provided through the JTAG interface. This allows for cloning (cf. Section 4.4.1) if this functionality is not disabled in final products. Moreover, the malicious modification of the existing configuration data may be performed utilizing tools, such as TORC [SWS[+]11] to include a hardware rootkit as presented by Kucera and Vetter in [KV07]. A dump of the configuration data may include sensitive data, giving the attacker the opportunity for *bitstream reverse engineering* (see Section 4.4.2).

Only the reliable reporting of current configuration data guarantees a qualified assessment of the overall trustworthiness of the system. However, none of the FPGA vendors is providing procedures to obtain cryptographically ensured integrity information. The integrity of the configuration data is only controlled by error-detecting codes, such as CRC [PB61]. The main purpose of these integrity measurements, present in current FPGAs, is the protection against misconfiguration, which may damage the device.

The *TinyTPM* architecture mitigates most of the TPM specific attacks outlined in Section 4.6. Attacks exploiting the system bus are not applicable to the *TinyTPM* as it does not implement the LPC bus interface, nor it is attached as an external device. The evil maid scenario is also out of scope, as the configuration data of the *TinyTPM* may be encrypted and additionally authenticated. Moreover, the *TinyTPM* thwarts the issues of other implementations, such as the tamper resistant package in [GKS+08a].

5.2.3 Freshness of Configuration Data

Reconfigurable systems face the treat of configuration roll-back. Thus, the configuration data shall include some indication on the freshness of the data. If an adversary is able to load outdated configuration data onto the FPGA, the adversary may be able to exploit security vulnerabilities, which have already been corrected in the design. Such an indication of freshness may be realized using a monotonic counter. Whenever an updated design is provided the counter will be incremented and a signature combining the configuration data and the counter value is generated. A design is only configured if the counter value stored in the device is greater or equal to the value provided with the signature over the configuration data.

Kucera and Vetter raised the issue of FPGA-rootkits, representing malicious modifications of configuration data in [KV07]. They also pointed out that a freshness guarantee of the configuration data is required to prevent replay attacks. In current FPGAs, this protection mechanism is missing, such that outdated configuration data may be used to reconfigure the a device.

For the implementation of these freshness guarantees, several possibilities have already been presented in literature. The major difficulty is that FPGAs in general do neither feature monotonic counters directly, nor a secure storage which can be exploited emulate the behavior of monotonic counters. Drimer and Kuhn defined a security protocol for the remote update of FPGA configuration data in [DK09]. Their approach requires a tamper-proof package for the FPGA and an external NVM. Using this, it can be guaranteed that a genuine configuration is present after power-up. Moreover, their approach can be applied to any FPGA available today.

Kepa et al. advocate a similar approach [KMK09], but they require the extension of the underlying FPGA fabric. This extension includes the authenticated configuration at power-up and the exclusive access to security-sensitive information during power-cycles. However, this approach does not include any freshness guarantees.

5.2 Trustworthy Reconfigurable Systems

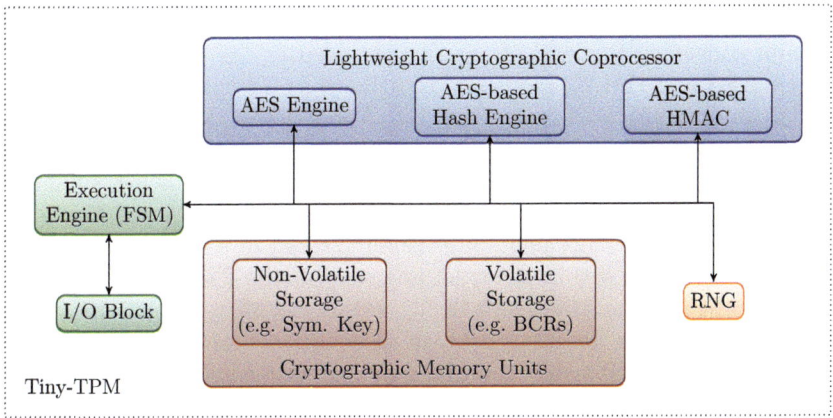

Figure 5.1: TinyTPM Architecture [FMMH11]

An alternative implementation to equip SRAM-based FPGA with an authenticated and encrypted storage has been proposed by [STP08]. This approach has been exploited to realize the secure storage in the *TinyTPM* and hence can be exploited to store monotonic counters according to the various device configurations. The number of counters is virtually unlimited using this approach, however to simplify implementation of the *TinyTPM*, the number of counters is fixed to one. With this mechanism in place, it is further possible to disable a particular core during the lifetime of the device.

5.2.4 TinyTPM Architecture

The overall architecture of the *TinyTPM* is very similar to the conventional TPM architecture outlined in Chapter 2. The fundamental building blocks of the *TinyTPM* architecture, as depicted in Figure 5.1, are cryptographic memories, a cryptographic coprocessor, and an execution engine. This altogether is conceived as a single hardware component. The cryptographic coprocessor performs encryption and decryption operations, as well as hash and HMAC [NIS08] computations. To cut down resource consumption, the cryptographic operations are all based on a single block cipher, i.e. AES. Hash and HMAC functions are realized by applying the block cipher-based Matyas-Meyer-Oseas hashing scheme, as presented in [MMO85]. This is in contrast to the cryptographic engines (RSA, SHA-1, HMAC) used in conventional TPMs [TCG11c]. Thus, in comparison to a conventional TPM, the *TinyTPM* is perceived as a lightweight module consuming less resources, without conceding the level of security provided.

The AES and HMAC modules are utilized in a generic composition to realize an authenticated encryption (cf. Appendix A.5). As both modules are based on a single AES implementation the authenticated encryption functionality is realized as a two-pass encrypt-then-MAC scheme, similar to other patent free approaches.

The integrity measurements are usually stored in a set of volatile configuration registers within the trust anchor. For the *TinyTPM* this is not different; the so called Bitstream Configuration Registers (BCRs) are providing volatile storage for integrity measurements (i.e. hash values) of the configuration data. Hence, the BCRs represent the equivalents of the PCRs in conventional TPMs. Upon each update of the configuration data, the contents of the BCRs are also updated.

An FPGA may contain multiple partially reconfigurable regions, therefore the *TinyTPM* provides a BCR for each of these regions. An additional register is available to store the initial configuration data, i.e. the static logic. If necessary, these registers may be combined or additional registers may be introduced to support more complex configurations. Furthermore, the software configuration may be recorded in individual registers, as well. The increased flexibility of this approach enables the customization of the system to meet the specific requirements.

The keys for encryption and for message authentication shall be stored in a non-volatile memory, which is only accessible from within the *TinyTPM* (cf. Section 3.1.1). Since only very few FPGAs provide user accessible non-volatile storage, different approaches have to be considered. For this purpose, the approach proposed by Schellekens et al. [STP08] is exploited providing key storage and access to an external authenticated non-volatile memory. This external memory is then used to host the updated configuration data and other non-volatile system parameters, such as monotonic counters. Moreover, Maes et al. presented a cryptographic key generator based on PUFs in [MVHV12]. These authors evaluated their implementation using FPGAs and thereby present a reference implementation for the generation of cryptographic keys on reconfigurable devices.

Utilizing a PUF derives a unique device dependent key from the physical characteristics of the device. By doing so, the impact of a possible key extraction is limited, as the adversary is only able to mimic a single device. The successful extraction of a single key does not affect other devices. Invalidating this particular key renders the attack of the adversary useless.

5.2 Trustworthy Reconfigurable Systems

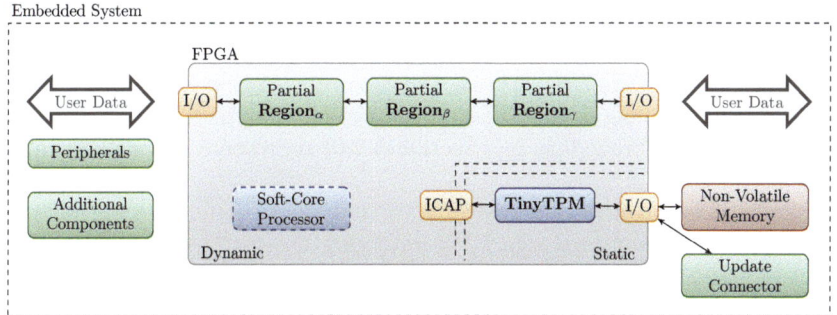

Figure 5.2: System View of TinyTPM Architecture [FMMH11]

For real world applications, keys shall be supplied for each IP provider individually.

The execution engine of the *TinyTPM* is triggered by external commands and enables access to the security functions. Providing trustworthy reconfiguration is its main purpose. Two fundamental methods are required to ensure trustworthiness, namely *measurement* and *attestation*. The execution engine therefore supports the commands `TinyTPM_Extend` and `TinyTPM_Quote`, respectively. Platform integrity measurement and system integrity reporting are performed analogously to the procedures described in Section 2.2.3 and Section 2.2.7.

The update protocol detailed in Section 5.2.7 mainly utilizes the `TinyTPM_Quote` command to assess the platform state before updating. Additionally, it makes use of a RNG to realize a mutual authentication that relies on rolling nonces. The actual update is carried out by utilizing the ICAP to overwrite the active configuration.

At system start-up and also during updates, platform integrity measurements are performed to reflect the system state of all configurations (hardware and software). During the attestation procedure the signed BCR contents are provided to the challenger for verification. The minimalistic requirements in designing trustworthy reconfigurable devices are reflected in the *TinyTPM* architecture.

An example of a complete system exploiting the *TinyTPM* as a Root-of-Trust is depicted in Figure 5.2. It includes an FPGA as the main functional element and features a set of partial configuration regions realizing the core functions of the system. This enables the realization of IP protection schemes by providing dedicated configuration regions for every IP-Core. For this, the *TinyTPM* provides means to attest the current state of each of these regions to a remote requester. Nevertheless, the proposed architecture also supports the extreme case that no reconfigurable region is utilized. In this case, the whole configuration is static and the measurement after the self-test in the bootstrap procedure (cf. Section 5.2.6) represents the initial system configuration.

The hereinafter proposed *TinyTPM* architecture should provide remedies against the following attacks. The intended use for the *TinyTPM* is in SRAM-based FPGAs. Since these devices do not feature a non-volatile storage for configuration data, this data has to be stored in an external memory. Even if the communication between this external NVM and the system is eavesdropped, the attacker should not be able to gain any knowledge on the keys stored in the NVM. Schellekens et al. advocated in [STP08] that authentication and encryption keys should be generated by PUFs. As a further solution they proposed to include the keys as a device ID into the configuration data. One of these measures for key storage may be selected according to the required protection profile of the final design. Moreover, including the microprocessor into the FPGA by means of a soft-core processors protects the communication to internal peripherals and memory from bus probing (cf. Section 4.4.2). Hence, this increases the attack resistance, as an adversary is not able to monitor unencrypted communication. Probing the memory bus and cold boot attacks [Sko02] are effectively mitigated if all security sensitive components are included in a single chip package. Protocol related issues, such as impersonation attacks and attacks on weak authorization data are also thwarted as detailed in Section 5.2.7.

5.2.5 Life-Cycle

The Life-Cycle of the *TinyTPM* consists in general of four subsequent phases. An generic overview is given in Figure 5.3

During the development phase the actual implementations of the PUF and its respective implementation parameters have to be selected. Further, the requirements on the configuration speed determines the type of the block cipher implementation. Dependent on the application scenario a customized solution may be provided. In general, the *TinyTPM* utilizes a block cipher as its main cryptographic primitive. For this reason, any AES variant may be implemented without any major modifications of the proposed architecture.

Realizing a PUF-based key storage requires a set-up phase, in which the helper data, to extract the key material from noisy PUF responses,

5.2 Trustworthy Reconfigurable Systems

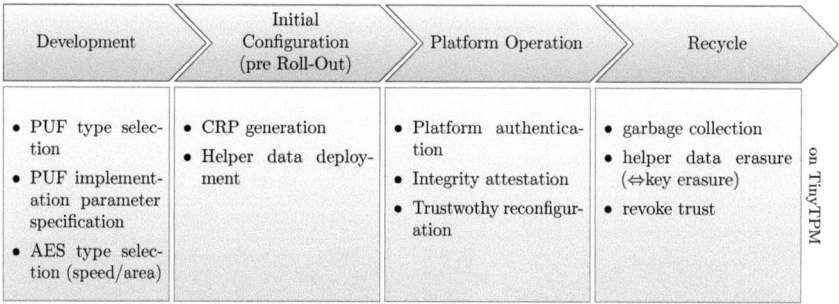

Figure 5.3: TinyTPM Life-Cycle

is generated. Authentication and encryption keys for later updates are implanted in the device, while it is still in a trustworthy environment, i.e. the IT-Department. These implanted keys are used to authenticate the update server and for the encryption of the update data. The internally generated keys are then exchanged with the update server to enable authenticity verification and encryption. Consequently the direct access to these internal keys has to be locked down by using non-volatile system parameters.

In the operational phase of the platform, all services provided by the *TinyTPM* are usable. The final recycling phase includes mainly the invalidation of key material and the revocation of this platform. Since reconfigurable platforms are exploited, the implementation of the *TinyTPM* may be adjusted to accommodate the new requirements and the life-cycle can be restarted.

5.2.6 Bootstrapping

Due to the volatile nature of SRAM-based FPGAs, the previous configuration is lost, as soon as the FPGA is powered down. Accordingly, their state is uninitialized during power-up. A *TinyTPM* enabled system reaches the operational mode by following the steps of the bootstrap procedure illustrated in Figure 5.4. Similar to the CRTM, the configuration data of *TinyTPM*, realizing all measurement capabilities of the system, is loaded into the static part of the FPGA's logic. This constitutes the `TinyTPM INIT` step in the bootstrap procedure.

Subsequently to the initial configuration of the FPGA, a system self test is executed as first operation. Utilizing the previously recorded reference values of the initial configuration, the integrity of the loaded configuration data is

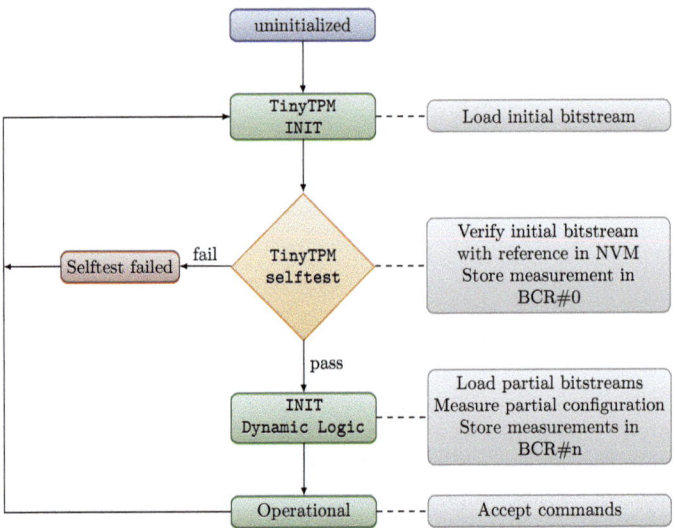

Figure 5.4: Bootstrapping Scheme [FMMH11]

verified, thus building the Root-of-Trust. The integrity measurements are stored in BCR#0 for later reference. The access to the PUF and therefore the access to the NVM is granted iff the initial configuration data is authentic. Note, during the initialization sequence all BCRs have been reset.

Depending on the results of the self-test, the bootstrap scheme continues either with the INIT Dynamic Logic step if the result was positive or it stops operation if the self-test failed. Different security requirements may prohibit the bootstrapping scheme from being restarted after a certain number of failures. This may be accommodated by additional fail states.

Once the initialization procedure is successfully completed, the partial configurations are initialized subsequently. At first they are measured and then loaded into the dynamic logic section on the FPGA during the INIT Dynamic Logic phase. The results of the integrity measurements are stored in individual BCRs for each of the partial regions. For later reference, a history of the measurements is kept in a log file similar to the SML in current TPMs. As already indicated above, the number of BCRs may be adjusted according to the application requirements.

The bootstrap procedure of the *TinyTPM* ends after the configuration data of all static and dynamic regions are measured and configured. During this operational state, commands are accepted by the *TinyTPM* either from

5.2 Trustworthy Reconfigurable Systems

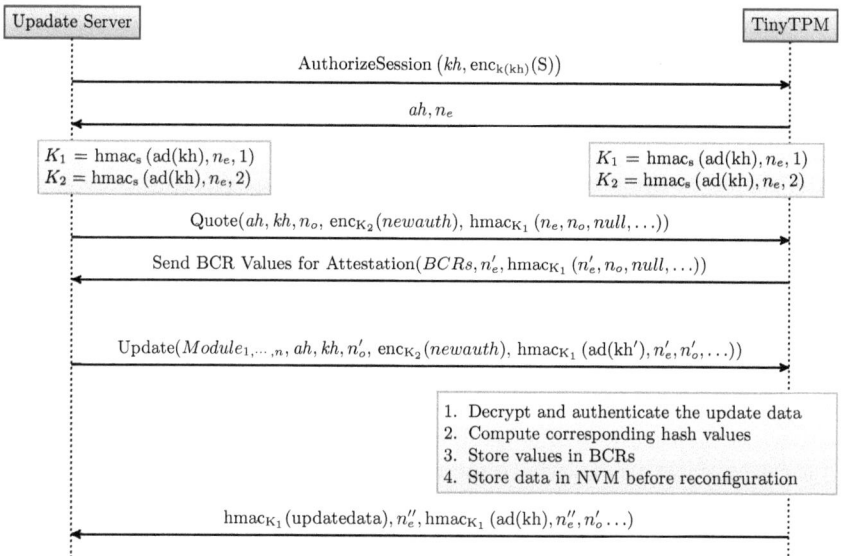

Figure 5.5: TinyTPM Update Protocol [FMMH11]

an external update server or from within the system. The configuration of the device is now valid and the overall system can be used accordingly.

Attacks trying to replay outdated configurations are effectively thwarted, using monotonic counters as detailed in [DK09]. Furthermore, Güneysu et al. advocate in [GMW12] that the configuration of an FPGA has to be monitored continuously, which can be easily adapted to the *TinyTPM* concept.

5.2.7 Update Protocol

A secure update of a reconfigurable cyber-physical system requires a protocol supporting mutual authentication of the communication partners. New configuration data from an update server has to be authenticated prior to configuration. Additionally, only authenticated remote entities should be able to issue commands on the *TinyTPM*. Thus, the protocol for providing secure updates mainly relies on the Session Key Authorization Protocol (SKAP) advocated by Chen et al. [CR10]. This protocol was proposed to mitigate the deficiencies in the protocols specified by the TCG.

Currently available authorization protocols for TPMs, such as OIAP, OSAP and the subsequent SKAP, support the following features. A remedy for replay attacks is provided by the rolling nonce scheme included in all of the above mentioned protocols. Two nonces are exploited and updated during the execution of the protocol, one side updates the *even* nonce n_e while the other updates the *odd* numbered nonce n_o. An ephemeral secret, by means of a session key, is used to protect a series of subsequent commands while the secret is supplied only once. The exposure of authorization values is therefore limited to a short period of time. In general, these protocols are used to proof the knowledge of authorization data to the TPM and do not supply the authorization values directly.

The SKAP has been designed to mitigate the cases of offline-dictionary attacks and impersonation attacks as detailed in [CR09, CR10]. Its main purpose is the secure session establishment between a user process seeking to access a TPM to execute commands. Therefore, this protocol has been adapted to accommodate the *TinyTPM* requirements as depicted in Figure 5.5. Note that the high-entropy session secret S is encrypted by a device dependent symmetric key. The π-calculus descriptions introduced by Chen et al. in [CR10] have been exploited to formally verify the modifications in the protocol. Moreover, the SKAP is considered for the follow-up TPM specification by the TCG.

Prior to starting the update process, an authorized session is initiated between the update server and the cyber-physical system by means of creating a secure communication channel, as depicted in Figure 5.5. The proof-of-concept implementation realizes communication using the UART protocol. The communication medium, however, is not fixed and may be altered according to specific capabilities of the system.

The update process is initiated by the update server using the `Quote` command, requesting an attestation of the system integrity measurements. The response of the *TinyTPM* includes in turn a set of BCR values authenticated by an HMAC, representing the previously recorded measurements of the system configuration. The successful verification of the attestation data is followed by issuing an `Update` command. The configuration data for specific partial regions is thereby sent to the system. Consequently, the data is first authenticated and then decrypted by the corresponding engines of the *TinyTPM* architecture. The AES-based HMAC engine and the AES engine are used for authentication and encryption, respectively. The update data, recorded in the BCRs of the *TinyTPM*, is computed by the AES-based hash engine.

5.2 Trustworthy Reconfigurable Systems

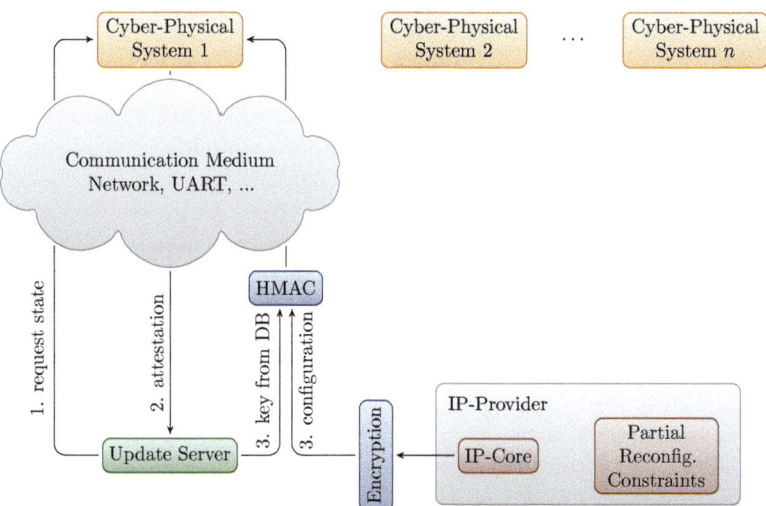

Figure 5.6: Hardware Configuration Update Flowchart [FMMH11]

These values are later used for attestation of the system. Before the actual reconfiguration takes place, the updated configuration data is stored in the NVM. The result of the update process is reported back to the update server by means of authenticated platform configuration data, indicating success or failure.

Every system features an unique key to protect other systems from replaying configuration data, which was not intended for this system. The update server facilitates a database of all these keys. Systems may be grouped together if they are intended to always share the same configuration. To this end, the same keys may be used for the whole group to simplify the handling of devices. This group key shall be only be used to decrypt configuration data from the update server.

In the sequel the proposed architecture and the update protocol are assessed by means of a proof-of-concept implementation. The previously outlined approach heavily relies on the Partial Reconfiguration (PR) feature present in current SRAM-based FPGAs. Further details on PR are provided in the Appendix B.2.

5.2.8 Proof-Of-Concept Implementation

The feasibility of the *TinyTPM* approach has been evaluated by a proof-of-concept implementation on a Xilinx Virtex-5 LX110T FPGA. Without loss of generality, the implementation has been simplified considering only the measurement and update of hardware configurations. If there is a need to further measure software configurations, they can be easily considered by adding more BCRs. Of course, slightly modified commands for updating software have to be accommodated as well. The additional implementation effort of adding software configuration registers is quite low, since the implementation of the *TinyTPM* is already providing the same measures for hardware assessments. In some sense, the software may be considered as an additional reconfigurable region. Hence, this case is conceptually covered by the proposed architecture.

For simplicity reasons, the proof-of-concept implementation only supports a single pre-shared key for all HMAC functions. Consequently, real-world implementations should at least support a minimum of two keys. Both, signature creation and the verification of authenticity requires separate keys.

The proof-of-concept implementation provides only a limited set of reconfigurable modules. These modules realize simple logic functions, such as **and**, **or**, and **xor**. The modules are dynamically exchanged using the partial reconfiguration features of the system.

The trustworthy reconfiguration provided by the *TinyTPM* is implemented using finite state machine, mainly consisting of the following four states: `IDLE`, `SELFTEST`, `QUOTE`, and `RECONFIGURE`. Initiating with the `SELFTEST` state after the initial configuration, the state machine proceeds to `IDLE` if the self-test was successful. The `QUOTE` and `RECONFIGURE` states for attestation and reconfiguration are reached upon external request. Thus, the `INIT Dynamic Logic` phase of the bootstrap procedure has to be triggered manually in our proof-of-concept implementation. The transition between the latter two states issues a signal to acknowledge communication. Results are then reported back to the requester, as seen from Figure 5.5.

As outlined before, at every system start-up a `SELFTEST` is conducted by applying a set of commands to the ICAP interface and measuring the active configuration data present in the FPGA's configuration memory. To this end, the output is grouped in blocks of 128 bits, consequently hashed by the AES-based hash module and the result is stored for later reference in a BCR.

The realization of trustworthy system integrity reporting is represented by the `QUOTE` state. Gathering a set of recorded BCR values and creating

5.2 Trustworthy Reconfigurable Systems

an authentication tag for these, compiles the system integrity report. As authentication tag an HMAC is computed sequentially for all BCR values in the set, before this set of BCR values together with the authentication tag is sent to the requester.

The reconfiguration of one of the partial regions is carried out in sequel to loading authenticated and integrity verified configuration data. Hence, the validity of the HMAC-based authentication tags is verified in the RECONFIGURE state while the data is transmitted to the system. The configuration data is transferred in blocks of 128 bit matching the block cipher construction. Since the HMAC construction utilizes inner and outer padding the message size has to be known in advance. Therefore, the number of blocks is reported at the beginning of each data transfer.

The two pass process of the authenticated encryption requires the incoming blocks to be stored. In the proof-of-concept implementation, these blocks are stored in a temporary memory location, whereas real-world applications would store the configurations directly in the NVM. The block-by-block transfer additionally enables the verification of the HMAC on the fly. Consequently, the HMAC computation is finalized after the last block of the configuration data has been transferred. The result is then compared to the last transferred block, which finalizes the HMAC computation. In case of a successful validation, the resulting HMAC value is extended into BCR prior to applying the configuration via the ICAP.

This concludes the measurement of the configuration and implicitly executes the TinyTPM_Extend function during the reconfiguration procedure. Instead of implementing the extend functionality directly, it has been simplified to only store the measurement results in the BCRs. This additionally allows to omit keeping records of the stored measurements. However a history of the measurements is required to exploit the full potential of the proposed architecture. Currently available TPMs facilitate a log file (i.e. the SML) to keep a history of integrity measurements for later reference.

5.2.9 Evaluation

The paramount requirement for an implementation supporting trustworthy reconfiguration is to use only a small amount of resources. Moreover, the time it takes to issue a configuration is also of importance. For some applications it is crucial that the reconfiguration is finished in a constraint amount of time.

The overall system design was evaluated by a specially developed control application. This application provides means for preprocessing of the

Table 5.1: Comparison of SHA-1 and AES-based Hardware Implementations of Cryptographic Hash Functions [FMMH11].

	Reg.	LUT	BRAM	latency [cycles]	max Freq. [MHz]	Throughput [Gbit/s]
AES-128	524	899	5	24	308.347	1.645
AES-Hash	813	1037	5	26	308.015	1.516
AES-HMAC	1107	1238	5	27	308.347	1.462
overhead Hash	289	138	0	2	~ 0	0.129
overhead HMAC	583	339	0	3	~ 0	0.183
SHA-1	1013	1754	0	83	193.445	1.193
AES-CCM	1035	2632	0	12	224.707	2.397

configuration data and performing a series of updates. The configuration data, as provided by the synthesis tool, contains further information that is not required during partial reconfiguration. Prior to the encryption and the generation of the HMAC, this additional header information is truncated. The resulting update may then be sent to the *TinyTPM*. Malicious modification of the update data results in inconsistent HMAC values, which in turn lead to the rejection of the update. During the evaluation the system integrity is verified before and after an update. This setup has been utilized for functional testing of the proposed proof-of-concept implementation.

Another important fact is the measurable performance of the system. Considering the implementation of the hash function, a comparison to other implementation variants is an interesting fact. In principle, any hash function is sufficient to provide system integrity measurements. Therefore, a comparison to the widely accepted SHA-1 function is carried out. Table 5.1 highlights the fact that an AES-based hash function is superior to a SHA-1 function in both, resource utilization and throughput performance. Looking at the numbers reveals that the AES-based approach with a straight-forward implementation already features a throughput advantage of more than 25%. The throughput optimized version (cf. Appendix A.3) using distributed logic, is estimated to outperform the SHA-1 by a factor of almost two.

The results displayed in Table 5.1 emphasize that the AES-based approach performs at almost the same speed as the underlying block cipher. Protecting the confidentiality of the configuration data already requires a block cipher, only the overhead for building the hash and HMAC functions should be

5.2 Trustworthy Reconfigurable Systems

Table 5.2: TinyTPM Hardware Resource Utilization Separated into Individual Components [FMMH11]

	Reg.	LUT	36Kbit BRAM
AES-128	524	899	5
Hash-Core	289	138	0
HMAC-Core	294	184	0
Execution Engine	662	453	0
PR ICAP	170	168	2
TinyTPM	1939	1842	7
TinyTPM incl. UART	2481	2595	7

taken into account. The SHA-1 function was selected for comparison, as current TPMs exploit it as their core hash function. An optimization, which is detailed in Section 5.3, further increases the overall reconfiguration performance. Note that the S-Box implementation in the AES-CCM requires 1152 LUTs but additionally saves 5 BRAMs.

The overall resource consumption of the *TinyTPM* is denoted in Table 5.2. The two most complex modules are the command execution engine and the AES block cipher. By means of the computation of the hash function, the AES, hash, and HMAC cores consume as much resources as a SHA-1 implementation. Whereas a current TPM consists of many other modules apart from the SHA-1, it can be concluded that the proposed *TinyTPM* only requires a fraction of the resources.

In its current implementation, the proof-of-concept ensures authenticity and integrity of the configuration data only. Although confidentiality is not covered in the implementation it is intrinsically present in the concept itself. The implementation overhead to include confidentiality in the design is negligible. The generic composition of the authenticated encryption utilizes a two pass scheme. Hence, decryption may be performed just before the configuration data is passed to the ICAP immediately before reconfiguration.

The proof-of-concept utilizes only two 36Kbit Xilinx Block RAM Modules (BRAMs) for storage within the ICAP module as the current application only considers a minimal amount of configuration data. Real-world applications shall facilitate NVM directly to store the configuration data. In conclusion, the resource utilization of the complete *TinyTPM* is slightly lager than the SHA-1 hash function. The *TinyTPM* can therefore be conceived as a lightweight implementation providing trustworthy reconfiguration.

The major goal of trustworthy reconfiguration has been presented by Eisenbarth et al., by including a complete TPM implementation on an FPGA. These authors estimate in their work [EGP+07] that this implementation requires roughly 3000 Logic Elements (LEs). Whereas an LE consists of a 4-input LUT and a single bit flip-flop. This corresponds to the resource consumption of the implementation presented in Table 5.2. The estimation of Eisenbarth does not include any figures regarding the reconfiguration time of their solution.

From the Figures 5.7 it can be seen that the overall resource consumption for the targeted FPGA architecture is very low. Even the smallest FPGA it is as low as 10% of the resources assuming that a real-world implementation may save two BRAMs. The histogram depicted in the Figures 5.8 illustrate the distribution of the maximum achievable frequency after synthesis. The Xilinx synthesis tools allow for various options, influencing the synthesis results.

Two different approaches have been chosen for the evaluation. The first approach evaluates the effects of applying all possible input combination of most of the synthesis parameters. The second approach uses the different cost tables, which represent different start values and weights for the place and route tools. This approach is also used by the Xilinx SmartXplorer tool and has also been exploited by Drimer in [Dri09]. The results of 4368 synthesis and place and route runs for the exhaustive method and 2626 for the cost-table based evaluation with differing parameters are depicted in Figure 5.7. The maximum achievable frequency of 235.018 MHz has been found using the exhaustive method.

Anti-Tamper security IP-cores, such as [Xil12d], require 1% to 8% of the, which is comparable to the advocated architecture hereinbefore.

Configuration Times

The partial reconfiguration of an FPGA is a time consuming task, which is dependent on the size of the reconfigured area. To estimate the time required for reconfiguration, a set of equations is presented in the following.

C_{BC} Clock cycles used to complete one block cipher operation.

$Blocks_{HMAC}$ Additional blocks used to generate an HMAC digest.

5.2 Trustworthy Reconfigurable Systems

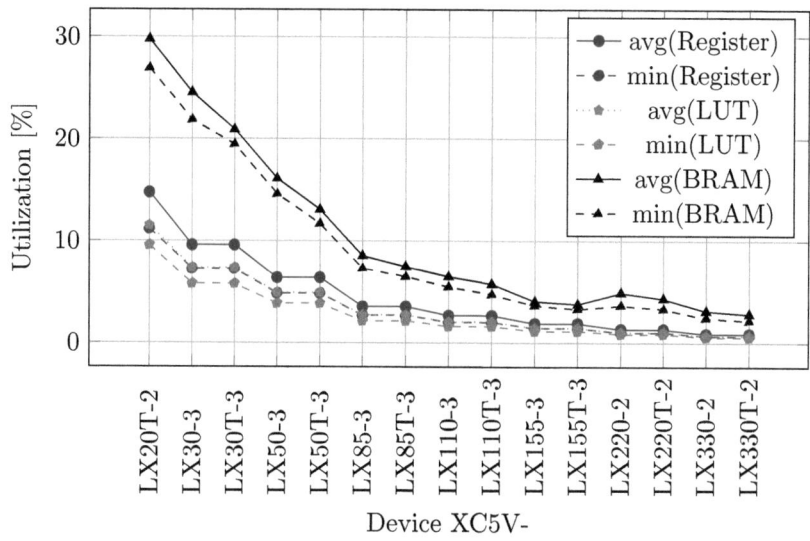

(a) Exhaustive Evaluation

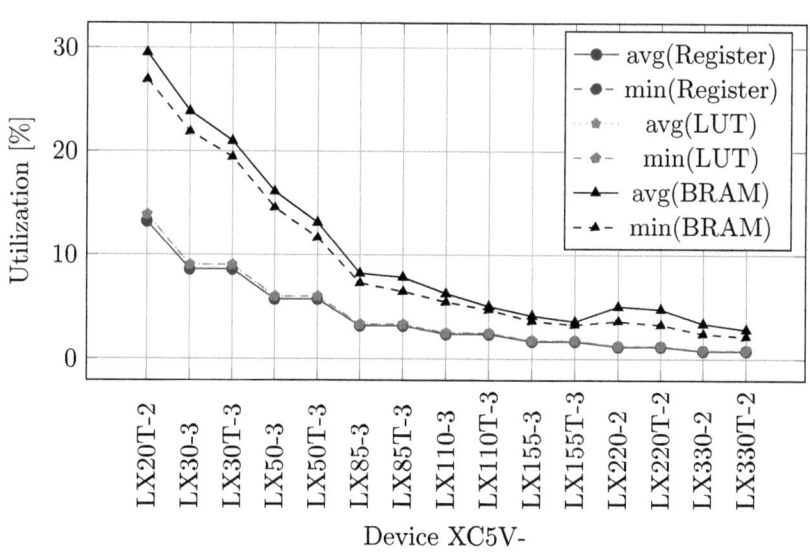

(b) Cost-Table Evaluation

Figure 5.7: Resource Utilization of the Proposed IP-Protection Scheme on Various Devices of the Virtex5-Family

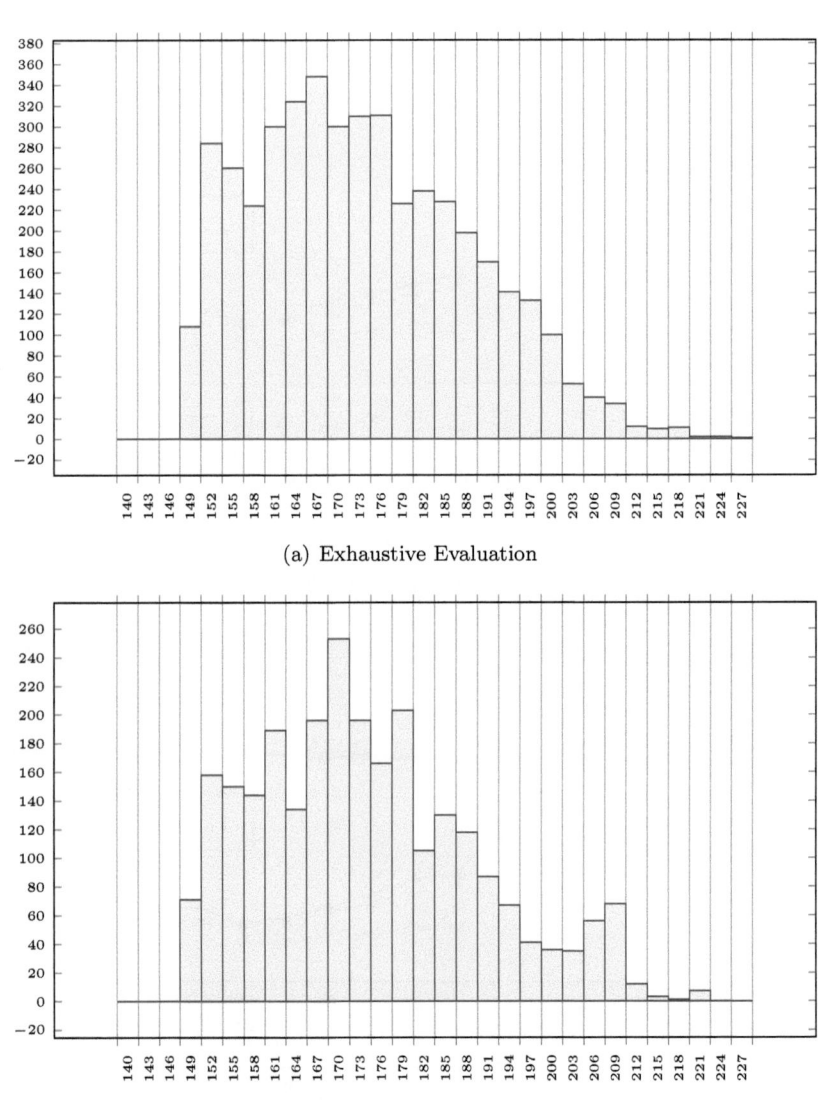

Figure 5.8: Frequency Histogram for the TinyTPM for all Virtex5 Family Devices

5.2 Trustworthy Reconfigurable Systems

$C_{Decrypt}$ Clock cycles used for decryption of all blocks

$C_{Command}$ Clock cycles used to process a *TinyTPM* command.

C_{two_pass} Overall number of clock cycles for a two pass authenticated encryption.

$Blocks_{ENC}$ Number of processed blocks for encryption.

$Config_{size}$ The size of the configuration data.

Since the *TinyTPM* decrypts the configuration data using AES, the number of encryption blocks $Blocks_{enc}$ can be derived by (5.1). Equation (5.2) denotes the number of cycles for an HMAC operation. Using the Matyas-Meyer-Oseas HMAC construction, the number of cycles for the block cipher and the block length of the message determine the number of cycles C_{HMAC} for the HMAC computation. After the successful authentication of the message, the decryption is performed in a second pass. The number of cycles for a decryption $C_{Decrypt}$ is denoted in (5.3). In summary the execution time for the complete two-pass scheme is given in (5.4). Equation (5.5) reflects the additional overhead for the command execution itself. The total reconfiguration time can be derived from (5.6).

$$Blocks_{enc} = \lceil Config_{size}/128 \rceil \tag{5.1}$$

$$C_{HMAC} = C_{BC} * (Blocks_{Enc} + Blocks_{HMAC}) \tag{5.2}$$

$$C_{Decrypt} = C_{BC} * Blocks_{Enc} \tag{5.3}$$

$$C_{two\_pass} = C_{BC} * (2 * Blocks_{Enc} + Blocks_{HMAC}) \tag{5.4}$$

$$C_{TinyTPM} = C_{two\_pass} + C_{Command} \tag{5.5}$$

$$t_{reconfig} = \frac{C_{TinyTPM}}{f_{max}} \tag{5.6}$$

The implementation dependent parameters for the previously proposed metric are given in Table 5.3. Due to the utilization of BRAMs an SBox-retrieval requires 2 clock cycles, which slows down the block cipher performance C_{BC}. The HMAC requires two additional blocks $Blocks_{HMAC}$ as the ipad and opad have to be included in the authentication code. The number of cycles for the AES in the original [FMMH11] implementation required 24 clock cycles. However, in Appendix A.3 an interface compatible implementation optimized for performance is presented.

Table 5.3: Proof-of-Concept Parameter Values

Parameter	Value
C_{BC}	24 cycles
$C_{Command}$	1 cycle
$Blocks_{HMAC}$	2 blocks

To give an estimation of the reconfiguration times, the typical sizes of the configuration data and the corresponding reconfiguration time $t_{reconfig}$ are detailed in the following. A comprehensive list of the configuration data sizes for all Virtex-5 devices is given in Table 5.4. Note that the size of the configuration data is denoted for the whole FPGA, which is not required for most applications. The time $t_{reconfig}$ represents the reconfiguration time for a single encryption block, performed by a *TinyTPM* design operating at 100 MHz.

5.3 TinyTPM Optimizations

Although it was not part of in the original contribution specified in [FMMH11], a measured boot (cf. Section 2.2.4) may be implemented with a negligible overhead. In addition to the mere recording of the HMAC, the configuration of the device is stopped as soon as a missmatch between the expected and the actual value is detected.

The configuration scheme in [FMMH11] uses a 2-pass encryption and authentication scheme, which doubles the reconfiguration time since the configuration data has to be processed twice. Additionally, the reconfiguration speed itself may be improved by applying some of the concepts summarized in Section 5.3.2.

5.3.1 Authenticated Encryption

The original approach presented in [FMMH11] is utilizing a block cipher based hashing and HMAC scheme. The generic composition (cf. Appendix A.5) of an AES-based encryption and the Matyas-Meyer-Oseas Hash is exploited to realize the encrypt-then-MAC function. There exist various schemes to realize authenticated encryption, which can be implemented more efficiently. A comprehensive summary of existing approaches is given in [vT05, Authenticated Encryption].

5.3 TinyTPM Optimizations 111

Table 5.4: Typical Size of Virtex-5 Configuration Data [Xil11d] and Estimated Reconfiguration Times (TinyTPM@100MHz).

Device Name	Size [bits]	#enc. Blocks	$t_{reconfig}[\mu s]$
XC5VLX30	8,374,016	65,422	314.0306
XC5VLX50	12,556,672	98,099	470.8802
XC5VLX85	21,845,632	170,669	819.2162
XC5VLX110	29,124,608	227,536	1,092.1778
XC5VLX155	41,048,064	320,688	1,539.3074
XC5VLX220	53,139,456	415,152	1,992.7346
XC5VLX330	79,704,832	622,694	2,988.9362
XC5VLX20T	6,251,200	48,838	234.4274
XC5VLX30T	9,371,136	73,212	351.4226
XC5VLX50T	14,052,352	109,784	526.9682
XC5VLX85T	23,341,312	182,354	875.3042
XC5VLX110T	31,118,848	243,116	1,166.9618
XC5VLX155T	43,042,304	336,268	1,614.0914
XC5VLX220T	55,133,696	430,732	2,067.5186
XC5VLX330T	82,696,192	646,064	3,101.1122
XC5VSX35T	13,349,120	104,290	500.597
XC5VSX50T	20,019,328	156,401	750.7298
XC5VSX95T	35,716,096	279,032	1,339.3586
XC5VSX240T	79,610,368	621,956	2,985.3938
XC5VFX30T	13,517,056	105,602	506.8946
XC5VFX70T	27,025,408	211,136	1,013.4578
XC5VFX100T	39,389,696	307,732	1,477.1186
XC5VFX130T	49,234,944	384,648	1,846.3154
XC5VFX200T	70,856,704	553,568	2,657.1314
XC5VTX150T	43,278,464	338,113	1,622.9474
XC5VTX240T	65,755,648	513,716	2,465.8418

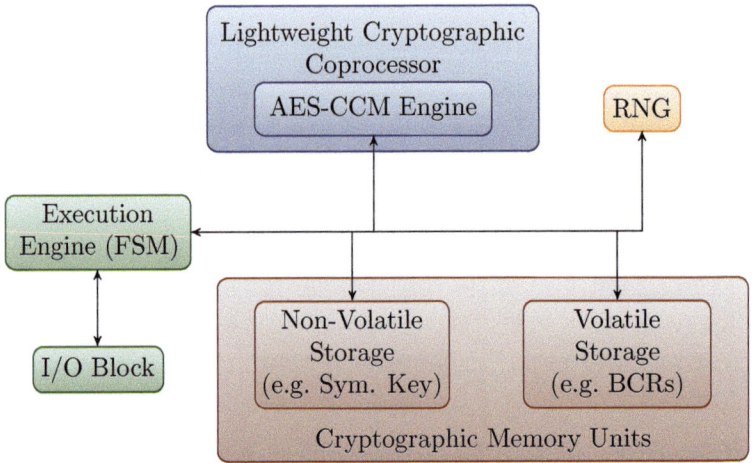

Figure 5.9: AES-CCM-based TinyTPM Architecture

Drimer proposed in [Dri07] to use two parallel AES cores to realize configuration data protection for FPGAs. This concept uses one AES for encryption and the other for authentication to realize a 1-pass generic composition approach. He did not include performance or resource utilization figures and related his decision to use two parallel to the implementation results presented by Parelkar [Par05]. Furthermore, this approach requires two separate keys for encryption and authentication. The resource utilization for Drimer's approach is expected to be twice as much as a single AES implementation with an additional 128-bit comparator.

The optimization of the *TinyTPM* should reflect the shortcomings of the 2-pass generic composition approach exploited in [FMMH11]. Since most of the existing single pass schemes are protected by patents (cf. [vT05]) an open solution has been considered. Schemes, such as CCM have been approved by NIST [Dwo07] but are based on a 2-pass authenticated encryption. The OpenCores AES-CCM implementation [dlP12] utilizes an amount of resources comparable to the *TinyTPM* approach as seen from Table 5.5. However, the throughput of the CCM variant is not comparable to the *TinyTPM* implementation.

Black stated in [vT05] that the generic composition of authentication and encryption schemes may be straightforward but it may not always be secure. The particular properties of the overall encryption scheme will depend on how the data will be encoded and which authentication and encryption schemes

5.3 TinyTPM Optimizations

Table 5.5: Comparison between Authenticated Encryption Schemes

Name	Reg.	LUT	BRAM	latency [cycles]	max. Freq. [MHz]	Throughput [Gbit/s]
AES-HMAC [FMMH11]	1107	1238	5	27	308.347	1.462
AES-CCM [dIP12]	1096	1274	5	33	231.59	0.890
AES-CCM (this work)	1035	2632	0	11	237.53	2.764 (1-pass)

have been selected. Thus, the careful selection of the authentication and encryption schemes is necessary. A widely accepted authenticated encryption scheme shall be considered to support this issue. Moreover Black states that there is no parallel implementation of the AES-CCM scheme available.

To mitigate the shortcomings of the 2-pass approach and to reflect the optimizations possible for AES-based schemes a novel parallel AES-CCM scheme has been implemented. This parallel authentication and encryption scheme almost doubles the throughput of the straight forward implementation.

The analysis of the AES-CCM scheme has shown that a rescheduling of the encryption part enables the parallel execution of authentication and encryption. Table A.4 denotes the scheduling of the parallel approach. The major difference is that the encryption and authentication in step three are executed in parallel. Moreover, most implementations require the encrypted data to be supplied twice to the core, first for the authentication of all blocks and second for the encryption of the payload. Hence, a novel 1-pass authenticated encryption scheme is presented in the following.

$Blocks_{auth}$ Associated data section, which is not encrypted.

$C_{AES-CCM}$ Clock cycles used to complete one block cipher operation.

C_{one_pass} Overall number of clock cycles for a one pass authenticated encryption.

$$C_{AES-CCM} = C_{BC} * (Blocks_{auth} + Blocks_{enc} + 1) \tag{5.7}$$
$$C_{one\_pass} = C_{AES-CCM} + C_{Command} \tag{5.8}$$

Table 5.6: AES-CCM Parameter Values

Parameter	Value
C_{BC}	11 cycles
$C_{Command}$	1 cycle

Using this optimization, the number of processed blocks is cut in halve. The comparison of the *TinyTPM* and the proposed implementation can be clearly derived from the Equations (5.5) and (5.7), which shows the benefit of the CCM approach. The CCM scheme requires a single key for authentication and encryption, and the AES is only used in forward/encryption mode for both encryption and decryption. This allows to combine the two independent keyschedules for the two parallel AES instances into shared resource.

An additional asset of the AES-CCM approach is the possibility to include associated data with every encryption cycle. Thus, the message may be composed of an unencrypted and an encrypted part; both these parts are authenticated. For the application of the AES-CCM in the *TinyTPM* this can be carried out to the two extremes. Authentication commands often only require the verification of authentication codes, this may be implemented with AES-CCM computations that only use the associated data section and no encrypted data at all. The AES-CCM mode of operation allows all possible combinations of associated data and encrypted data (cf. [Dwo07]).

Figure 5.10 presents the improved architecture realizing a pseudo single-pass implementation. The parallel execution of the encryption and authentication enables this improvement in speed. For resource efficiency, not the complete AES cores are parallelized. The key schedule was extracted from the datapath operations of the scheme, since both cores use the same roundkeys and this information is then shared between both AES cores. Further details on the implementation results can be found in the Appendix A.5.2.

Evaluation

The performance of the advocated AES-CCM scheme is evaluated against different measures. First, a comparison to the original *TinyTPM* is given and second, the scheme is compared to well-known implementations in the literature.

The reconfiguration times of the CCM-based solution and the original generic composition approach of the *TinyTPM* is depicted in Figure 5.11.

5.3 TinyTPM Optimizations

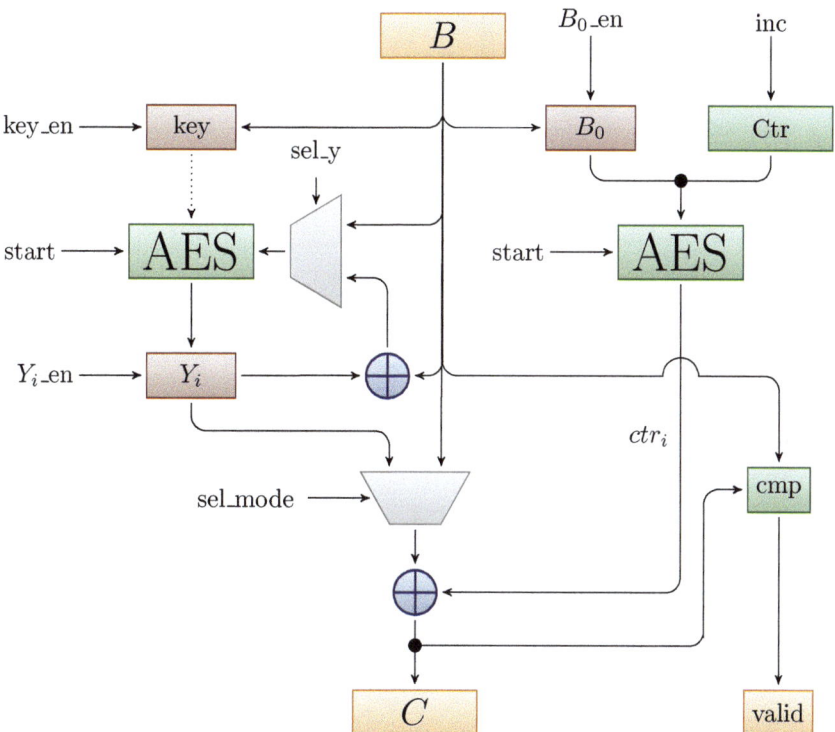

Figure 5.10: Datapath of the AES-CCM Architecture

It is clearly visible that the CCM approach features the lower configuration times. The direct comparison of the underlying data shows that the CCM approach is 4.3 times faster than the original *TinyTPM*. This performance benefit is achieved by using only twice as much LUTs and without using any BRAMs, as denoted in Table 5.5.

A comparison of various CCM implementations is given in Table 5.7. The throughput column has been divided to reflect the fact that the effective throughput of 2-pass schemes is only half of the AES throughput. If the whole authenticated encryption scheme is concerned, both passes have to be taken into consideration to calculate the throughput. The 1-pass column denotes the throughput values with regard to the overhead of the second pass. Missing values, that have been derived from existing values, are denoted in brackets.

Table 5.7: Comparison of AES-CCM Hardware Implementations on Various Xilinx Device Families

(a) Virtex5-LX110T-3

Name	# Pass	Reg.	LUT	Slices	BRAM	latency [cycles]	max. Freq. [MHz]	Throughput [Gbit/s] 2-pass	1-pass
[dIP12]	2	1096	1274	–	5	33	231.59	0.890	(0.449)
[Hel11]	2	–	–	490	–	23	274	1.525	(0.763)
AES-CCM	1	1035	2632	793	0	11	237.53		2.764

(b) Virtex4-LX60-11

Name	# Pass	Reg.	LUT	Slices	BRAM	latency [cycles]	max. Freq. [MHz]	Throughput [Gbit/s] 2-pass	1-pass
[Par05]	2	2830	3308	2799	14	22	87.5	(0.5091)	0.255
[AFCM08]	2	–	1995	1200	18	(13)	152.42	1.951	(0.976)
AES-CCM	1	1037	8005	4690	0	11	133.65		1.5552

(c) Spartan3-4000-4

Name	# Pass	Reg.	LUT	Slices	BRAM	latency [cycles]	max. Freq. [MHz]	Throughput [Gbit/s] 2-pass	1-pass
[AFCM08]	2	–	1661	1041	18	(13)	86.34	1.087	(0.544)
[LTRHDP06]	2	–	–	2154	106	12	100.08	1.051	(0.503)
AES-CCM	1	1374	7934	4115	0	11	81.1		0.9437

5.3 TinyTPM Optimizations

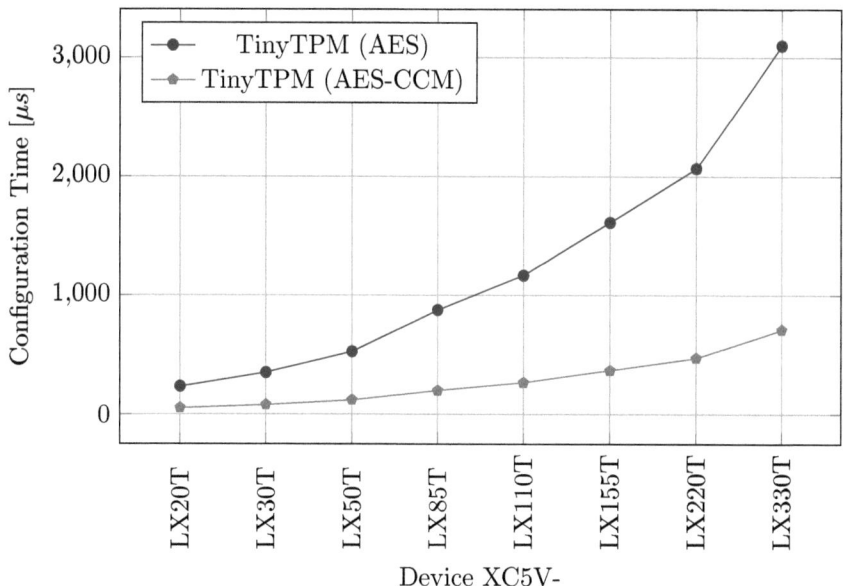

Figure 5.11: Reconfiguration Time Comparison Between the Original TinyTPM [FMMH11] and a CCM-based Implementation on Various Devices of the Virtex5-Family

The Virtex-5 implementation results in Table 5.7(a) include the synthesis results of a AES-CCM core by de la Piedra in [dlP12]. This realization requires 33 clock cycles for each AES encryption. The throughput values of this implementation have been directly derived from the synthesis results of the implementation. A commercially available AES-CCM module from Helion Technology as stated in [Hel11] has been included. Although it does not include all the information available from the other sources, it still represents a common yardstick for the throughput.

As Parelkar already pointed out in [Par05], authenticated encryption is perfectly feasible to protect the configuration data of reconfigurable devices. The throughput of the Parelkar variant of the AES-CCM variant on a Virtex4 device, as denoted in Table 5.7(b), already includes the 2-pass structure of the implementation. In contrast, the implementation results presented by Algredo-Badillo et al. in [AFCM08] denote the throughput without taking the 2-pass structure into account. Although the herein presented implementation exceeds the resource requirements of the other two as it

Table 5.8: Partial Reconfiguration Throughput for Xilinx Devices

	Device	Design	ICAP [MHz]	Throughput [MB/s]	[Gbit/s]
[CZS+08]	Virtex-2Pro	PLB	100	89.9	(0.7192)
[CZS+08]	Virtex-4 FX	PLB	100	295.4	(2.3632)
[CAAS10]	Virtex-2Pro	PLB	100	93.94	(0.75152)
[CAAS10]	Virtex-2Pro	PLB	150	136.8	(1.0944)
[CAAS10]	Virtex-4	MPMC	100	400	(3.200)
[CAAS10]	Virtex-4	MPMC	140	560	(4.480)
[CAAS10]	Virtex-5	MPMC	100	400	(3.200)
[CAAS10]	Virtex-5	MPMC	200	800	(6.400)
[CAAS10]	Virtex-5	MPMC	300	1200	(9.600)
[LKLJ09]	Virtex-4 FX	DMA	100	82.6	(0.6608)
[LKLJ09]	Virtex-4 FX	MST	100	235.2	(1.8816)
[LKLJ09]	Virtex-4 FX	BRAM	100	372.4	(2.9792)
[HKT11]	Virtex-5 LX110T		500	2000	(16.000)
[HKT11]	Virtex-5 LX110T		533	2132	(17.056)
[HKT11]	Virtex-5 LX110T		550	2200	(17.600)
[BCB+12]	Virtex-4 FX12	SEDPRC	220	838	(6.704)

does not use BRAMs. Not using BRAMs increases the number of 4-Input LUTs by 4608. The AES-CCM variant outperforms the implementations of Parelkar and Algredo-Badillo by a factor of at least 1.5 as it requires only one pass of the AES-CCM scheme.

Table 5.7(c) has been included to estimate the feasibility of the herein advocated approach for the cost efficient implementations. Depending on the requirements of the application, the AES-CCM core is implemented without the usage of BRAMs. Again, it can be seen from equation (A.3) that 4608 LUTs may be replaced by BRAMs to realize the SBox functionality (cf. Appendix A.3.2).

5.3.2 Partial Reconfiguration Performance

Initially the partial reconfiguration was limited to eight bit transfers at an ICAP frequency of 100 MHz [Xil07c]. In more recent devices the ICAP access

5.3 TinyTPM Optimizations

width is supported up to 32 bit. [Xil12c] specifies the maximum throughput of an Virtex-5 ICAP to achieve a maximum throughput of 3.2Gbit/s. However, using encrypted configuration data the access to the ICAP is often limited to the eight bit parallel mode [Xil11d]. Since this significantly increases the configuration time, the *TinyTPM* can be used to effectively mitigate this performance limitation.

The reconfiguration time may be a key factor some applications, as it indirectly defines the switching frequency of partially reconfigured hardware tasks. In the set-top-box application example, as outlined in Section 6.3, the reconfiguration of the encryption scheme has to be completed within the channel switching cycle. To support these and other applications, research strives in pushing the reconfiguration performance of FPGAs to its limits. Table 5.8 compiles the recent achievements for Xilinx devices. The throughput denoted in the last column has been derived from the results stated in the corresponding work to enable the comparison to other throughput values stated in this work.

To match even with the highest available reconfiguration approaches the encryption of data may be realized using a pipelined AES variant, as presented in [Hut12]. This implementation provides a throughput higher than 33Gbit/s, which exceeds even the implementations, which are overclocking the ICAP.

The sequential structure of most hashing algorithms limits the application of pipelined implementations. However, such a solution is only feasible, if a minimal reconfiguration time is one of the required design goals. In this case the additional cost of a parallel hash function to improve the performance of this part is required.

The figures shown in Table 5.8 mainly show the measurements of small configuration data packets. Hansen et al. [HKT11] and Claus et al. [CZS+08] raised the issue of sustainably supplying configuration data, even from the DDR2 memory. For an improved resource-performance ratio, the maximum speeds achievable for memory transfers have to be taken into account.

Even at the highest configuration frequencies, the *TinyTPM* is still able to compete with the current solutions. This is due to the fact that the ICAP access for encrypted reconfiguration is limited to eight bit. The highest reconfiguration design [HKT11] is in this case only twice as fast as the CCM-based approach. Moreover, it is not clear that the encryption hardware in the FPGA device is capable of decrypting the incoming data stream at the same speed, as it is provided by the ICAP.

5.4 Physical Attack Resistance

Physical attacks have already become a common threat, as the cost for analysis equipment is constantly dropping. The physical attack resistance of current FPGA devices is under investigation in academia. The protection mechanisms provided by the FPGA vendors have been successfully circumvented using side-channels. In [MBKP11, MKP11, MKP12] Moradi et al. were able to demonstrate the results of side-channel attacks on these protection mechanisms. Therefore an effective protection mechanism for partial reconfiguration in regard to physical attacks is required.

Whenever an adversary is able to extract the authentication and encryption keys from an FPGA device, the adversary is gaining the ability to clone the device functionality. Furthermore, the configuration data may then be analyzed to extract parts of the design.

This optimization had been taken into account as it was expected to improve two properties of the already existing design. On the one hand, the lightweight PRESENT algorithm improves the resource footprint of the *TinyTPM* implementation. On the other, the resulting side-channel aware implementation was expected to consume as much resources as the original implementation.

5.4.1 Side-Channel Aware TinyTPM Architecture

In order to provide a side-channel aware implementation of the *TinyTPM* two steps have been performed. First, a lightweight block cipher has been introduced to reduce the amount of resources required by the protection scheme. Second, the block cipher has been equipped with a masking function to improve its resistance against side-channel attacks.

The PRESENT block cipher [BLK+07] has been chosen for the implementation because of its resource footprint. This cipher has been designed by Bogdanov et al. in [BLK+07] to be resource efficient and its implementations require only a fraction of standard AES implementations. The architecture of the PRESENT block cipher is similar to the AES and also consists of a substitution permutation network. The cipher has been specified to operate on blocks of 64 bits and uses 80 bit or 128 bit keys for encryption. In contrast to the 10 to 14 rounds of the standard AES [NIS01], the PRESENT cipher requires 31 rounds for each encryption cycle. The evaluation of the side-channel properties has been presented in [SFH11], thus the following compares the architecture to the previously specified *TinyTPM*.

5.4 Physical Attack Resistance

In [SFH11] three different basic implementation variants of the PRESENT block cipher have been considered. The two standard variants using 80 and 128 bit keys on blocks of 64 bits and a throughput optimized variant which consists of two parallel datapaths of the PRESENT cipher using 128 bit keys. This PRESENT variant operates on blocks of 128 bits, which makes it a straight forward replacement for the block cipher used in the *TinyTPM*. The major drawback of the resource efficient implementation using the PRESENT cipher is the throughput of the overall system.

The number of clock cycles required for reconfiguration using the PRESENT-based approach can also be derived from 5.1 to 5.6. The parameters in comparison to the original *TinyTPM* implementation only differ in the number of clock cycles required for one block cipher encryption $C_{BC} = 33$.

5.4.2 Evaluation

Figure 5.12 denotes the resource utilization of the side-channel aware implementation of the *TinyTPM*. 2626 individual synthesis runs had been completed to compile the information summarized in Figure 5.12. It can be seen from this figure, that it was possible to reduce the amount resources consumed by the *TinyTPM* and at the same time improve its side-channel characteristics. The highest frequency resulting from all these synthesis runs was 264.201MHz. The side-channel analysis results have been presented in [SFH11].

The AES block cipher is heavily investigated in terms of its side-channel properties. Apart from the replacement of the AES block cipher with a side-channel aware PRESENT variant, it is straightforward to include a side-channel aware implementation of AES.

5.4.3 Tamper Protection

The protection against tampering plays a crucial role for the overall resistance against physical attacks provided by a solution. Hence, most SmartCards provide measures to protect against these kind of attacks. The FPGA vendors already provide solutions for their products (cf. [Alt08, Xil11b]).

Current devices feature voltage and temperature sensors to identify a tampering of the operating conditions. Moreover, the multiple unsuccessful programming attempts of the FPGA can also lead to the zeroization of key material and/or FPGA configuration data. For solutions using battery backed-up keys to protect configuration data, it may be as simple as setting a special pin to zero to activate key zeroization.

122 5 Towards Trustworthy Cyber-Physical Systems

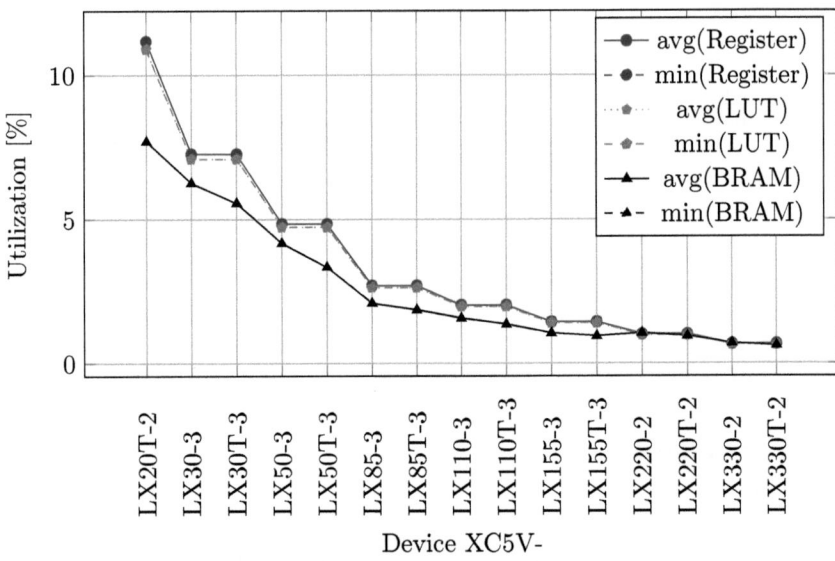

(a) Cost-Table Evaluation – Resources

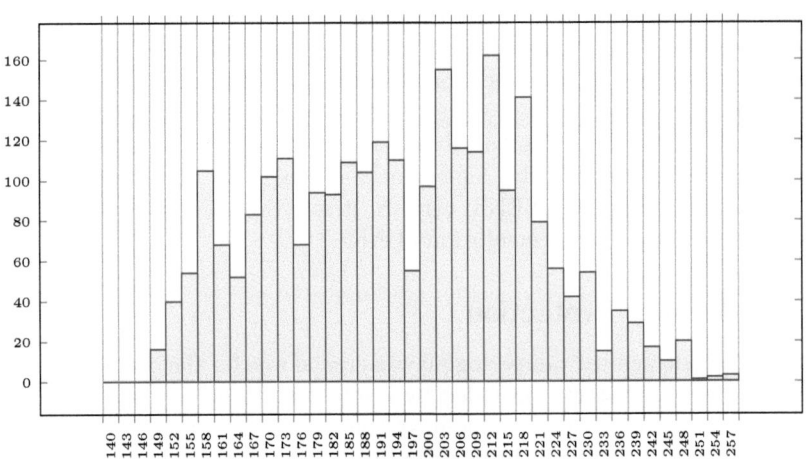

(b) Cost-Table Evaluation – Frequency Histogram

Figure 5.12: Resource Utilization of Various Implementation Variants for the Proposed IP-Protection Scheme on Different Devices of Virtex5-Family

For special application scenarios the key data residing in the device can be protected further by introducing a tamper resistant coating. Certain vendors support this kind of protection for their devices (cf. [Alt08]). Similar simple but effective measures can be introduced in the architecture at almost no additional cost.

5.5 Supporting Multiple Stakeholders

The requirements for trustworthy systems are constantly changing with the emergence of new technologies. The TPM has been specified to mitigate the weaknesses of commodity computers to securely store security-sensitive data. Thus, these modules have currently to cope with issues, they have not been designed for. Applications such as mobile computing, cloud services, and even IPTV require protection mechanisms to protect the individual assets of various stakeholders. Thus, the incapability of TPMs in supporting multiple stakeholders by means of sharing the resources of a single platform is considered as one such shortcoming.

If the emerging market of mobile platforms is considered, device manufacturers, application service providers, cellular service providers, and the user himself act as stakeholders. Thus, several entities share a single resource constraint device and require mutually isolated execution environments for each of their applications. These stakeholders shall not be required to establish trustworthy relationships beforehand. Trustworthy attestation of the current state for each stakeholder shall be available independently of any other stakeholder. Ekberg et al. have proposed and implemented the Mobile Trusted Module (MTM) in [EK07] representing the first approach to the multiple stakeholder problem.

A similar situation is present in cloud computing applications, especially raising concerns in regard to the visibility of sensitive data. Eguro and Venkatesan propose the usage of FPGAs to provide multiple stakeholders with the ability of secure computations even within the virtualized cloud environments in [EV12]. Their approach foresees that the security-sensitive operations are offloaded to trustworthy reconfigurable devices. By doing so, the data is only present in its readable plaintext within the device. This approach is providing a highly secured computing environment for the actual data processing task, but it does not take tampering of the software configurations into account.

Of utmost importance is therefore to support trustworthy computing for an arbitrary number of stakeholders. Furthermore, each stakeholder needs to be enabled to select the actual implementation of the TPM according to his security requirements. The architecture advocated hereinafter additionally supports high performance implementations as well as full custom designs that fit the TPM command structure.

Note that the term context is used to refer to the data representing the security-sensitive data usually stored in a TPM. By combining this context data with the required capabilities, the TPM functionality is provided to a specific stakeholder. To represent the physical realization of a given context, the term *Trust Compartment* is used. As detailed in the following, various *Trust Compartment* realizations may be used. Since the *Trust Compartments* are implemented using the partial reconfiguration technology, they may be considered as a placeholder for their implementation. Partial reconfiguration enables the time shared usage of hardware resources on the FPGA. An novel architecture, called the Dynamic-Context TPM (dcTPM) to mitigate the aforementioned issues is detailed in the following (cf. [FMKH11]).

5.5.1 Dynamic Context Management Concept

The basic idea of the Dynamic Context Management concept is to provide trustworthy computing resources to multiple entities. By exploiting the partial reconfiguration technology these computing resources are provided by means of hardware resources on an FPGA. The actual TPM functionality is then provided by a dedicated TPM instance.

The dcTPM manages the exclusive access to a dedicated TPM instance with integrated security and authorization mechanisms. This concept provides three flavors of TPM implementations, namely off-the-shelf TPMs, hardware implementation of the TPM functionality on an FPGA, and a software based implementation. Hence, the usage of a hardware based TPM for every stakeholder becomes possible. The underlying hardware resources are scheduled among the stakeholders by time-slicing the configuration of their individual contexts. Further, in the cloud computing context the dcTPM serves as the security anchor by enabling both the users and the providers to flexibly exploit trustworthy TPM instances. Thus, by using a dcTPM architecture it is possible to design secure and highly available systems, which are adaptable to the individual needs of various stakeholders.

Supporting mutually isolated execution environments, which are unique to each stakeholder, represent the core of the Dynamic Context Management concept. The general case considered hereinafter is based on a plurality of parallel execution environments for various stakeholder contexts. Access to the specific contexts is governed by the Context Manager, granting

5.5 Supporting Multiple Stakeholders

access to context resources (i.e. a TPM) and forwarding communication. Stakeholders therefore request access for data related to one exclusive TPM. The implementation may be transparent to the user process, while handling resource identifiers for individual contexts is provided by modified TPM drivers. Especially in cloud computing and – more generally – in virtualization scenarios, requests of stakeholders may be forwarded transparently by the VMM similar to vTPM approach [BCG+06].

The essential security-sensitive information, such as cryptographic keys, system parameters, and the system state, for executing the TPM functions is referred to as a context. In relation to Dynamic Context Management, such a context is represented as a set of data stored in memory. The protection of the stakeholder data on the platform is of paramount importance for scenarios which require support for multiple stakeholders. A current TPM may provide a single context to a number of stakeholders, but this situation would require mutual trust among the stakeholders, which is rarely a practical approach.

In general, the cryptographic keys and system parameters are being used similarly to the MTM concept proposed by Ekberg et al. in [EK07]. In contrast to the concept proposed by Stumpf and Eckert [SE08], the implementation outlined below is independent of the processor architecture and additionally supports multiple active TPM contexts at the same time. The degree of parallelism is limited by the utilized FPGA and the amount of resources required for every context implementation. Together with a decent scheduling scheme, the performance of the system can be improved N-fold in comparison to the approach presented in [SE08].

Security Assumptions for Dynamic Context Management

Some features considered for the *dcTPM* architecture, especially the support for generic TPMs, lead to weaker security assumptions. The Trust Compartments are realized to comply to the TCG specification [TCG11c], which does not consider physical attacks of any kind. In particular, man-in-the-middle attacks via bus probing (cf. Section 4.4.2) and TPM reset attacks [Kau07] are not considered within the scope of the *dcTPM* architecture. Since the proposed architecture supports to plug-in commercially available TPMs, it cannot supply higher security levels than the ones provided with these modules. The partial configuration data, representing the Trust Compartment implementations, and the additional security-sensitive data of the context, are protected by the *TinyTPM* (cf. Section 5.2.4). However, if the usage of external TPMs is not required, these attacks are effectively mitigated by

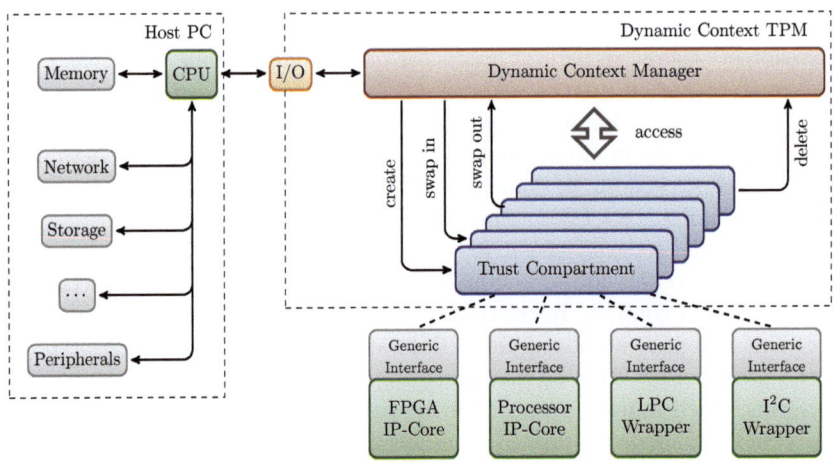

Figure 5.13: dcTPM System Architecture [FMKH11]

the proposed architecture. In cloud computing scenarios, these issues may be successfully thwarted using physical access control mechanisms to the hardware itself.

The integrity and authenticity of the configuration data is verified, prior to loading the Trust Compartments into the allocated reconfigurable regions. Utilizing the *TinyTPM* [FMMH11] or similar approaches [STP08], cover classical Dolev-Yao [DY83] assumptions of man-in-the-middle attacks during memory access. Thus, the malicious modification of Trust Compartments is protected against adversaries. With this protection of the Trust Compartments in place, attacks on the Dynamic Context Manager fall into the class of denial-of-service attacks, which are out of the scope of this work. The adversary is therefore not able to yield any useful information from the Dynamic Context Manager. Moreover, the above mentioned approaches provide means for the protection of both, the Dynamic Context Manager and the Trust Compartments. The underlying FPGA architecture is supporting the separation of memory areas and thus it complies to the security standards as required by the TCG. Apart from the ICAP, which is controlled by the *TinyTPM*, there is no way for data to migrate between memory areas.

5.5 Supporting Multiple Stakeholders

Key Components of the Generic Architecture

The generic architecture for Dynamic Context Management is comprised of two parts, namely the host PC and the *dcTPM*. An illustration of the generic architecture is given in Figure 5.13. On the host PC the applications are executed or virtual machines are provided by a VMM for various stakeholders. Access to the Dynamic Context Manager is provided by the host PC. The *dcTPM* contains multiple Trust Compartments hosting the stakeholder contexts. The dynamic context management firmware provides measures for allocation and scheduling of these compartments. Allocated Trust Compartments provide the functionality of a trust anchor for each stakeholder, by means of a hardware realization.

Running programs on the host PC may access stakeholder data by issuing commands to the Dynamic Context Manager. Authentication protocols similar to the TCG specifications are used in this case (cf. Section 5.5.3). The execution of TPM commands is provided by the cryptographic engines included in the Trust Compartments. Each hardware realization configured in a Trust Compartment complies with the TCG specifications [TCG11c]. This compliance may be verified in the usual manner, well-known from the commercially available TPMs. For simplicity Figure 5.13 does not depict the NVM used to store the context data.

Stakeholders decide on the realization of the their particular compartment upon creation. In general, three different realization variants may be distinguished: *i*) processor IP-Cores emulating trust anchor functionality in software; *ii*) hardware-based TPMs by means of FPGA-based implementations; and *iii*) interface wrappers for commercially available trust anchors. These variants are briefly outlined in the following.

Processor IP-Core: This Trust Compartment embodies the TPM functionality in software by means of an emulation as provided by Strasser in [SS08]. A softcore processor needs to be configured in this compartment, executing one or more TPM emulators. The Dynamic Context Manager guards the essential security-sensitive information of each compartment by mapping this data to the NVM.

FPGA IP-Core: An FPGA-based hardware implementation of the trust anchor is provided by this variant, deploying the cryptographic engines as hardware modules directly. As in the Processor IP-Core, the security-sensitive information is mapped to the NVM.

LPC & I^{2}C Wrapper: Interfaces to access commercially available ASIC TPMs offered by various vendors, are provided by these variants. Depending on the actual interface the appropriate wrapper is selected to accommodate the connection to devices, such as LPC TPMs or upcoming Soft-I^{2}C TPMs (e.g., Infineon SLB 9635 TT 1.2).

In addition to a TPM-like implementation supporting trustworthy operation of the stakeholder software, specialized IP-cores may also be configured. The reconfigurable technology exploited in this approach allows for a flexible usage of the available resources. Even multiple Trust Compartments can be available to a single stakeholder, which supports concepts as presented in [EV12]. Hence, not only the software configuration is constantly monitored, but all operations on unencrypted security-sensitive data are performed in a sealed trusted computing environment.

Management of Trust Compartments

The process of creating, swapping, and deleting trust anchor instances is illustrated in the following. Goldman and Berger have defined a similar process for their vTPM architecture in [GB08], however, the *dcTPM* creates, swapps, and deletes instances autonomously. If a stakeholder is requesting the Dynamic Context Manager to create a context, one of the previously outlined Trust Compartment variants is configured according to the requirements of the stakeholder. This newly created instance behaves exactly like a newly shipped TPM. Once it is assigned to the stakeholder, an endorsement key certificate has to be created and the stakeholder takes ownership of the device. In the case of a wrapper-based realization, the endorsement key may be supplied with the TPM, which in turn only requires the verification of the certificate provided by the TPM vendor. The scheduling of the access to the available Trust Compartments is carried out by the Dynamic Context Manager.

If more instances of trust anchors are active at the same time then there are Trust Compartments available in the system, the scheduler begins swapping of the least frequently accessed instances. Of course other scheduling approaches than round robin may be provided by the dynamic context management firmware. In general, swapping of Trust Compartment instances is always possible for FPGA IP-Core and Processor IP-Core realizations. In this case the relevant context data is stored in a NVM. Only the amount of non-volatile memory and the number of externally available TPMs limits the available Trust Compartments. Although the TPM also features volatile memory regions, the complete context data is stored. Suspending and resuming of virtual machines is supported, as the status of the virtual machine is provided. Furthermore, this supports the live migration of virtual machines as detailed

5.5 Supporting Multiple Stakeholders

in Section 5.5.5. The number of parallel active Trust Compartments is restricted by the available resources on the FPGA.

The deletion of contexts is essentially a two step process depending on the Trust Compartment realization. In case of a wrapper instance which embodies an off-the-shelf hardware module, the stakeholder needs to execute the `TPM_OwnerClear` to remove the key hierarchy storing the stakeholder secrets. In contrast, if the compartment variant is not realized using an interface wrapper, the Dynamic Context Manager is informed of the deletion of the context and releases the corresponding memory area. Additionally, as a second step all residues of stakeholder data can be removed from the surrounding infrastructure. In example, the endorsement key certificates, which are specific to the user, shall be removed.

5.5.2 dcTPM Proof-of-Concept

The main goal of the *dcTPM* architecture is to provide trust anchors to multiple stakeholders. According to their needs, the stakeholders select an appropriate implementation, which is then configured in a Trust Compartment. The overall architecture, therefore supports a generic interface to dynamically replace Trust Compartment instances. Based on the generic concept for dynamic context management, a proof-of-concept, implementing a subset of the architectural features, is outlined in the following.

Naïve Approach of Providing Multiple Contexts

In commodity computer systems a TPM is connected to the LPC-bus (cf. [TCG11c]). Since the bus architecture allows for attaching multiple devices, a naïve approach of realizing a *dcTPM* would be to simply connect multiple TPMs directly to the LPC bus. In order to simplify the BIOS implementation and hence enable the measured boot of the system, the LPC bus address of the TPM has been fixed to `0xFED40000` by the TCG specification. Connecting multiple off-the-shelf TPMs to the LPC bus directly leads to obvious address conflicts.

Proof-of-Concept Implementation

The proof-of-concept implementation outlined in this section is depicted in Figure 5.14. An FPGA hosts the prototype implementation and provides interfaces to the host, memories, peripherals and the individual TPMs. The implementation utilizes softcores on the FPGA by means of providing a CPU

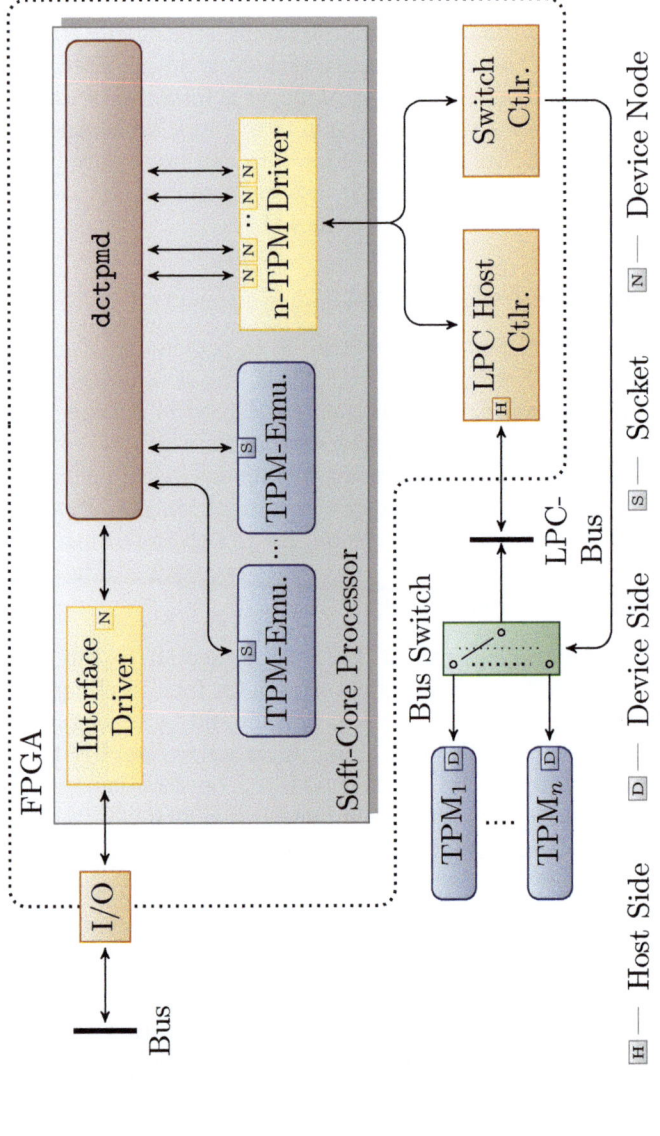

Figure 5.14: Simplified View of the dcTPM Proof-of-Concept Implementation [FMKH11,Dei10]

5.5 Supporting Multiple Stakeholders

(e.g. a MicroBlaze [Xil12b]), a memory controller, diverse I/O controllers. Furthermore, a single host controller for the LPC-bus is implemented on the FPGA, to which the hardware TPM is connected. A peripheral interface controller is supporting the connections to the host PC side of the *dcTPM*. The bus switch to connect multiple TPMs to one LPC-bus is realized by a custom made PCB using a Texas Instruments (SN74CBTLV3245A) bus switch IC [Tex05].

The address conflicts of the naïve approach are managed by introducing a bus switch to make use of multiple off-the-shelf TPMs in one system. A direct connection to the switch ensures the isolation between the TPM instances by design, hence making their access mutually exclusive. Commonly available busses, such as PCI Express [PCI12] or even LPC [Int02] may be used to establish the connection to the host system. However, for simplicity, the proof-of-concept realizes the host interface using the LPC-bus. TPMs are asynchronous passive components and therefore the results of executed commands are polled by the TSS. Hence, a TPM may be disconnected from the bus during computation. The proposed proof-of-concept implementation instantiates only two hardware TPMs, nevertheless it is not limited to this number.

At the heart of the *dcTPM* architecture beats a MicroBlaze Soft-Core processor [Xil12b] running a PetaLinux [Wil] operating system. Figure 5.14 illustrates the internal components of the PetaLinux. The drivers for the peripheral interface controller, the switch controller, and the LPC host controller have been implemented as uClinux kernel modules. Access to the hardware TPMs using the n-TPM driver is done via the respective device nodes, such as /dev/tpm0 and /dev/tpm1. It is only limited by the physical interface present on the PCB. If a device is accessed, the n-TPM driver controls the switch to attach a specific Trust Compartment to the bus. In short, the n-TPM driver manages the communication to externally attached hardware TPMs by means of implementing a LPC wrapper.

An variant of a processor IP-Core is implemented using the Linux kernel module presented by Strasser et al. [SS08]. Some minor modifications of the TPM emulators to fix some issues regarding the memory alignment were necessary for the PetaLinux implementation. New software TPMs are instantiated according by creating multiple instances of the emulator kernel module. Each kernel module is then accessed using UNIX sockets. Note that, a software-based TPM instance does not provide the same security properties as a hardware implementation. Therefore, these instances can be used for applications with lower security requirements. The number of software-based TPMs is only limited by the available memory in the system.

Table 5.9: Resource Utilization of dcTPM Prototype Implementation [FMKH11, Dei10]

Module	Register	LUT	BRAM	DSP48Es
MicroBlaze CPU	2326	2704	4	6
DDR2 Controller	5857	4673	15	0
Network Interface	939	849	0	0
LPC Host Controller	478	428	1	0
Switch Controller	66	38	0	0
Addl. Peripherals and Buses	1012	1139	2	0
Overall dcTPM	10678	9831	22	6

The dctpmd (dcTPM Daemon) connects to the host PC driver using the device node of the interface driver. Commands from the host PC are received through these device nodes. These *dcTPM* commands are first authenticated and then decapsulated into native TPM commands, which are in turn forwarded to the respective TPM instances. The actual context data and a list of the active sessions linking to these contexts is stored in two separate arrays.

With reference to the generic system architecture, various Trust Compartment instances have been implemented, namely software-based Processor IP instances and physical hardware TPMs using LPC wrapper. According to the requirements of the stakeholders, the emulators may run on dedicated softcore processors if this implementation is applied to enterprise environments. Currently all software components of the proof-of-concept implementation a running on a single processor. Consequently these kinds of adjustments to the *dcTPM* architecture represents one of the tasks to be completed to develop a product out of the existing implementation.

Evaluation

The overall resource utilization of the *dcTPM* proof-of-concept implementation is summarized in Table 5.9. The MicroBlaze [Xil12b] Soft-Core processor is running the PetaLinux operating system. To support the instantiation of multiple software TPMs, a large amount of memory is required. The utilization of a DDR2 memory controller provides this memory, but additionally requires a huge amount of resources itself. As visible from Table 5.9,

5.5 Supporting Multiple Stakeholders

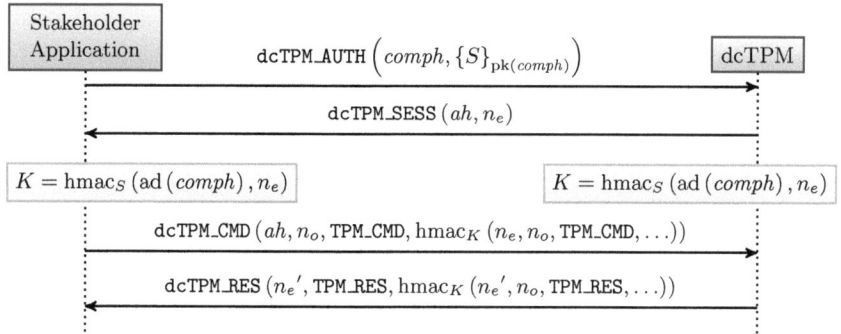

Figure 5.15: Context Authorization Protocol [Dei10]

this memory controller consumes roughly the half of the utilized *dcTPM* prototype resources.

For rapid prototyping during software development, a network interface has been included to supply a network file system. Other distinct purposes of the network interface are to issue commands and to display debugging information through a remote console. The necessary interfaces for the n-TPM driver are available through the LPC host controller and the switch controller implementation. In summary the *dcTPM* prototype consumes 30% of the available resources on a Xilinx Virtex-5 LX110T FPGA, which in turn ensures enough space for additional realizations of Trust Compartments.

5.5.3 Context Authorization Protocol

The Dynamic Context Manager of the *dcTPM* controls all available Trust Compartments and incoming commands are forwarded to the addressed instances. An authorized session has to be established by the stakeholder application before the particular Trust Compartment may be accessed. As only authenticated commands shall be forwarded to the Trust Compartments, the issued commands are encapsulated using the protocol, depicted in Figure 5.15. The encapsulation of packages is preferably included on a layer below the TSS [Tru07] to ensure transparent communication between the stakeholder applications and the related Trust Compartments.

A modified version of the SKAP [CR10] protocol is utilized to authenticate and to select particular Trust Compartments. Any stakeholder application requesting the exclusive access to a Trust Compartment hosted on the *dcTPM*, is sending a dcTPM_AUTH packet over the communication channel.

A publicly known compartment handle *comph* and a high entropy session secret S, encrypted by the compartment's public key ($pk(comph)$), comprise a dcTPM_AUTH packet. The *dcTPM* returns a dcTPM_SESS packet containing the authorization handle, which is used as a session identifier for the context, and the first nonce n_e. Both entities, the stakeholder application and the *dcTPM* can independently derive the session key K from the already known information. Every context features authorization data for identification of the compartments. Together with the nonce n_e, this authorization data $ad(comph)$ is used for the HMAC calculation of the parameters, which results in the session key K.

The actual encapsulation of TPM commands to a specific Trust Compartment uses the dcTPM_CMD being sent to the *dcTPM* for further processing. Therefore, the authorization handle ah, reused to identify the session, a new nonce n_o, an HMAC digest, and the actual TPM command, are compiled in this packet. For authentication of the message, the HMAC digest is computed over the TPM command data and the parameters n_e and n_o using the session key K. In return, the result replied by the context TPM_RES is encapsulated in the dcTPM_RES packet, which is authenticated using the same digest. A new nonce n'_e or n'_o is included with every command that is issued by means of realizing a rolling nonce scheme(see [TCG11c]).

5.5.4 dcTPM-Commands

In comparison to the conventional TPM specification, a new set of commands is required in order to implement the proposed architecture and the aforementioned protocol. These newly specified *dcTPM* commands are similar in structure to the commands specified by the TCG. Hence, for simplicity, the same algorithms are used for the implementation of the *dcTPM* commands and their responses. Additionally, it is assumed that the sequence of the TPM commands and responses is fixed, such that the *dcTPM* responses to previously issued commands, can be easily identified. A summary of the requirements for the *dcTPM* commands is given in Table 5.10.

With reference to Figure 5.15 it can be seen that the communication with the Trust Compartments is essentially established using four *dcTPM* commands. The dcTPM_AUTH and the dcTPM_SESS commands are used for authentication and session establishment, respectively. TPM commands are sent to the Trust Compartments by encapsulation with the dcTPM_CMD. A respective response is carried out by the dcTPM_RES command.

An example for the composition of one of the *dcTPM* commands is detailed in Table 5.11. The dcTPM_RES command encapsulates a Trust Compartment

5.5 Supporting Multiple Stakeholders

Table 5.10: Requirements for the dcTPM Commands [FMKH11]

Description	Specification
Hash-Algorithm	*SHA*-1
Hash-Length	160 Bit / 20 Byte
Encryption Algorithm	RSA
Key Length	2048 Bit / 256 Byte
Public Exponent e	65537
Encryption Scheme	TPM_ES_RSAESOAEP_SHA1_MGF1 [TCG11c]
Nonce- and Seed-Length	160 Bit / 20 Byte

Table 5.11: Composition of the dcTPM_RES-Response [FMKH11]

Offset	Length	Description	4 Byte Data	Value
0	4	Parameter Size	UINT32	$n + 48$
4	4	Return Code	dcTPM_RESULT	...
8	20	Nonce even	...	...
28	n	TPM Result	...	...
$n + 28$	20	Digest	...	see Figure 5.15

response, which results from a stakeholder request. Since the *dcTPM* is not able and also not aimed to make meaningful conclusions of the TPM commands, the return code is always set to dcTPM_SUCCESS if the Trust Compartment instance sends any reply. Otherwise the return code is set to dcTPM_FAIL, similar to the process in conventional TPMs. Therefore, only the status of the *dcTPM* is reflected in the return codes. The status replies of the TPM commands are forwarded to the stakeholders TSS for further processing.

5.5.5 Multi-Context Trust/Live Migration

In cloud computing scenarios the VMs are often shifted between several hosts to maximize utilization of the available resources. This Live Migration process is usually transparent to the VM and it is initiated by the cloud provider. In case of a maintenance of a given platform, all VMs are migrated to other hosts to eliminate side-effects. If commercial available TPMs are used within this process, the migration is not as straight forward as it is with the main memory occupied by the VM. None of the central keys in a TPM can be migrated and therefore other measures are required. However, this limitation is subject to change in future developments of the TCG standard.

Furthermore, the platform configuration records (i.e. PCRs) are stored in volatile memory and they are lost if the TPM is migrated physically. The physical migration of the TPM requires a reboot of the VM and is therefore no longer transparent to the VM user and partly exposes the background processes of the cloud provider.

In a nutshell, this process requires the Live Migration procedure to handle the trustworthy computing part in parallel. The migration may be generally similar to the key migration protocol specified by the TCG. The fundamental difference to this protocol is the requirement that a TPM shall not be executed within two platforms at the same time.

Stumpf and Eckert have comprised a Live Migration protocol in [SE08]. Their concept guarantees that a dynamic context is not executed on two platforms at the same time by using synchronized monotonic counters. The *dcTPM* architecture fulfills all the requirements Stumpf and Eckert state in their work, thus being a feasible platform for the implementation of their approach. Moreover, Goldman and Berger have applied a Live Migration protocol to their vTPM approach, which can be directly applied to the dcTPM proof-of-concept implementation. The handling of off-the-shelf TPMs requires a special treatment and represents the only limitation of the *dcTPM*.

6 Application Scenarios

In this chapter several case studies are presented to highlight the potential of the aforementioned trustworthy architectures. Current protection mechanisms for FPGA configuration data lack the ability to actively monitor configurations. Having that said, the main application for the *TinyTPM* becomes obvious. Hence, this chapter starts with the IP protection features provided by this approach.

By establishing this enabling technology for trustworthy configuration, many areas of application may benefit from these services. After the generic description of the IP protection services, two additional examples are given to highlight the feasibility of the presented solution. Providing transparent hard disk encryption of Serial-ATA (SATA) devices represents the first example application. A novel Set-Top Box (STB) architecture supporting flexible Common Access Module (CAM) implementations is representing the second.

6.1 IP-Protection for Partial Reconfiguration

The flexibility gained by the reconfiguration of FPGAs opens various possibilities on the one hand, but also makes systems prone to attacks on the other. FPGA vendors strive for effective protection mechanisms of configuration data to protect against attacks. The IP protection problem has been tackled only to a certain extent by the FPGA vendors (cf. [Xil11d, Alt09]). Mainly they include the encryption of static configuration data, but they lack effective measures verifying the integrity and authenticity, or even metering correct platform behavior.

The complexity of current systems is constantly growing and more and more system designers tend to use IP cores to realize functions, instead of designing them from scratch. The functional blocks used in hardware designs, are included in IP libraries being similar to software libraries. These IP cores contain highly optimized implementations of the required functions and are required for the realization of complex systems. As previously pointed out, the major threat when using current FPGAs, is cloning of these IP cores without the reimbursement of licensing fees (cf. Section 4.4.1).

The major challenges in IP protection for reconfigurable devices are the following: i) The IP in a given design has to be protected from disclosure. ii) Malicious code execution as a part of the overall design has to be omitted. iii) The device needs to provide a trustworthy update procedure for configuration data to enable the external assessment of the device.

6.1.1 Trustworthy Reconfiguration enforcing IP-Protection

Most low-cost FPGAs do not provide protection mechanisms of the configuration data. Other FPGAs require that the configuration data protection is disabled as soon as partial reconfiguration is exploited [Xil11d]. The partial reconfiguration technology is especially useful for smaller FPGAs, as the limited resources are used efficiently. This raises the threat of overproduction, since FPGAs are inexpensive standard catalogue devices that may be purchased and cloned without the knowledge of the system developer. To mitigate this weakness, the *TinyTPM* provides measures for these devices to support trustworthy configuration of reconfigurable devices by consuming only a minimal amount of resources, as outlined in Section 5.2.4. Even if encryption and authentication are available on larger and thus more costly hardware, the concept is still providing further features to the system. The *TinyTPM* enables the assessment of the current active configuration on a particular reconfigurable hardware device. Moreover, by exploiting measures similar to the secure boot procedure (cf. Section 2.2.5), a protection against the malicious modifications of the device configuration data is achieved.

Whenever an adversary is able to extract unencrypted configuration data from a reconfigurable device, the embodied Intellectual Property (IP) is at risk. Several methods, as presented by Note and Rannaud [NR08] enable the transition from configuration data to netlist implementations. The extraction of netlist information does not necessarily enable the adversary to modify the design, as she still has to handle the complexity of the optimized logic structure. Moreover, she has to reverse engineer the complex optimizations and the mapping of the original design to fit into the FPGA resources. These steps, performed by current synthesis tools, are themself non-deterministic, further complicating the reverse engineering procedure. Although, the process of reverse engineering the configuration data may be complex, the extraction of parts of the functions may not be too hard. The *TinyTPM* enables the authenticated encryption of configuration data to cryptographically to thwart these extraction mechanisms of FPGA designs.

The security services provided by the *TinyTPM* implementation are given in Table 6.1. Trustworthy reconfiguration is the result of a compilation of

Table 6.1: Security Services Provided by the TinyTPM (based on [GKST07])

Security Service	Description
Trustworthy reconfiguration	Secure update of the existing platform configuration.
Platform authentication	The platform is able to generate qualified signatures for authentication.
Configuration data authenticity	Only authenticated designs are configured ensuring platform integrity.
Platform IP lock	Hardware designs may be locked to a specific platform.
Remote (de-)activation	The design may require an on-line activation procedure to protect against overproduction.
Design confidentiality	The system integrator is only in possession of the black box interface description. The actual implementation is only available for the hardware IP owner.

measures and enables the secure usage of reconfigurable platforms. The authenticity of the active configuration data is assessed to ensure platform integrity. Device individual keys allowing for platform authentication and the confidentiality of design data are other measures proclaimed by trustworthy reconfiguration. Furthermore, certain IP configurations may be locked to a specific platforms as this has been defined in [GKST07].

Similarly to the encryption features provided by the FPGA vendors, the *TinyTPM* realizes design confidentiality and authenticity. A step beyond this state can be achieved by supplying placement constraints to black box interface definitions, enabling the system integrator to use the actual hardware IP without knowing any implementation details. By doing so, licensed IP is usable without disclosure of implementation details, protecting the IP against counterfeiting. The service of remote activation of devices incorporates the protocol provided in [GKST07] and enables the IP owner to keep track of devices actually in use. This protocol effectively mitigates the risk of overproduction by only activating features if the rightful ownership has been verified. Figure 6.1 summarizes the threats, concepts, and measures

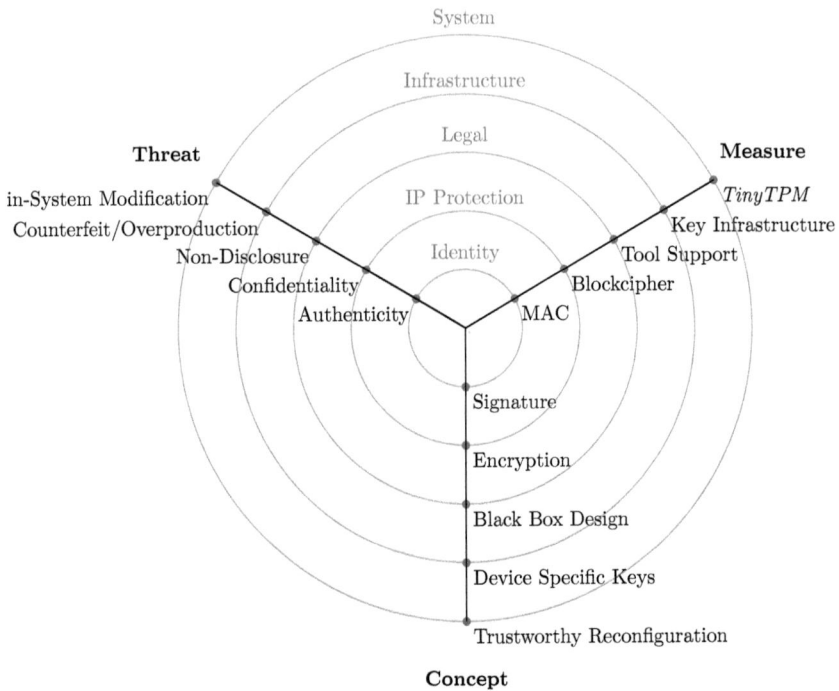

Figure 6.1: Y-Diagram of Cyber-Physical Design Security

incorporated in a cyber-physical design flow for building secure systems. This figure depicts the hierarchical requirements for any cyber-physical design and further it highlights the different levels of abstraction that need to be considered in providing trustworthy systems. In contrast, Shoufan and Huss have presented a similar diagram in [SH09] that has also been conveyed from the representation by Gajski et al. in [GDWL92]. The focus of their Y-Diagram is the representation of information security in a broader sense. However, Figure 6.1 details the specific security requirements of hardware design projects.

To prevent cloning of an FPGA during the production phase, an approach similar to the remote activation scheme by Alkabani et al. [AKP07] may be exploited. This approach delays the activation of the complete function until the activation of the particular IP has been requested. This delayed activation of the FPGA configuration is achieved by supplying a minimal test configuration with the required functions for printed circuit board production testing. Later, the final product is activated within a secure environment by replacing this test configuration with the final implementation. Since the test configuration will not contain valuable IP no additional protection is required.

Moreover, intelligent pay-per-use models for IPs are needed, as FPGAs are not used in the same large quantities as ASICs. Tom Kean advocated in [Kea02] to adapt existing ASIC IP-core business models reflecting these requirements. The *TinyTPM* may be modified to include this usage monitoring approach to support these requirements. This approach can be seen as a generalization of the delayed activation mechanism presented by Alkabani et al. [AKP07]. Furthermore, Maes et al. advocate a pay-per-use licensing model for reconfigurable architectures in [MSV12] reaching a step further in the usage of FPGAs. Apart from the already presented update protocols in Section 5.2.7, the protocols outlined hereinbefore can be harnessed with just minor modifications to the *TinyTPM*.

6.1.2 Configuration Management

The *TinyTPM* enables the configuration management of the cyber-physical system by means of a versioning mechanism. Cryptographic signatures and monotonic counter values provide the necessary information to derive a versioning mechanism similar to the approach presented by Drimer and Kuhn [Dri07]. The secure boot performed by the *TinyTPM* makes sure that only authenticated configurations come to execution. Former versions of system functions are no longer accepted by the *TinyTPM* as the monotonic counter values are used to invalidate the cryptographic signatures of older configurations.

In case of a malicious configuration attempt, the secure boot is immediately aborted and the system enters an untrusted state. Depending on the actual requirements, the *TinyTPM* is adapted to either signal the failure of the secure boot or to just deny the access to the *TinyTPM*. The overall system architecture is required to take care of this matter and it has to define procedures to handle the consequences.

6.2 Hard Disk Encryption

Current hardware based solutions for encrypted data storage on hard disks usually employ a *full disk encryption* scheme. This approach is feasible for mobile devices, such as laptops but of limited use in environments with multiple users, which not necessarily trust each other. As long as the device is unlocked, any user of the system is able to access the data. Especially in scenarios exploiting virtualization, the data is most likely not encrypted using the hardware based functions but a software based solution, to allow for encryption on a per user basis. This contributes to the fact that these environments are prone to software attacks.

Even in single user environments certain limitations are present. The migration of data from one device to another without decrypting data is not possible, since the cryptographic keys are stored within the device and shall never leave it. A key migration scheme, similar to the one available for TPMs is not available.

Commercially available hard disks provide in general an AES based encryption as required by the TCG Storage Security Subsystem Class Opal [TCG12a]. Some devices furnish additional features, such as fast key erasure and hardware accelerated data deletion [Mic12d]. The hardware support for encryption is currently available for many devices, however it is limited to support full disk encryption only. If encryption schemes other than AES or authenticated data regions shall be exploited, the off-the-shelf solutions are no longer feasible. In addition to using various encryption schemes the transparent hard disk encryption feature, as depicted in Figure 6.2, may also be included in a larger security subsystem. This subsystem may then contain the data encryption facilities along with basic security anchor functions as provided by the *TinyTPM* or the *dcTPM*.

6.2.1 Proof-of-Concept Implementation

The generic concept of such a transparent encryption scheme is depicted in Figure 6.2. This scheme embodies an FPGA in between the host PC and the hard disk to realize the encryption function. In practice the setup for the proof-of-concept implementation is comprised of an off-the-shelf PC being hooked up to one of the SATA ports present on the Xilinx XUPV5-LX110T development board. The second SATA port is connecting the FPGA with the actual SATA device, which was in this case a usual hard disk. This allows for the manipulation of the data stream while it is transmitted from the host PC to the hard disk.

The proof-of-concept implementation, detailed in [Hut12], is depicted in Figure 6.3. At the physical layer the incoming data stream is buffered deserialized and then analyzed to determine the further processing steps. During transmission, the data are scrambled and 8bit/10bit encoded to ensure

6.2 Hard Disk Encryption

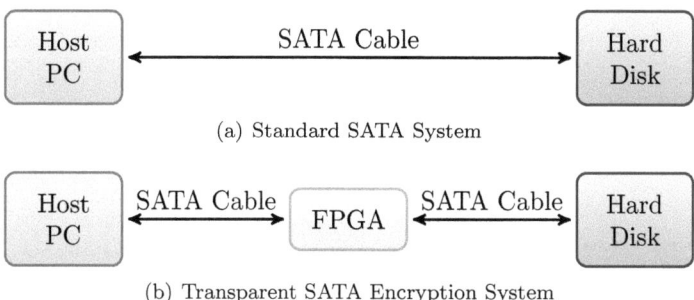

(a) Standard SATA System

(b) Transparent SATA Encryption System

Figure 6.2: System Overview of Transparent Hard Disk Encryption

integrity over the high frequency serial bus on the link layer. The resulting link layer packet header is analyzed to identify user data, represented by the data Frame Information Structure (FIS). If this is the case, the data is buffered in the encryption pipeline. As soon as 128 bit of data have been buffered, the data is encrypted. This process needs to be preserve the order of the data packets, therefore all non-data FIS packets are also buffered in a delay buffer. Consecutively, the data is then processed through link layer and physical layer to be forwarded to the hard disk. The lower part of Figure 6.3 indicates the reverse process to decrypt data while it is transferred from the hard disk to the host PC.

The initial implementation of this scheme is using a null cipher [GK98] and a simple XOR encryption to test the feasibility of this approach. By doing so it was possible to apply arbitrary patterns to the written data prior to propagating it to the hard disk. Since SATA is asynchronous by nature and the transfer speeds of devices differ, measures to control data flow are indispensable. The HOLD/HOLDA FIS primitives are providing the facilities to indicate the need for pausing the FIS delivery and to acknowledge this pause, respectively (cf. [And07]). This function is directly related to the fill levels of input and output buffers and therefore either side has to timely acknowledge a pause during transfer. For this purpose the turnaround time of the HOLD/HOLDA primitives is constraint to the transfer time of 20 data words.

Due to this turnaround time limitation of the HOLD/HOLDA primitives, the overall latency of this encryption architecture is limited to 10 data words. The processing of data through the physical layer and the link layer delays the transfer by 2 data words at each side, which leaves 6 data words for the encryption buffers (see Figure 6.3). The AES requires 128 bit or

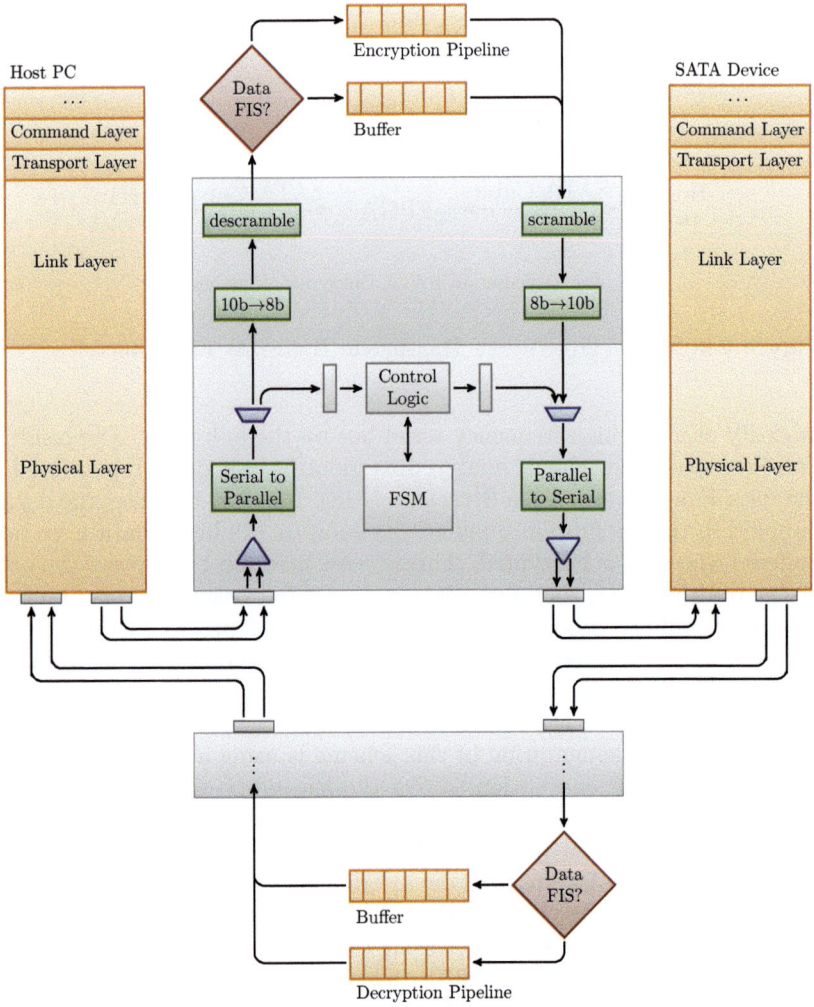

Figure 6.3: System Architecture of Transparent Hard Disk Encryption [Hut12]

6.2 Hard Disk Encryption

four data words for encryption, which results in a buffer length of at least four data words. Having that said, the incapability of including encryption schemes with a bit width larger then 64 bits at the link layer is obvious. The major issue in this approach is the in-order execution of the encryption scheme to simplify the overall approach. Huth highlights the requirement of the implementation of a handling mechanism for these primitives at the transport layer. However, he has shown that it is possible to include hardware encryption mechanisms in the lower levels of the SATA protocol. Table 6.2 depicts the resource utilization of the approach advocated by Huth [Hut12].

Together with the hereinbefore advocated *TinyTPM* approach, the encryption schemes used by the transparent hard disk encryption can be exchanged on the fly. Moreover, each of these partitions may use a different hardware accelerated encryption scheme. This is achieved my multiplexing the encryption/decryption pipeline depicted in Figure 6.3 in case of multiple partitions using several encryption schemes. Partial reconfiguration of the encryption scheme is applied if the system needs to migrate from one encryption scheme to another.

The key material for each partition may also be migrated using the procedures defined by the TCG. This feature additionally allows to copy only the encrypted data, as the encryption keys are present at the target host. The data itself may also be copied offline to the target, however this obligates an authentication to access the data on the disk.

This scheme additionally mitigates the risk of *warm-replug* attacks, as the hard disk does not contain any unencrypted data. Müller et al. presented an attack on common FDE devices which demonstrates a weaknesses of this approach in [MLF12]. Access to the data on a FDE device is granted only after successful authentication. Moving this device to another host without cutting power supply allows for the successful extraction of data. Most of the systems evaluated by Müller et al. were prone to this attack and modifications in the interface connections are almost impossible to detect while the system is powered down.

6.2.2 Multi-User Environments

The transparent encryption of data with multiple different keys and various encryption schemes is impossible to realize with currently available full-disk encryption schemes. Most systems available today use AES to encrypt data directly before it is written to the disk. These hardware accelerated systems mainly target the mobile/laptop market segment that does not require any multi-user capabilities.

Table 6.2: Resource Utilization of the Transparent Hard Disk Encryption Proof-of-Concept [Hut12]

	AES-based		XOR/Null		Available
Register	7032	10%	893	1%	69120
LUTs	20856	30%	1221	1%	69120
IOBs	27	4%	27	4%	640
BUFG/BUFGCTRLs	7	21%	7	21%	32
DCM_ADVs	1	8%	1	8%	12

In cloud computing scenarios users may require a separation of data from other users. Only software-based solutions accommodate measures flexible enough supporting this requirement. An extension to the previously presented hard disk encryption scheme allows for the application in multi-user environments.

By emulating a SATA port multiplier, an existing hard disk is partitioned for different users providing user specific cryptographic algorithms. According to the SATA standard, such a port multiplier can host 15 different devices and hence every device may utilize a different cryptographic scheme for data encryption. Moreover, the access control mechanisms and authentication schemes may be different for each of these multiplier ports providing maximum flexibility. By using this methodology the operating system is unaware of the physical organization of hard disk sectors and the virtual machine host can map any combination to its virtual machine guests.

6.3 Pay TV Content Protection

Current pay TV content is protected by provider-specific proprietary encryption schemes. In general, the scrambled data stream is forwarded to a special hardware device realizing the decryption of the video content. A common interface has been defined to foster flexibility of content providers in selecting encryption schemes. The implementation of the decryption scheme is then packed into an access module that is inserted into the Set-Top-Box. Therefore, most Set-Top-Box architectures feature a hardware interface for a so called Common Access Module (CAM) to make the Set-Top-Box usable independently from the particular content provider.

6.3 Pay TV Content Protection

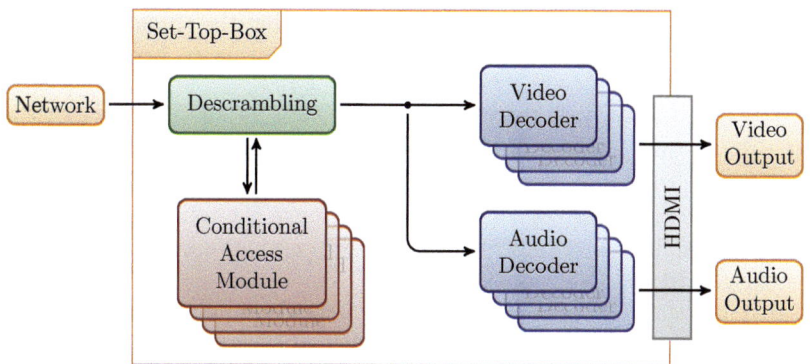

Figure 6.4: Functional View of Reconfigurable Set-Top-Box Architecture

In order to decrypt pay TV content correctly the Set-Top-Box has to be equipped with cryptographic secrets. The most commonly used method to deliver these secrets to the subscribers is achieved by shipping smart-cards to the users or bundling the smart-card directly with the Set-Top-Box. The smart-card is configured by the content provider in a confined environment to protect the security-sensitive data.

The generic CAM is not obligated to feature a smart-card interface, however most of them do. Different encryption schemes and smart-card types are supported by this approach. With this flexibility provided, the requirements of content providers are met. Moreover, this open standard liberates the provider to be independent on a single source for Set-Top-Boxes.

6.3.1 Reconfigurable Security

The CAM performing the descrambling procedure of the content is depicted in Figure 6.4. For the purpose, an encryption algorithm using the security-sensitive key material stored inside the smart-card is exploited. Set-Top-Boxes and especially the CAM and the smart-cards used therein have been a target for the hacker community for over a decade. Among other publications, Weinmann and Wirth in [WW05] and later Tews et al. in [TWW12] have shown that the commonly used Common Scrambling Algorithm (CSA) is no longer effective. Moreover, Chris Tarnovsky of Flylogic[1] was able to demonstrate hardware attacks on smart cards[2]. These facts are

---
[1] http://www.flylogic.net
[2] http://www.wired.com/politics/security/news/2008/05/tarnovsky

demonstrating that this scenario is actively facing the threat of counterfeit smart cards and hence this confirms the obligation to provide a flexible encryption scheme for pay TV content protection.

The well established CAM system enables content providers to timely change the subscriptions of users. This is either performed by shipping new smart-cards to new users or by updating the subscriptions in the sub-channel data. However, in case of a CAM system change the roll-out procedures are cumbersome, since not only the smart-cards or smart-card software needs to be exchanged.

Relying on the *TinyTPM* scheme, the partial reconfiguration feature may be utilized to build FPGA-based, reconfigurable security module for use in Set-Top-Boxes, to replace the common CAM implementation. Depending on the pay TV providers requirements, different hardware implementations of the CAM are available to be used within the Set-Top-Box. In the same case of a compromise in the CAM system the CAM is replaced by invoking the remote update procedure. The dynamic reconfiguration times estimated in Table 5.4 indicate the feasibility to reconfigure the CAM during channel switching. Reconfiguration of the CAM is possible within a few milliseconds, thus it does not significantly contribute to the channel switching time. Key storage may be realized by continuing to use smart-cards or by using the *TinyTPMs* internal PUF-based storage.

Regardless of the actual implementation, by enabling the reconfigurable Set-Top-Box architecture implementation, not only the CAM may be reconfigured but also any audio/video decoder present in the system. Drawbacks in the CAM implementation can be timely mitigated, as well as, the performance of decoders can be improved to match future standards.

If a separation of execution environments, between the content provider and the Set-Top-Box manufacturer is required, separate *TinyTPMs* may be instantiated to facilitate mutually exclusive environments. As a step beyond this state, supporting multiple stakeholders required by future applications may also be supported by using a *dcTPM*-based concept. Hwang leaps a step further by stating a generic relationship between the four entities involved in Internet Protocol television (IPTV), namely the content provider, the service provider, the network provider, and the customer [Hwa09]. These multiple stakeholders share a common platform and require the separation of data to fulfil their individual security goals. When looking at the STB itself, it additionally consist of two stakeholders, the STB manufacturer and the CAM provider. In general, the separation is not that strict as services are partitioned into three individual hardware devices; the STB, the CAM, and the smart card containing the service provider secrets.

6.3 Pay TV Content Protection

Combining these three devices in a single reconfigurable security architecture enables pay TV service providers to also combine their security architecture. A generic CAM implementation may be modified to support upcoming changes in the security protocols. Moreover, the components may be simplified as no generic interfaces are necessary to support various products. The hardware implementation is tailored to the special requirements of each service provider. Thus the flexibility of exchangeable CAMs is even further extended, since updates of reconfigurable devices are available on demand and can be immediately rolled-out through remote update procedures. Every content provider is able to change the behavior of the CAM on a regular basis without the need to ship new tokens to the subscribers.

6.3.2 Proof-of-Concept Implementation

A proof-of-concept implementation for the video stream encryption has been presented in [Sol12]. This proof-of-concept exploits the implementation presented in [KN08] to realize descrambling and audio/video decoding. Since Kinsman et al. have used a development board especially built for media processing applications, several fast SRAM memories are exploited to buffer the processing steps. The approach presented in [Sol12] uses a completely different memory architecture and makes use of the more recent Xilinx Spartan-6 FPGA architecture. Therefore, a sophisticated DDR2-based buffer design has been developed to accommodate the architectural changes.

Table 6.3 summarizes the resource utilization of this proof-of-concept implementation. The decryption of the video stream data has been performed prior to descrambling, however this may also be offloaded to an FPGA implementation of a Common Access Module (CAM).

The generic architecture depicted in 6.4 indicates the usage of the Partial Reconfigurable Region (PRR) feature to realize different CAMs. Moreover, the video and audio decoders may also be reconfigured to the need of the content providers. Solis Vasquez has further extended the initial approach to include a AES-based encryption of the video stream data, as detailed in [Sol12]. This proof-of-concept enables a simple encryption system for content protection in an IPTV environment.

Table 6.3: Proof-of-Concept Resource Utilization [Sol12]

	Slice			Frequency	
	LUTs	FF	BRAM	Max.	Actual
AES Core	1338	397	0	140.385	54
Sequence Decoder	4103	1015	13	62.884	54
DDR2					
YUV2DDRAddr	545	102	0	184.362	54
Sector Decoder	22	7	0	389.955	54
Write	102	96	0	319.223	300
FWD Read	161	171	1	266.912	54, 250
BWD Read	161	171	1	266.912	54, 250
Y Read	106	76	0	217.009	40
Cr Read	145	76	0	210.675	40
Cb Read	141	77	0	215.633	40
DVI					
TX Interface	337	186	0	199.718	40, 80, 400
Linebuffer YCbCr	593	266	0	265.305	40
Full STB	7000	2940	18		

7 Summary

Several architectures for trustworthy reconfigurable systems, mitigating the shortcomings of existing trust anchors in various areas of application, have been presented within this thesis. The basics of trustworthy computing platforms have been outlined in respect to the hereinbefore advocated architectures. This synopsis included a specific life-cycle definition and the generic concepts for platform integrity measurements. The unique requirements of computing platforms, operated by multiple stakeholders, have been outlined.

Further, a summary of the generic requirements for building trustworthy systems has been given. This included the common definitions for the central aspects in providing trustworthy systems, namely key storage and authentication. The design security aspects of current reconfigurable cyber-physical systems along with typical threats have been analyzed.

The *TinyTPM* architecture is perceived as the paramount concept enabling the design of trustworthy reconfigurable systems. Together with the authentication and integrity measurement facilities, it is providing the fundamental building block for trustworthy reconfiguration. In addition, measures to protect Intellectual Property (IP) of partial hardware configurations have been accommodated in this architecture.

A thorough analysis of this basic building block has been conducted, demonstrating the feasibility of the approach for various applications. The resource utilization of the proof-of-concept implementation has been minimized to provide most of the reconfigurable logic resources to the user. A product life-cycle has been defined for the *TinyTPM*, as this is required for security evaluations, such as FIPS140-2 or Common Criteria.

The comparison to a lightweight derivative of this building block has been presented, illustrating the possibility to further reduce hardware resources and to furnish additional means to counter side-channel attacks. The resource utilization of the *TinyTPM* and it's lightweight side-channel aware counterpart has been thoroughly evaluated. For this a special automated synthesis flow has been developed exploiting numerous combinations of synthesis arguments and parameters. The gathered synthesis results underscore the feasibility in building a trustworthy basis for reconfigurable architectures.

Although, the resource utilization shall be kept at a minimum, the performance of a trustworthy reconfigurable system is crucial for it's acceptance. The central components of the hereinbefore advocated architectures are the MAC supporting integrity measurement as well as authentication, and the block cipher encryption algorithm providing means to ensure confidentiality. The original authenticated encryption scheme has been investigated to increase performance. In view of this, a novel hardware architecture for the AES-CCM authenticated encryption scheme has been investigated. The reorganization incorporated in this novel approach, allows the conceptually sequential two-pass algorithm to be executed in parallel. Thus, this solution is providing royalty-free authenticated encryption on a single-pass performance level. The comparison of the parallel AES-CCM clearly shows the advantage over the generic composition used within the original *TinyTPM* approach.

This building block supports the implementation of additional services for more complex applications. The fact that multiple stakeholders are using the same architecture obligates mutually exclusive protection techniques. The *dcTPM* is envisioned to build the foundation for a dynamic management of mutually exclusive trust anchors. Each of these trust anchors is configured on demand into one of the available Trust Compartments. The Trust Compartments may host different kinds of trust anchor implementations ranging from wrappers for commercially available TPMs, to customized hardware implementations. Using the hardware-based trust anchor support for multiple stakeholders pushes the limits of cloud and mobile computing scenarios.

The applicability to real-world problems of this architectures for trustworthy reconfigurable systems has been outlined by two case studies. The proof-of-concept implementations cover the trustworthy reconfiguration of central functions of the architecture. In the case of the reconfigurable Set-Top Box (STB) not only the media decoding scheme may be reconfigured, but also the content protection scheme being the most crucial part of this architecture.

The current proof-of-concept implementation of the *TinyTPM* is rather static. There are various design decisions to be clarified upfront prior to roll-out. To increase the flexibility in this case, the static Finite State Machine (FSM) may be replaced by a small (8-bit) microcontroller. The implications on the device firmware and the overall security architecture are demanding further investigation and are considered to be part of future work.

A very promising approach to realize the *TinyTPM* functions for additional hardware platforms, is an implementation using the TrustZone architecture.

7 Summary

The most recent reconfigurable devices from the Zynq FPGA family [Xil12e] already include mechanisms for the protection of configuration data in its BootROM; shipping the devices with a modified version of the internal BootROM image would provide a feasible solution. Different flavors of implementations may be provided using an approach similar to the Intel TXT late launch capability, by using a signed executable to bootstrap the whole security subsystem. When applied to the Zynq architecture this can be provided by a different First Stage Boot Loader (FSBL) running within the TrustZone environment.

The concepts presented in this thesis rely, among others, on the stability of PUF implementations for FPGAs. The construction of a PUF is rather fragile and depends on subtle differences in the physical properties of the particular device. The effects of reconfiguration on the PUF implementation itself has not been investigated in detail. Having that said, a comprehensive study on the influence of placement and routing and the reconfiguration of surrounding logic is required in further research. This may include measures to intermix the PUF implementation realizing the authentication of a device with the core functions of the trust anchor architecture. Any modification performed by an adversary, either on the PUF itself or on the surrounding logic, shall lead to a failure in authentication.

A Cryptographic Primitives

The realization of trustworthy architectures requires the implementation of various cryptographic primitives. In particular, the facts and figures of the implementations of hash algorithms for integrity verification, symmetric encryption schemes and message authentication codes are detailed in the following. This chapter provides a reference for the implementations used within this work and compares them to existing approaches. Due to the complexity of random number generators, especially the assessment of the quality of random numbers, only a brief summary of existing approaches is given.

A.1 Selection of Algorithms

The level of trustworthiness provided by a given architecture is determined by the selected algorithms. The selection process for the architectures advocated herein is detailed and an overview of the available algorithms is given. Moreover, the resource utilization of various algorithms is presented in the following.

The higher the cryptographic strength of an algorithm, the more users can rely on the security provided by it, and the more users can trust a given device. However, the algorithms utilized within the concepts presented in herein have been selected according to best practices and commonly accepted recommendations. The amount of resources consumed by a given algorithm is an additional requirement for the selection. The application of asymmetric cryptography in resource constraint systems is legitimate, although its usage may not be reasonable in general. In contrast, asymmetric schemes not only require more resources for implementation, but additionally require higher execution times for each operation.

If cryptographic algorithms are considered, the strength of the algorithm may be mapped to the number of bits utilized within the algorithm. The computational complexity of an exhaustive key search (cf. [vT05]) is taken as a common yardstick to determine the cryptographic strength of an algorithm. Depending on the requirements for the resulting system, a so called security margin is added to the required strength of the algorithm to make it suitable for longer periods of time. A very large security margin has been included in the design of the SHA-1 hash algorithm design. However, the security quickly fell with the discovery of Wang et al. when figuring out how to attack [WYY05]. The major difficulty solved by Wang et al. was how the design has to be analyzed, the security margin claimed by the design was giving a false sense of strength. Hence, the realization shall not solely rely on good security margins.

Several metrics for cryptographic algorithms have been presented in literature. A commonly accepted recommendation by the NIST on the usage of cryptographic algorithms is presented in [BREK11]. Similar to most other recommendations, the NIST relates symmetric schemes, asymmetric schemes and hash functions to a level of security provided by a symmetric algorithm (i.e. AES). In order to do this, the computational complexity of a brute force attack on these ciphers is compared. Additionally, a time frame is provided in which the algorithms under consideration shall be used with certain key lengths. An interactive comparison[1] of key length recommendations has been summarized by Giry and Quisquater.

Most of the recommendations put measures into place, which relate the key length of a given algorithm with its level of security provided. Grigg and Gutman elaborate in their article [GG11] on the reliance on this numerical properties. These authors call this numerical properties a curse, as designers often only concentrate on the cryptographic strength of the algorithm, not on the security of the resulting system. Moreover, they argue that the mere focus on the brute force success on one particular key does not threat the millions of other keys. Especially if the successful attack requires vast amount of resources and time. Although Grigg and Gutman recognize the necessity of strong cryptographic algorithms for certain applications, they call on the common sense of the designers to choose appropriate implementations.

In the following possible algorithms providing certain security objectives for cyber-physical systems are outlined. Where appropriate, the recommendations for the usage of cryptographic algorithms are detailed. In general, the recommendations by NIST are used as a baseline for the selection of algorithms.

---

[1]http://www.keylength.com

A.1 Selection of Algorithms

A.1.1 Providing Integrity

The protection of data integrity may be provided using a variety of algorithms. Error detection and error correction measures, such as CRC or Viterbi [Vit67] encoding are not of primary interest, as they are not able to detect malicious modifications. Integrity protection in the cryptographic sense, which is addressed in this section, requires collision resistance of the computed integrity values. Collision resistance describes the complexity of finding two arbitrary different messages m_1 and m_2 such that:

$$H(m_1) = H(m_2) \tag{A.1}$$

Where $H(x)$ denotes the particular hash function. Prominent representatives of cryptographic hash functions are MD5, the SHA-Family, Wirlpool, and RIPEMD. The most commonly used function is SHA-1.

As aforementioned, Wang et al. have presented an approach to find collisions for the SHA-1 hash algorithm [WYY05]. Hence, the NIST recommends not to use SHA-1 after 2010 and mandates the same for 2013 [BREK11]. For newer systems the designers are beginning a transition to SHA-2 or SHA-3 hash algorithms. The NIST recently announced the selection of the follow-up SHA-3 candidate in [NIS12b]. It is expected that the provided security margins and the corresponding key-length of the follow-up SHA-3 algorithm KECCAC will be included in an updated recommendation.

A.1.2 Providing Authenticity

The authenticity of data is usually guaranteed by a cryptographic signature appended to the message. In principle, there are two types of procedures to provide authenticity, being digital signatures and MACs. A summary of the main properties of these two is given by Goldreich in [Gol04]. In a nutshell, asymmetric cryptography additionally provides non-repudiation (see Section A.1.4), as the private key is only known to one unique entity. In comparison to message authentication, the key used for signing and verification has to present at all communication partners.

In the asymmetric case, the authenticity of a message is provided by a digital signature on the hash value of the message. A well-known representative of an asymmetric cryptography scheme is RSA [RSA78]. It uses the computationally complex modular exponentiation for encryption and decryption of a message. For this reason, asymmetric schemes are not applied to encrypt larger messages directly, as the amount of processed data exceeds feasible computation times. To mitigate this issue, asymmetric cryptography is usually only applied for message integrity values or symmetric encryption keys in case of signature generation and encryption, respectively.

Therefore, they are in general not utilized to encrypt/sign large messages but indeed the representation of the message integrity (i.e. hash value) is exploited. Message authentication using keyed hash functions (i.e. HMAC), a representative of symmetric cryptography, is often favored in cyber-physical systems for efficiency reasons. Simple authentication schemes, are generating a MAC of a nonce, which in turn is verified by the communication partner. The authentication is successful if and only if the computation on both sides match.

A.1.3 Providing Confidentiality

Confidentiality is, as aforementioned, provided by encryption of data. The class of encryption algorithms is divided into two subgroups, namely symmetric and asymmetric encryption. For practicality reasons, symmetric encryption schemes are preferred as they benefit from a lower computational complexity. The most commonly used symmetric encryption scheme today is the AES. It has been selected in a public competition by the NIST and was standardized in the NIST FIPS-197 in 2001 [NIS01].

A.1.4 Providing Non-Repudiation

The term *non-repudiation* is usually used in legal settings, which question the authenticity of a digital signature. Some constructions using public-key cryptography hinder the repudiation of signatures. In summary, these systems have to ensure the confidentiality of private keys, usually achieved by generating the key within the system itself. For most problems cyber-physical systems have to face, non-repudiation is not necessary, however it has been included for completeness.

A.1.5 Providing Long-Term Security

Data which needs to be protected for a longer period of time, a whole new class of algorithms come into play. In this case the terms *long term usage* and *long term security* are often used. Usually *long term* meaning something equal or longer then a lifetime ($\xi 100$ years). A prominent example for data which needs to be protected for such a long time would be the genome data of a human being. In a case of a compromise, genetic illnesses or defects come to be known publicly, this may lead to the rejection of a life insurance or

Table A.1: Comparison of SHA-1 Hardware Module Implementations.

	Reg.	LUT	BRAM	latency [cycles]	Freq. [MHz]	Throughput [Gbit/s]
SHA-1 [FMMH11]	1013	1754	0	83	193.445	1.193
SHA-1v2	874	1353	0	80	166.661	1.067
SHA-256v2	1067	1699	0	64	169.262	1.354
SHA-512v2	2123	3435	0	80	148.660	1.903

similar for the affected persons. For such long periods of time measurements for security do not exist, therefore alternate security backgrounds to factoring and discrete logarithm problems have been exploited, as the latter two face the threat of a quantum computer.

A.2 Secure Hash Algorithm

The Secure Hash Algorithm (SHA) was developed and standardized by the NIST in [NIS12a] and includes a family of cryptographic hash functions. These functions take arbitrary length inputs to produce a unique output, which is often referred to as the message digest. This fixed length message digest is a representation of the input and allows for integrity verification. A small change in the input of the function result in a significant change of the output, which is know as diffusion [Sha49] or the avalanche effect [Fei73].

Table A.1 denotes the implementation results of various SHA function implementations. Note that SHA-224 and SHA-384 are based on the SHA-256 and SHA-512 implementation variants, respectively. The implementations presented in this table are more or less exact implementations of the NIST standard [NIS12a].

The security of the SHA family has been discussed in [Dan09]. It summarizes the security strengths of each SHA variant in terms of collision and preimage resistance. [BREK11] further states that SHA-1 shall not be used for signature generation after 2013, since the collision resistance of SHA-1 is not clear after the attack presented by Wang et al. [WYY05].

A.3 Advanced Encryption Standard

The Advanced Encryption Standard (AES) is the most widely used algorithm providing symmetric cryptography. It has been selected in a public competition as a successor of the DES and 3DES. The algorithm is patent free and can be used without licensing. AES is approved by the US government for confidential federal documents.

The AES cypher is based on a substitution-permutation network and uses four modules during encryption, namely *SubBytes*, *ShiftRows*, *MixColumns*, and *AddRoundkey*. It uses the 128-bit input as a 4x4 matrix of bytes, referred to as the state. AES is carried out by the repetition of these main modules in a number of rounds.

The *SubBytes* function represents the non-linear substitution of bytes, needed to eliminate simple algebraic attacks. The cyclic shifting of the rows in the state variable is realized using the *ShiftRows* function. The *MixColumns* is realizing a permutation of the columns in the state variable and provides the necessary diffusion [Sha49] of the cypher. Initially only one key supplied to the cipher. A new key for every round is derived using the first three modules. This roundkey is added/XORed to the state value during the *AddRoundKey* function.

The hardware implementation of the *ShiftRows* and *MixColumns* functions boils down to some wires. The bitwise addition in the *AddRoundKey* function is realized using XOR functions. In general, there are no decisions when implementing this functions in hardware other then the bit-width of the individual operations.

A.3.1 Low Latency AES Implementation

Figure A.1 depicts the timing diagram of the low latency AES implementation (AES-128 v2). An overview of various implementation variants is given in Table A.2. The two implementation variants AES-128 and AES-128 v2, mainly differ in the realization of the sub-bytes implementation. The first variant uses BRAMs for implementation while the second variant uses a straight-forward distributed logic implementation. A comparison of different sub-bytes implementations is denoted in Section A.3.2.

A.3 Advanced Encryption Standard

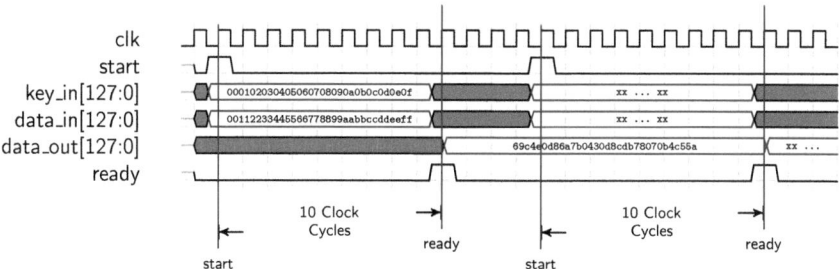

Figure A.1: Timing Diagram of Low Latency AES Implementation.

The last two variants have been included for comparison. Note, the latency values for the latter two have been estimated as the latency has not been stated in the references.

Table A.2: AES Hardware Implementation Variants

	Reg.	LUT	Slices	BRAM	latency [cycles]	Freq. [MHz]	Throughput [Gbit/s]
AES-128 [FMMH11]	524	899	–	5	24	308.35	1.645
AES-128 v2	392	1327	369	0	11	234.58	2.729
Iterative [Hut12]	270	1196	417	2	11	204.81	2.622
Pipeline [Hut12]	2827	5434	2257	57	20	150.08	19.211
AES-Fast [Hel09]	–	–	342	0	(11)	363	4.224
Bulens et al. [BSQ+08]	–	–	400	0	(11)	350	4.1

A.3.2 Sub-Bytes Implementations

The substitution of bytes (sub_bytes, or more often SBox) is an integral part of the AES algorithm to guarantee the non-linearity of the result. In

Table A.3: Resource Utilization of Different SBox Implementations for Virtex-5 Devices

Name	distributed logic	distributed logic [BSQ+08]	BRAM	composite field
Register	0	0	0	0
LUT-6	1152	540	0	1000
BRAM	0	0	5	0
Delay[ns]	5.332ns	–	(1.818ns)	9.194ns
Delay[clk]	0	0	1	0
Style	combinatorial	combinatorial	synchronous	combinatorial

general, there exist two major implementation variants, namely memory based approaches and logic for the composite field implementation. The implementation of distributed logic, which mainly exploits the LUTs as memory, and a BRAM-based implementation are both memory based. The authors of [BSQ+08] discriminate between, logic, algorithmic and RAM based approaches, representing a similar taxonomy. An overview of several implementation variants for the SBOX is given in Table A.3. The first distributed logic variant represents a straight-forward, but also portable implementation, whereas the approach presented by Bulens et al. exploits architectural properties of certain FPGAs.

Many implementations utilize BRAMs to realize the SBOX, as this is an straight forward implementation of look-up tables. To enable a comparison between approaches using distributed logic and BRAMs, the equivalent of both realizations is denoted in the following. An SBOX is generally specified by a look-up-table of 256 x 8 bit values. If encryption and decryption shall be provided simultaneously, the resources required by the SBOX doubles for all memory based variants. Although, this is also true for the BRAM implementation, the actual number of BRAMs will not increase in this case, as one BRAM provides enough memory resources for both, encryption and decryption look-up tables.

Utilizing distributed logic, the implementation of one SBOX requires 64 6-input LUTs. The full-parallel look-up of a 128 bit AES input block is provided by 16 of these SBOX instances. Together with the 4 encryption-only instances required by the key-schedule it summarizes to 16 full and 4 half instances, which in total requires 1152 6-input LUTs. An efficient approach for implementing the SBox has been presented by Bulens et al. in [BSQ+08]. They use only eight slices to implement a single SBox, such that their implementation only requires 512 LUTs for the encryption and 128 LUTs for the key schedule. Additionally the depth of the logic is reduced, which improves overall performance. This optimization is achieved by grouping four 6-input LUTs together with two multiplexer stages to perform a 256 x 1 bit look-up.

$$(16\text{SBox} + \frac{4\text{SBox}}{2}) * \frac{256 * 8\text{bit}}{\text{SBox}} * \frac{\text{LUT-6}}{64\text{bit}} = 1152 \text{ LUT-6} \qquad (A.2)$$

$$(16\text{SBox} + \frac{4\text{SBox}}{2}) * \frac{256 * 8\text{bit}}{\text{SBox}} * \frac{\text{LUT-4}}{16\text{bit}} = 4608 \text{ LUT-4} \qquad (A.3)$$

If an SBox is implemented in a BRAM, usually four of these are combined to match with the 32 bit inputs of the BRAM. To enable the look-up of a full 128 bit AES input block, usually 4 of these BRAMs are utilized. An additional BRAM is required to implement the key-schedule.

A.4 Message Authentication Codes (MAC)

A Message Authentication Code (MAC) is an authentication tag that is appended to a message. This authentication tag needs to be created by an irreversible process. Cryptographic hash functions are one-way functions, which are used to produce such a tag. Since the sole creation of a cryptographic hash only provides integrity of the data, a secret key is used to create MACs to additionally provide the authenticity. The construction of the MAC has to ensure, that secret cannot be derived from the output in computationally feasible time.

Two common methods to create these authentication tags are: HMACs and block ciphers using CBC modes. The HMAC construction by Bellare et al. [BCK96], a widely adapted standard for authentication, is outlined in the following. Block ciphers in CBC mode xor the output of the cipher and the message to create the next input. The output of the last message block represents the authentication tag.

The verification of the authentication tag is done by computing the MAC again followed by the comparison of the result with the supplied value. The message is authenticated if these two values match. A comprehensive overview of these and various other MAC constructions is given in [PP10, Chapter 12].

A.4.1 Hash-based Message Authentication Codes (HMACs)

Bellare et al. not only give a definition ot the HMAC function in their work [BCK96], but also analyze the security other MAC constructions. Later this proposal has been described as an RFC [KBC97] and it has been approved by the NIST [NIS08]. Currently the HMAC standard is widely used, for example to realize the access protocols in current TPMs (cf. Section 2.2.6).

Mathematically the $HMAC(K,m)$ function under key (K) of message (m) to yield the signature (σ) is defined by:

$$\sigma = HMAC(K,m) = H\left((K \oplus opad) || H((K \oplus ipad) || m)\right). \qquad (A.4)$$

Where $H(x)$ denotes to a cryptographic hash function and —— represents the concatenation operation. A generic property of HMAC is that the overall cryptographic strength of the HMAC function is depending upon the underlying hash function [KBC97].

The upper bound for the HMAC throughput, is the underlying hash-function, e.g. HMAC-SHA cannot be faster than the SHA function itself. In addition to the time required to compute the hash of the message (Blocks = $\lceil length(m)/512 \rceil$ for SHA-1), the HMAC includes two additional blocks, which adds two hash iterations to the required time. To mitigate this issue, the results of $H(K \oplus ipad)$ and $H(K \oplus opad)$ may be precomputed to improve performance. These values need to be stored in the same manner as secret keys.

As an implementation example the HMAC function, as it has been presented in [FMMH11] is given. This exploits an AES-based Matjas-Meyer-Oseas [MMO85] hash function, which is also widely known as Davies-Meyer scheme (cf. [PGV94]) This hashing scheme is then embedded in the general HMAC function. The resource consumption of the HMAC scheme is denoted in Table 5.1.

A.5 Authenticated Encryption

The term generic composition refers to the composition of an authentication scheme and an encryption scheme to realize authenticated encryption. Simply selecting algorithms for both authentication and confidentiality seems straightforward and secure, but a number of pitfalls have been discovered [vT05].

A.5 Authenticated Encryption

To ensure authentic and confidential data, both mechanisms need to utilize independent keys, K_1 and K_2 respectively. In general, there exist three common schemes for *authenticated encryption* as detailed in the following:

Encrypt-then-MAC The message M is encrypted $C \leftarrow E_{K_2}(M)$ and the resulting ciphertext is computed by applying $\sigma \leftarrow MAC_{K_1}(C)$ to generate the ciphertext/signature pair.

MAC-then-Encrypt First the authentication code σ of the message M is generated by $\sigma \leftarrow MAC_{K_1}(M)$ and then the resulting pair is encrypted by $C \leftarrow E_{K_2}((M, \sigma))$.

Encrpyt and MAC Both operations utilize only the message M as an input to yield the ciphertext/signature pair, by applying $C \leftarrow E_{K_2}(M)$ and $\sigma \leftarrow MAC_{K_1}(M)$, respectively.

Decryption and verification are executed intuitively by reversing the order of the operations.

A comprehensive list of the available *authenticated encryption* schemes is compiled in [vT05]. The authors categorize single-pass and multi-pass schemes, and whether the scheme is patented or not.

A.5.1 AES Counter Mode with CBC-MAC – AES-CCM

AES-CCM is a common *authenticated encryption* scheme used in several applications, e.g. it is a mandatory standard for 802.11 [IEE12]. Additionally, the scheme is patent free and a proof of its security has been presented. The implementation of this scheme for FPGAs is presented in the following.

The AES-CCM scheme is generally using two passes, the first one being the MAC generation and the second the actual encryption of the data. If the scheme is implemented in Hardware, both passes can be carried out in parallel as stated in [WHF03]. As an additional asset, the CCM scheme utilizes only one key for both passes, being especially useful as the two key-schedules may be merged.

Table A.4 lists the parallel execution steps of the AES-CCM implementation. The parameters used within this table are detailed in the following.

t length of the MAC in bytes.

Q the length of the Payload in Bytes.

N a Nonce.

P The payload represents the data being encrypted.

A The associated data corresponds to the unencrypted but authenticated data within the scheme.

q the byte representation of the payload length (Q).

B_0 contains the configuration flags of the algorithm (t,q), the nonce for this encryption step (N), and the length of the number of bytes in the payload (Q).

B_i Input data of the algorithm.

u the number of associated data blocks.

r the total number of data blocks ($Q + u + 1$).

A commonly used value for the parameter t is 8 bytes. The parameter q is often selected to be 2 bytes in length, which is relatively small but it allows the nonce to be 15-q bytes in length. Moreover, with 2 bytes representing the octet length, a total of $2^{16} * 8 = 64$Kbyte defines the maximum payload length. This notation corresponds to [Dwo07]. In general, the scheme allows both, authentication data and payload to be of zero length, resulting in a pure authentication mode.

A.5.2 Hardware Implementation

In general, AES-CCM schemes use 2-pass approach, as it has been specified in [NIS08]. Hence, a parallel scheme as visualized in Figure 5.10 mitigates this drawback and implements the authenticated encryption scheme within a single pass. This is achieved by the parallel execution of two AES encryption cores. The keyschedule has been extracted from both AES cores to efficiently use the resources. Only the datapath has been replicated to enable the parallel execution.

A general timing diagram of the AES-CCM implementation is depicted in Figure A.2. The next_data signal has been delayed by one clock cycle for simplification of the visual representation. In the implementation the next data value may be presented after 11 clock cycles. The implementation presented in this thesis, not only requires a minimum of 11 clock cycles for each AES encryption, it further exploits the parallel structure of the CCM scheme. The required number of AES encryption iterations in this implementation is represented by:

A.5 Authenticated Encryption

Table A.4: Scheduling of Internal Operations in AES-CCM Implementation

Step	Input	Internal Signals	AES #1	AES #2	Output
Init & $MAC(B_0)$	$B_0(Flags, N, Q)$	$B'_0 \Leftarrow (Flags, N); i, j = 0$	$Y_0 = CIPH(B_0)$		
$MAC(Assoc.Data)$	$B_1 \cdots B_u$	$i++$	$Y_i = CIPH(B_i \oplus Y_{i-1})$		
$MAC(Payload)$	$B_{u+1} \cdots B_r$	$i++, j++$	$Y_i = CIPH(B_i \oplus Y_{i-1})$	$S_j = CIPH(Ctr_j)$	$C_j = B_{u+j+1} \oplus S_j$
$MACoutput$		$T = MSB(Y_r)$		$S_0 = CIPH(Ctr_0)$	$C_j = T \oplus S_0$
$VerifyMAC$	$MAC = T' \oplus S_0$	$T = MSB(Y_r)$		$S_0 = CIPH(Ctr_0)$	valid

$$\text{\# assoc. data blocks} = \lceil u*8/128 \rceil \tag{A.5}$$
$$\text{\# message blocks} = \lceil Q*8/128 \rceil \tag{A.6}$$
$$\text{\# AES encryptions} = \text{\# assoc. data blocks} + \text{\# message blocks} + 1 \tag{A.7}$$
$$\text{throughput} = \frac{\text{\# AES encryptions} * \text{Frequency}}{11} \tag{A.8}$$

In short, the authenticated encryption realized by the presented hardware module, processes one 128 bit block of data within 11 clock cycles.

At the end of each authenticated encryption, the calculated MAC may be compared to the supplied value T. The output function of the *valid* signal is denoted in (A.9). If the verification is not necessary, especially if data is encrypted, this last step may then be omitted.

$$valid = \begin{cases} 1 \Leftrightarrow & T = T' \\ 0 \Leftrightarrow & T \neq T' \end{cases} \tag{A.9}$$

A.6 Random Number Generators

Random Number Generator (RNG) play an integral role of every security protocol. New random numbers (nonces) are needed for every authentication procedure to guarantee the freshness of the reply. This freshness can only be guaranteed, if the random numbers produced by the RNG fulfill certain quality requirements. In contrast to other functions, it is not possible to evaluate the correctness of the RNG output, as it should be unpredictable by nature. Hence, the non-determinism of RNGs is tested using statistical methods as it has been compiled in the DieHarder[2] test suite.

Usually, non-deterministic RNGs often produce random bits at a very low rate. To reach the required bitrates, they are often combined with pseudo-random generators. A pseudo-random number generator is a deterministic function that uses diffusion to create new numbers from a given seed. For example block ciphers provide the necessary diffusion to realize this. However, the overall quality of the random numbers is determined among others by the quality of the seed. A non-deterministic seed may be produced by measuring

---

[2]http://www.phy.duke.edu/~rgb/General/dieharder.php

A.6 Random Number Generators

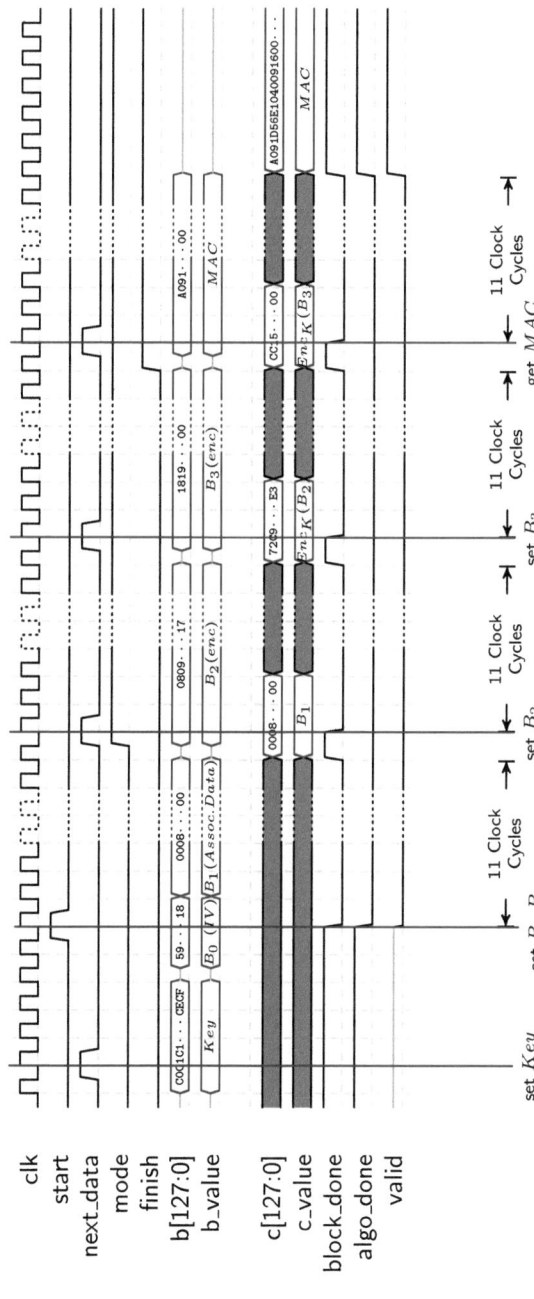

Figure A.2: AES-CCM Timing Diagram

unpredictable physical phenomena and exploit the results as a source of entropy.

An FPGA-based true RNG exploiting the metastability of storage elements (flip-flops) was introduces by Majzoobi et al. in [MKD11]. These authors use the programmable delay lines to introduce signal transitions during setup and hold times of the flip-flops embodied in the FPGA. This puts the flip-flops into a metastable state to produce unpredictable outputs as needed for RNGs. In practice, random sources often show defects (cf. [vT05, p.512]), such as correlations between bit values. To overcome these issues, the random bit streams are post-processed to hide these defects. These post-processing mechanisms range from scrambling to hash algorithms or block ciphers in certain modes.

The current advancements in the design and implementation of PUFs is also beneficial for the application of random number generation. A certain amount of all PUF implementations provide random bit values, which in turn can be exploited as entropy sources for RNGs. Despite the approach presented by Majzoobi et al., various other approaches have been presented in literature.

Self-oscillating structures provide random bits whenever they are measured. This principle has been applied by Kohlbrenner and Gaj in [KG04]. Varchola and Drutarovski presented an advanced ring oscillator based approach by exploiting the transition effects in [VD10]. Their approach shows a higher variance, uncorrelated random bits and is almost independent from working conditions.

The start-up noise of on-chip memories is another physical property that is utilized to implement random bit generators. Güeneysu et al. and later van der Leest et al. exploit this feature in [Gün10] and [LSS$^+$12], respectively.

As a step beyond this state Maes et al. include a key generator into their PUF design. Thereby they provide a key generator together with a secure storage element in [MVHV12].

Attacks on RNGs, such as frequency injection [MM09], have to be considered if one of the herein outlined schemes is put into practical use.

B FPGA Technology

FPGAs allow the implementation of a self contained digital system. The three basic components of a digital system, namely logic functions, interconnection, and external interfaces, are fully programmable in an FPGA. Logic functions are provided by the LUTs in the FPGA, which currently feature up to six inputs. This enables the realization of logic functions with six literals. Additionally, the results may be retained using storage elements, such as flip-flops or latches. In recent devices, four LUTs are grouped together with four flip-flops and additional adder logic to form a basic logic component, often referred to as Configurable Logic Block (CLB).

The interconnection between CLBs and the external I/Os is realized by switching matrices, to realize every possible combination of input and output connections for each CLB. The connection to external devices is provided by I/O blocks supporting the electrical characteristics required by various standards. Furthermore, there are special I/O ports available for the realization of serial high-speed protocols, such as SATA, PCIe, just to name a few.

The functions realized by an FPGA are determined by the configuration data present on the device. This configuration data is generated from a hardware description language representation, specifying the desired functionality of the device. From this description a netlist representation is deducted by the synthesis tool. This netlist contains the logic function and their interconnection, which defines the digital system. Afterwards, this intermediate format is mapped to the target architecture creating the actual implementation. This implementation is then compiled into a configuration data stream, which is then loaded into the memory of the FPGA.

B.1 Configuration Technologies

In principle there are two distinct methods for the configuration of an FPGA, the external and the internal configuration. The external configuration is exploited by using the generic JTAG interface, while the internal configuration is using the internal configuration logic. For the case of the external

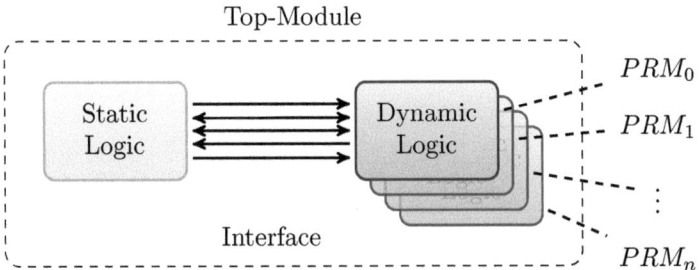

Figure B.1: Module Structure for Partial Reconfiguration

configuration, the data is transferred to the configuration memory and is consequently activated. SRAM-based FPGAs in general provide an internal logic for the configuration of the device. This logic accesses an external memory and transfers the configuration data to the device. Flash-based FPGAs use an internal non-volatile memory to store the configuration data and activate this configuration directly at power-up.

Additionally, most of the recent devices support an internal interface to access the configuration. For Xilinx devices this is referred to as Internal Configuration Access Port (ICAP). This interface may be used to reconfigure parts of the configuration data from within the system.

B.2 Partial Reconfiguration

Partial reconfiguration [Alt10, Xil12c] enables the selective modification of the functions provided by an FPGA. Parts of the configuration are thereby exchanged to realize a different function. The use of *partial reconfiguration* allows for time sliced resource sharing and enables to support a variety of algorithms for a certain task. If the reconfiguration is triggered by an internal event and carried out during the runtime of the device, it is referred to as *dynamic partial reconfiguration*. The *dynamic partial reconfiguration* requires measures to protect against data loss of the processed data. An often referred application scenario for *dynamic partial reconfiguration* is the processing of data streams (i.e. video, audio) as well as software-defined radio [DNLM09].

The *partial reconfiguration* technology is provided by multiple FPGA vendors. This special feature of current FPGAs enables the replacement of parts of the configuration data. If this feature is exploited, the configuration data is divided logically into two partitions, namely the static logic and the dynamic logic. The static logic partition contains configuration data, which is not modified throughout the lifetime of this product. The dynamic logic partition is utilized to realize changing functionality. Both of these partitions may contain as much logic resources as there are available. This consequently leads to the other partition being empty. If the dynamic logic is empty, the resulting system represents an equivalent to FPGA implementations without *partial reconfiguration* capabilities.

The dynamic logic partition may be divided into one or more Partial Reconfigurable Regions (PRRs). These regions define the position and size of the loaded Partial Reconfigurable Modules (PRMs) realizing the desired functionality.

B.2.1 Workflow

The partial reconfiguration workflow is represented in the following. For simplicity, the outlined workflow contains only one PRR in the design. If more than one PRR is used, the steps 3. to 8. have to be repeated for each of the regions.

1. Interface definition in top-module

2. Definition of the top-module functions

3. Instantiation of a PRM as a stub module

4. Definition of the available resources for the PRM

5. Synthesis and implementation of the top-module

6. Definition of the PRM functionality

7. Synthesis and implementation of the PRM

8. repeat 6. and 7. for all PRMs

In a first step, the interface of the PRM is defined in the top-level design. This interface is not reconfigurable and all partial modules have to share this common interface. The second step represents the definition of the overall top-module functions. The functions provided by the PRM are excluded in this definition. In the third step either a stub module of the PRM, or an initial implementation of the PRM is used to complete the overall system functions. Often the partitioning in static and dynamic regions is performed after the initial design and thus the PRM implementation can be used within this step. The resources available for the PRM are specified in the fourth step by defining the physical area on the FPGA. An actual implementation of the PRM helps in the definition of the required resources for the definition of the PRR. The fifth step is using the top-module description to create a representation of the static logic in the partially reconfigurable design. The steps six and seven consist of the definition and synthesis of the actual PRM, which have to be repeated for every PRM used in the design.

The common interface of the module on the one hand, or the resource requirements on the other may not match all future PRMs requirements and are therefore subject to change. In this case the top-module and/or resource requirements have to be changed accordingly, followed by a full synthesis of the overall design starting with the top-module. Of course all existing PRMs have to be synthesized again accommodating the changes in the top-module. The resulting full bitstream and all updated partial modules may then distributed to update existing implementations.

The so called partial configuration data of the PRMs are stored in the configuration memory and are configured upon request. Each partial bitstream is replacing all the content in the physical area defined in step 4. and thus occupying all the resources within this area. During the synthesis of the initial configuration data, the synthesis tool may also decide to use parts of the resources in the PRR. Consequently, these resources are not available for the realization of the PRM.

List of Publications

Stefan Nuernberger, **Thomas Feller**, and Sorin A. Huss. RAY – A Secure Microkernel Architecture. In *Eighth IEEE annual Conference on Privacy Security and Trust (PST)*, Ottawa, Canada, August 2010. doi:10.1109/PST.2010.5593231.

Thomas Feller, Sunil Malipatlolla, David Meister, and Sorin A. Huss. TinyTPM: A Lightweight Module aimed to IP Protection and Trusted Embedded Platforms. In *IEEE International Symposium on Hardware Oriented Security and Trust (HOST)*, San Diego, USA, CA, June, 2011. doi:10.1109/HST.2011.5954987.

Thomas Feller, Sunil Malipatlolla, Michael Kasper, and Sorin A. Huss. dcTPM: A Generic Architecture for Dynamic Context Management. In *IEEE International Conference on ReConFigurable Computing and FPGAs (ReConFig)*, Cancun, Mexico, December 2011. doi:10.1109/ReConFig.2011.23.

Sunil Malipatlolla, **Thomas Feller**, Abdulhadi Shoufan, Tolga Arul, and Sorin A. Huss. A Novel Architecture for a Secure Update of Cryptographic Engines on Trusted Platform Module. In *IEEE International Conference on Field-Programmable Technology (FPT)*, New Delhi, India, December 2011. doi:10.1109/FPT.2011.6132705.

Marc Stoettinger, **Thomas Feller**, and Sorin A. Huss. A Side-Channel hardened IP-Protection Scheme for FPGA-based Platforms. In *IEEE International Conference on Field-Programmable Technology (FPT)*, New Delhi, India, December 2011. doi:10.1109/FPT.2011.6269382.

Sunil Malipatlolla, **Thomas Feller**, and Sorin A. Huss. Partially Reconfigurable TPM Architectures as the Security Anchors of Future Embedded IT Systems. In *International Workshop on Cryptographic Architectures Embedded in Reconfigurable Devices (CryptArchi)*, Chateau de Goutelas, Marcoux, France, June, 2012.

Sunil Malipatlolla, **Thomas Feller**, and Sorin A. Huss. An Adaptive System Architecture for Mitigating Asymmetric Cryptography Weaknesses on TPMs. In *IEEE/ACM NASA/ESA Conference on Adaptive Hardware and Systems (AHS)*, Nuremberg, Germany, June 2012. `doi:10.1109/AHS.2012.6268654`.

Norman Goettert, **Thomas Feller**, Michael Schneider, Sorin A. Huss, and Johannes Buchmann. On the Design of Hardware Building Blocks for Modern Lattice-Based Encryption Schemes. In *Workshop on Cryptographic Hardware and Embedded Systems (CHES)*, Leuven, Belgium, September, 2012. `doi:10.1007/978-3-642-33027-8_30`.

Technical Reports

Thomas Feller and Aziz Demirezen. Hardware Trojans: Data Leakage Using General Purpose LEDs. TUD-CS-2010-2384, October, 2010.

Sami Alsouri, **Thomas Feller**, Sunil Malipatlolla, and Stefan Katzenbeisser. Hardware-based Security for Virtual Trusted Platform Modules, *arXiv preprint*, August, 2013, `arXiv:1308.1539`.

List of Supervised Theses

1. Erik Virctorsson. Encrypted Solid State Storage, November 2012. Master Thesis, ERASMUS - KTH Sweden.

2. Leonardo Solis Vasquez. Reconfigurable Security for IPTV Set-Top-Box Architectures on an FPGA, October 2012. Master Thesis, ERASMUS - Politecnico di Torino.

3. Christopher Huth. Design und Implementierung einer transparenten Verschlüsselung für SATA Festplatten, August 2012. Master Thesis.

4. Norman Göttert. Implementation of a Post Quantum Public-Key Cryptography Algorithm in Hardware, January 2012. Master Thesis.

5. David Meister. Realisierung der Kommunikation mit einem nichtflüchtigen Speicher auf Basis von Tree Parity Machines, September 2011. Master Thesis.

6. Mehmet Ariman. Automatic VHDL Testbench Generation, August 2011. Bachelor Thesis.

7. Octavio Gamero. Entwurf einer Auswertungsplattform für Seitenkanalanalysen, October 2010. Diplomarbeit.

8. Stefan Nürnberger. Secure Microkernel with Behaviour Deviation Detection, October 2010. Master Thesis.

9. Felix Deichmann. Architektur eines Multi Context TPM, March 2010. Diplomarbeit.

Other Student Works

1. Minakshi Karwa. Random Number Generatrors on FPGAs, November 2011. Internship, h_da.

2. Zuhaib Ahmed Chohan. High-Speed Video Processing on FPGAs, September 2011.

3. Suraj Das. IP-Core Library Framework for Cryptographic Modules, Juli 2011. Internship, DAAD WISE Scholarship Programme.

4. David Meister, Aziz Demirezen. Tiny TPM - reducing a TPM to its lightweight components, March 2011.

5. David Meister. AES Implementations for Resource Constraint Systems, September 2010.

6. Aziz Demirezen. Hardware Trojans, September 2010.

7. Joel Njeukam, Partielle Rekonfiguration für Virtex-5 FPGAs, April 2010. Internship.

8. Mahmoud Kamar, Hardware Trojans - State of the Art, February 2010. Internship.

Bibliography

[Ach12]   Achronix Semiconductor Corporation. *Speedster22i HD FPGA Family*, April 2012. DS004 Rev. 1.6. URL: http://www.achronix.com/wp-content/uploads/docs/Speedster22iHD_FPGA_Family_DS004.pdf.

[ADDS91]   D. G. Abraham, G. M. Dolan, G. P. Double, and J. V. Stevens. Transaction security system. *IBM Systems Journal*, 30(2):206 –229, 1991. doi:10.1147/sj.302.0206.

[AF08]   Jerome Azema and Gilles Fayad. *M-Shield^{TM} Mobile Security Technology: making wireless secure*. Texas Instruments, February 2008. White Paper. URL: http://focus.ti.com/pdfs/wtbu/ti_mshield_whitepaper.pdf.

[AFCM08]   Ignacio Algredo-Badillo, Claudia Feregrino-Uribe, René Cumplido, and Miguel Morales-Sandoval. FPGA implementation and performance evaluation of AES-CCM cores for wireless networks. In *International Conference on Reconfigurable Computing and FPGAs, 2008. ReConFig '08*, pages 421–426, December 2008. doi:10.1109/ReConFig.2008.54.

[AK96]   Ross J. Anderson and Markus Kuhn. Tamper resistance – a cautionary note. In *Proceedings of the Second USENIX Workshop on Electronic Commerce*, volume 2, pages 1–11, November 1996. URL: http://static.usenix.org/publications/library/proceedings/ec96/kuhn.html.

[AK07]   Yousra M. Alkabani and Farinaz Koushanfar. Active hardware metering for intellectual property protection and security. In *16th USENIX Security Symposium*, 2007. URL: http://static.usenix.org/events/sec07/tech/full_papers/alkabani/alkabani.pdf.

[AKP07]   Yousra Alkabani, Farinaz Koushanfar, and Miodrag Potkonjak. Remote activation of ics for piracy prevention and digital right management. In *Proceedings of the 2007 IEEE/ACM international conference on Computer-aided design (ICCAD)*, pages 674–677, November 2007. doi:10.1109/ICCAD.2007.4397343.

[Alt07] Altera. *An FPGA Design Security Solution Using a Secure Memory Device*, October 2007. White Paper WP-01033-1.0. URL: http://www.altera.com/literature/wp/wp-01033.pdf.

[Alt08] Altera. *Anti-Tamper Capabilities in FPGA Designs*, July 2008. White Paper WP-01066-1.0. URL: http://www.altera.com/literature/wp/wp-01066-anti-tamper-capabilities-fpga.pdf.

[Alt09] Altera. *Design Security in Stratix III Devices*, September 2009. White Paper WP-01010-1.5. URL: http://www.altera.com/literature/wp/wp-01010.pdf.

[Alt10] Altera. *Increasing Design Functionality with Partial and Dynamic Reconfiguration in 28-nm FPGAs*, July 2010. White Paper WP-01137-1.0. URL: http://www.altera.com/literature/wp/wp-01137-stxv-dynamic-partial-reconfig.pdf.

[Alt11a] Altera. *Cyclone III Device Handbook*, December 2011. CIII5V1-4.0. URL: http://www.altera.com/literature/hb/cyc3/cyclone3_handbook.pdf.

[Alt11b] Altera. *Stratix II Device Handbook*, April 2011. SII5V1-4.5. URL: http://www.altera.com/literature/hb/stx2/stratix2_handbook.pdf.

[Alt11c] Altera. *Stratix III Device Handbook*, March 2011. Version 2.2. URL: http://www.altera.com/literature/hb/stx3/stratix3_handbook.pdf.

[Alt11d] Altera. *Stratix IV Device Handbook*, March 2011. SIV5V1-4.5. URL: http://www.altera.com/literature/hb/stratix-iv/stratix4_handbook.pdf.

[Alt12] Altera. *Stratix V Device Handbook*, February 2012. SV5V3-1.8. URL: http://www.altera.com/literature/hb/stratix-v/stratix5_handbook.pdf.

Bibliography

[AMD12] Advanced Micro Devices, Inc. *AMD64 Architecture Programmer's Manual*, March 2012. URL: http://support.amd.com/us/Processor_TechDocs/24593_APM_v2.pdf.

[And07] Donovan Anderson. *SATA Storage Technology*. MindShare, Inc., April 2007.

[AR07] Tiago Alves and John Rudelic. *ARM® Security Solutions and Intel® Authenticated Flash – How to integrate Intel Authenticated Flash with ARM TrustZone® form maximum system protection*. Intel Corporation, 2007. URL: http://www.design-reuse.com/articles/16975/arm-security-solutions-and-intel-authenticated-flash-how-to-integrate-intel-authenticated-flash-with-arm-trustzone-for-maximum-system-protection.html.

[ARM09] ARM Ltd. *ARM Security Technology – Building a Secure System using TrustZone® Technology*, April 2009. URL: http://infocenter.arm.com/help/topic/com.arm.doc.prd29-genc-009492c/PRD29-GENC-009492C_trustzone_security_whitepaper.pdf.

[Atm12a] Atmel Corporation. *Atmel AT25DF641A Datasheet*, May 2012. Rev.: 8693B-DFLASH-5/12. URL: http://www.atmel.com/Images/doc8693.pdf.

[Atm12b] Atmel Corporation. *Atmel ATSHA204 Datasheet – Atmel CryptoAuthentication*, March 2012. Rev.: 8740D-CRYPTO-3/12. URL: http://www.atmel.com/Images/doc8740.pdf.

[BBK+08] Steven A. Bade, Linda N. Betz, Andrew G. Kegel, Michael J. Kelly, and William L. Terrell. Method and system for virtualization of trusted platform modules, May 2008.

[BCB+12] Sheetal Bhandari, Fabio Cancare, Davide Basilio Bartolini, Matteo Carminati, Marco Domenico Santambrogio, and Donatella Sciuto. On the management of dynamic partial reconfiguration to speed-up intrinsic evolvable hardware systems. In *Proceedings of the 6th HiPEAC Workshop on Reconfigurable Computing*, January 2012. URL: http://home.dei.polimi.it/bartolini/pub/workshops/bhandari-2012-wrc-dpr.pdf.

[BCG+06] Stefan Berger, Ramón Cáceres, Kenneth A. Goldman, Roland Perez, Reiner Sailer, and Leendert van Doorn. vTPM: virtualizing the trusted platform module. In *Conference on USENIX Security Symposium*, pages 305–320, August 2006. URL: http://static.usenix.org/event/sec06/tech/full_papers/berger/berger.pdf.

[BCK96] Mihir Bellare, Ran Canetti, and Hugo Krawczyk. Keying hash functions for message authentication. In Neal Koblitz, editor, *Advances in Cryptology — CRYPTO*, volume 1109 of *Lecture Notes in Computer Science*, pages 1–15. Springer Berlin / Heidelberg, 1996. doi:10.1007/3-540-68697-5_1.

[BCMV03] Roberto Bez, Emilio Camerlenghi, Alberto Modelli, and Angelo Visconti. Introduction to flash memory. *Proceedings of the IEEE*, 91(4):489–502, April 2003. doi:10.1109/JPROC.2003.811702.

[BDL97] Dan Boneh, Richard DeMillo, and Richard Lipton. On the importance of checking cryptographic protocols for faults. In Walter Fumy, editor, *Advances in Cryptology — EUROCRYPT*, volume 1233 of *Lecture Notes in Computer Science*, pages 37–51. Springer Berlin / Heidelberg, 1997. doi:10.1007/3-540-69053-0_4.

[BDWJ08] Robert M. Backus, Charles F. Duffey, Andrew C. Weil, and Swati V. Joshi. Non-imprinting memory with high speed erase, May 2008. URL: http://www.google.com/patents/US7379325.

[Ber07] Guido M. Bertoni. Secure non-volatile memory: is it a new trend for the security of embedded systems?, October 2007. Presented at the LSEC & IMEC Security Forum. URL: http://www.lsec.be/upload_directories/documents/6STM_Securenonvolatiememory_Bertoni_Guido.pdf.

[BET08] Benoit Badrignans, Reouven Elbaz, and Lionel Torres. Secure FPGA configuration architecture preventing system downgrade. In *Int. Conf. on Field Programmable Logic and Applications, FPL'08*, 2008. doi:10.1109/FPL.2008.4629951.

[BGPS10] Stefan Berger, Kenneth A. Goldman, Ronald Perez, and Reiner Sailer. Architecture for supporting attestation of a virtual machine in a single step, November 2010. US Patent 7840801.

[BKT+09] An Braeken, Serge Kubera, Frederik Trouillez, Abdellah Touhafi, Nele Mentens, and Jo Vliegen. Secure FPGA technologies and techniques. In *Field Programmable Logic and Applications, 2009. FPL 2009. International Conference on*, pages 560–563, September 2009. doi:10.1109/FPL.2009.5272414.

[BLK+07] Andrey Bogdanov, Gregor Leander, Lars R. Knudsen, Christof Paar, Axel Poschmann, Matthew J.B. Robshaw, Yannick Seurin, and Charlotte Vikkelsoe. PRESENT - An Ultra-Lightweight Block Cipher. In *Proceedings of CHES 2007*, number 4727 in Lecture Notes in Computer Science (LNCS), pages 450–466. Springer-Verlag, 2007. doi:10.1007/978-3-540-74735-2_31.

[BREK11] Elaine Barker, Allen Roginsky, Randall Easter, and Sharon Keller. *Transitions: Validation of Transitioning Cryptographic Algorithm and Key Lengths*. National Institute of Standards and Technology (NIST), February 2011. SP800-131b. URL: http://csrc.nist.gov/publications/drafts/800-131B/draft-SP800-131B_February2011.pdf.

[Bri12] Derek Brink. Endpoint security: Hardware roots of trust, June 2012. URL: http://www.aberdeen.com/Aberdeen-Library/7080/RA-trusted-computing-security.aspx.

[BSH12] Florian Benz, André Seffrin, and Sorin A. Huss. Bil: A toolchain for bitstream reverse-engineering. In *22nd International Conference on Field Programmable Logic and Applications (FPL)*, pages 735–738, August 2012. doi:10.1109/FPL.2012.6339165.

[BSI07] Federal Ministry of the Interior, Germany and Federal Ministry of Economics and Technology, Germany. *Key requirements on "Trusted Computing"*, September 2007. URL: https://www.bsi.bund.de/SharedDocs/Downloads/DE/BSI/SicherePlattformen/trusted-computing-key-requirements_pdf.pdf?__blob=publicationFile.

[BSI11]   Federal Office for Information Security, Germany. *Protection Profile for the Security Module of a Smart Metering System (Security Module PP)*, November 2011. V 0.8.3. draft. URL: https://www.bsi.bund.de/SharedDocs/Downloads/DE/BSI/SmartMeter/PP_Security_%20Module.pdf.

[BSQ+08] Philippe Bulens, François-Xavier Standaert, Jean-Jacques Quisquater, Pascal Pellegrin, and Gaël Rouvroy. Implementation of the AES-128 on virtex-5 FPGAs. In Serge Vaudenay, editor, *Progress in Cryptology – AFRICACRYPT*, volume 5023 of *Lecture Notes in Computer Science*, pages 16–26. Springer Berlin / Heidelberg, 2008.

[Buc04]   Johannes Buchmann. *Einführung in die Kryptographie*. Springer, 2004. doi:10.1007/978-3-662-06855-7.

[CA11]   J. Couch and P. Athanas. An analysis of implanted antennas in xilinx FPGAs. In *2011 International Conference on Reconfigurable Computing and FPGAs (ReConFig)*, pages 1–6, December 2011. doi:10.1109/ReConFig.2011.9.

[CAAS10] Christopher Claus, Rehan Ahmed, Florian Altenried, and Walter Stechele. Towards rapid dynamic partial reconfiguration in video-based driver assistance systems. In Phaophak Sirisuk, Fearghal Morgan, Tarek El-Ghazawi, and Hideharu Amano, editors, *Reconfigurable Computing: Architectures, Tools and Applications*, volume 5992 of *Lecture Notes in Computer Science*, pages 55–67. Springer Berlin / Heidelberg, 2010. doi:10.1007/978-3-642-12133-3_8.

[CC07]   *Common Criteria for Information Technology Security Evaluation – Evaluation Methodology*, September 2007. Version 3.1 Revision 2. URL: http://www.commoncriteriaportal.org/files/ccfiles/CEMV3.1R2.pdf.

[CC09a]   *Common Criteria for Information Technology Security Evaluation – Part 1: Introduction and general model*, July 2009. Version 3.1. URL: http://www.commoncriteriaportal.org/files/ccfiles/CCPART1V3.1R3.pdf.

[CC09b]   *Common Criteria for Information Technology Security Evaluation – Part 2: Security functional components*, July 2009. Version 3.1. URL: http://www.commoncriteriaportal.org/files/ccfiles/CCPART2V3.1R3.pdf.

[CC09c] Common Criteria for Information Technology Security Evaluation – Part 3: Security assurance components, July 2009. Version 3.1. URL: http://www.commoncriteriaportal.org/files/ccfiles/CCPART3V3.1R3.pdf.

[CDD+10] Stephen Checkoway, Lucas Davi, Alexandra Dmitrienko, Ahmad-Reza Sadeghi, Hovav Shacham, and Marcel Winandy. Return-oriented programming without returns. In *Proceedings of the 17th ACM conference on Computer and communications security*, CCS '10, pages 559–572, New York, NY, USA, 2010. ACM. doi:10.1145/1866307.1866370.

[CFK+09] Stephen Checkoway, Ariel J. Feldman, Brian Kantor, J. Alex Halderman, Edward W. Felten, and Hovav Shacham. Can DREs provide long-lasting security? the case of return-oriented programming and the AVC advantage. In *Proceedings of the 2009 conference on Electronic voting technology/workshop on trustworthy elections*, EVT/WOTE'09, pages 6–6, Berkeley, CA, USA, 2009. USENIX Association. doi:10.1145/1855491.1855497.

[Cha10] Rajat Subhra Chakraborty. *Hardware Security Through Design Obfuscation*. Phd thesis, Case Western Reserve University, US, May 2010.

[Com12] Committee on Armed Services. Inquiry into counterfeit electronic parts in the department of defense supply chain. Report 112-167, United States Senate, May 2012. 112TH Congress, 2nd Session. URL: http://www.armed-services.senate.gov/Publications/Counterfeit%20Electronic%20Parts.pdf.

[Coo06] Jim Cooke. Flash memory 101: An introduction to NAND flash. http://www.eetimes.com/design/memory-design/4009410/Flash-memory-101-An-Introduction-to-NAND-flash, March 2006. URL: http://www.eetimes.com/design/memory-design/4009410/Flash-memory-101-An-Introduction-to-NAND-flash.

[CR09] Liqun Chen and Mark Ryan. Offline dictionary attack on TCG TPM weak authorisation data, and solution. In David

Gawrock, Helmut Reimer, Ahmad-Reza Sadeghi, and Claire Vishik, editors, *Future of Trust in Computing*, pages 193–196. Vieweg+Teubner, 2009. doi:10.1007/978-3-8348-9324-6_20.

[CR10] Liqun Chen and Mark Ryan. Attack, solution and verification for shared authorisation data in TCG TPM. In Pierpaolo Degano and Joshua Guttman, editors, *Formal Aspects in Security and Trust (FAST'09)*, volume 5983 of *Lecture Notes in Computer Science (LNCS)*, pages 201–216. Springer Berlin / Heidelberg, 2010. doi:10.1007/978-3-642-12459-4_15.

[CSF+08] D. Cooper, S. Santesson, S. Farrell, S. Boeyen, R. Housley, and W. Polk. Internet X.509 Public Key Infrastructure Certificate and Certificate Revocation List (CRL) Profile. RFC 5280 (Proposed Standard), May 2008. URL: http://www.ietf.org/rfc/rfc5280.txt.

[CZS+08] C. Claus, B. Zhang, W. Stechele, L. Braun, M. Hubner, and J. Becker. A multi-platform controller allowing for maximum dynamic partial reconfiguration throughput. In *International Conference on Field Programmable Logic and Applications, 2008. FPL 2008*, pages 535–538, September 2008. doi:10.1109/FPL.2008.4630002.

[Dan09] Quynh Dang. *Recommendation for Applications Using Approved Hash Algorithms*. National Institute of Standards and Technology (NIST), February 2009. SP800-107. URL: http://csrc.nist.gov/publications/nistpubs/800-107/NIST-SP-800-107.pdf.

[Dei10] Felix Deichmann. *Architektur eines Multi Context TPM*. Diplomarbeit, Technische Universität Darmstadt, March 2010.

[DFG+11] Anupam Datta, Jason Franklin, Deepak Garg, Limin Jia, and Dilsun Kaynar. On adversary models and compositional security. *IEEE Security & Privacy Magazine*, 9:26–32, May 2011. doi:10.1109/MSP.2010.203.

[DK09] Saar Drimer and Markus G. Kuhn. A protocol for secure remote updates of FPGA configurations. In Jürgen Becker, Roger Woods, Peter Athanas, and Fearghal Morgan, editors,

5th International Workshop on Reconfigurable Computing: Architectures, Tools and Applications (ARC), volume 5453 of *Lecture Notes in Computer Science (LNCS)*, pages 50–61. Springer Berlin / Heidelberg, 2009. doi:10.1007/978-3-642-00641-8_8.

[dlP12] Antonio de la Piedra. Compact AES-CCM core, 2012. URL: http://opencores.org/project,aesccm.

[DNLM09] Julien Delorme, Amor Nafkha, Pierre Leray, and Christophe Moy. New OPBHWICAP Interface for Realtime Partial Reconfiguration of FPGA. In *International Conference on Reconfigurable Computing and FPGAs (ReConFig)*, December 2009. doi:10.1109/ReConFig.2009.69.

[DoD85] Department of Defence – Computer Security Center. *Trusted Computer System Evaluation Criteria*, December 1985. 5200.28-STD DoD.

[DPW11] Jean Paul Degabriele, Kenny Paterson, and Gaven Watson. Provable security in the real world. *IEEE Security & Privacy Magazine*, 9:33–41, May 2011. doi:10.1109/MSP.2010.200.

[Dri07] Saar Drimer. Authentication of FPGA bitstreams: why and how. In *Applied Reconfigurable Computing*, volume 4419 of *LNCS*, pages 73–84. Springer, March 2007. doi:10.1007/978-3-540-71431-6_7.

[Dri08] Saar Drimer. Volatile FPGA design security – a survey. http://www.saardrimer.com/sd410/papers/fpga_security.pdf, April 2008.

[Dri09] Saar Drimer. *Security for volatile FPGAs*. Phd thesis, University of Cambridge, Computer Laboratory, November 2009. URL: http://www.cl.cam.ac.uk/techreports/UCAM-CL-TR-763.pdf.

[dVM07] Ann de Vries and Yanjun Ma. A logical approach to nvm integration in soc design. Technical report, IMPINJ, January 2007. URL: http://www.impinj.com/pdf/EDN_NVMinSoC.pdf.

[Dwo07] Morris Dworkin. *Recommendation for Block Cipher Modes of Operation: The CCM Mode for Authentication* and *Confidentiality*. National Institute of Standards and Technology (NIST), July 2007. SP800-38C. URL: http://csrc.nist.gov/publications/nistpubs/800-38C/SP800-38C_updated-July20_2007.pdf.

[DY83] Danny Dolev and Andrew C. Yao. On the security of public key protocols. *IEEE Transactions on Information Theory*, 29(2):198–208, March 1983. doi:10.1109/TIT.1983.1056650.

[EA10] Jan-Erik Ekberg and N. Asokan. External authenticated non-volatile memory with lifecycle management for state protection in trusted computing. In Liqun Chen and Moti Yung, editors, *Trusted Systems*, volume 6163 of *Lecture Notes in Computer Science*, pages 16–38. Springer Berlin / Heidelberg, 2010. doi:10.1007/978-3-642-14597-1_2.

[EAK+08] Jan-Erik Ekberg, N. Asokan, Kari Kostiainen, Pasi Eronen, Aarne Rantala, and Aishvarya Sharma. Onboard credentials platform: Design and implementation. Technical Report NRC-TR-2008-001, Nokia Research Center, Helsinki, Finland, January 2008. URL: http://http://research.nokia.com/files/tr/NRC-TR-2008-001.pdf.

[ECG+09] Reouven Elbaz, David Champagne, Catherine Gebotys, Ruby B. Lee, Nachiketh Potlapally, and Lionel Torres. Hardware mechanisms for memory authentication: A survey of existing techniques and engines. In *Transactions on Computational Science IV*, volume 5430, pages 1–22. Springer Berlin Heidelberg, Berlin, Heidelberg, 2009. doi:10.1007/978-3-642-01004-0_1.

[EGP+07] Thomas Eisenbarth, Tim Güneysu, Christof Paar, Ahmad-Reza Sadeghi, Dries Schellekens, and Marko Wolf. Reconfigurable trusted computing in hardware. In *2nd Workshop on Scalable Trusted Computing (STC'07)*. ACM, 2007.

[EK07] Jan-Erik Ekberg and Markku Kylänpää. Mobile Trusted Module (MTM) - an introduction. Technical Report NRC-TR-2007-015, Nokia Research Center, Helsinki, Finland, November 2007. URL: http://research.nokia.com/files/NRCTR2007015.pdf.

[Els11] Data privacy & data security in german smart grids and smart meters, March 2011. URL: http://www.elster-instromet.com/en/download_magazines/Profiles_2011_03_DataSecurity.pdf.

[EV12] Ken Eguro and Ramarathnam Venkatesan. FPGAs for trusted cloud computing. In *2012 22nd International Conference on Field Programmable Logic and Applications (FPL)*, pages 63–70, August 2012. doi:10.1109/FPL.2012.6339242.

[FD10] Thomas Feller and Aziz Demirezen. Hardware Trojans: Data Leakage Using General Purpose LEDs. Technical Report TUD-CS-2010-2384, CASED - Center for Advanced Security Research Darmstadt, Darmstadt, Germany, October 2010. URL: http://www.informatik.tu-darmstadt.de/fileadmin/user_upload/Group_ISS/TUD-CS-2010-2384.pdf.

[Fei73] Horst Feistel. Cryptography and computer privacy. *Scientific american*, 228(5):15–23, 1973. URL: http://www.apprendre-en-ligne.net/crypto/bibliotheque/feistel/.

[FMKH11] Thomas Feller, Sunil Malipatlolla, Michael Kasper, and Sorin A. Huss. dcTPM: A Generic Architecture for Dynamic Context Management. In *IEEE International Conference on ReConFigurable Computing and FPGAs (ReConFig)*, pages 211–216, November 2011. doi:10.1109/ReConFig.2011.23.

[FMMH11] Thomas Feller, Sunil Malipatlolla, David Meister, and Sorin A. Huss. TinyTPM: A lightweight module aimed to IP protection and trusted embedded platforms. In *Hardware-Oriented Security and Trust (HOST), 2011 IEEE International Symposium on*, pages 6–11, June 2011. doi:10.1109/HST.2011.5954987.

[FS03] Niels Ferguson and Bruce Schneier. *Practical Cryptography*. John Wiley & Sons, Inc., New York, NY, USA, 2003.

[FS12] Bartol Filipowić and Oliver Schimmel. Protecting embedded systems against product piracy. Technical report, Fraunhofer Research Institution for Applied and Integrated Security, April 2012. Version 1.1 (eng).

[GB08] Ken Goldman and Stefan Berger. TPM main part 3 - IBM commands, January 2008. Revision 36.

	URL: http://researcher.watson.ibm.com/researcher/files/us-kgoldman/mainP3IBMCommandsrev36.pdf.
[GCvDD02]	Blaise Gassend, Dwaine Clarke, Marten van Dijk, and Srinivas Devadas. Silicon physical random functions. In *Proceedings of the 9th ACM Conference on Computer and Communications Security*, CCS '02, pages 148–160, New York, NY, USA, 2002. ACM. doi:10.1145/586110.586132.
[GDWL92]	Daniel D. Gajski, Nikil D. Dutt, Allen C-H Wu, and Steve Y-L Lin. *High-level Synthesis: Introduction to Chip and System Design*, volume 34. Kluwer Boston, 1992.
[GG11]	Ian Grigg and Peter Gutmann. The curse of cryptographic numerology. *IEEE Security & Privacy Magazine*, 9(3):70–72, May 2011. complete source. doi:10.1109/MSP.2011.69.
[GK98]	Rob Glenn and Stephen Kent. The NULL Encryption Algorithm and Its Use With IPsec. RFC 2410 (Proposed Standard), November 1998. URL: http://www.ietf.org/rfc/rfc2410.txt.
[GKMB09]	Benjamin Glas, Alexander Klimm, Klaus Müller-Glaser, and Jürgen Becker. Configuration Measurement for FPGA-based Trusted Platforms. In *20th IEEE/IFIP Int. Symp. on Rapid System Prototyping*, 2009. doi:10.1109/RSP.2009.28.
[GKS+08a]	Benjamin Glas, Alexander Klimm, Oliver Sander, Klaus Müller-Glaser, and Jürgen Becker. A System Architecture for Reconfigurable Trusted Platforms. In *Proceedings of IEEE/ACM Int. Conference on Design, Automation and Test in Europe*, pages 541–544, 2008. doi:10.1109/DATE.2008.4484907.
[GKS+08b]	Benjamin Glas, Alexander Klimm, David Schwab, Klaus Müller-Glaser, and Jürgen Becker. A Prototype of Trusted Platform Functionality on Reconfigurable Hardware for Bitstream Updates. In *19th IEEE/IFIP Int. Symp. on Rapid System Prototyping*, 2008. doi:10.1109/RSP.2008.24.
[GKST07]	Jorge Guajardo, Sandeep Kumar, Geert-Jan Schrijen, and Pim Tuyls. FPGA intrinsic PUFs and their use for IP protection. In Pascal Paillier and Ingrid Verbauwhede, editors, *Cryptographic*

Hardware and Embedded Systems (CHES), volume 4727 of Lecture Notes in Computer Science, pages 63–80. Springer Berlin / Heidelberg, 2007. doi:10.1007/978-3-540-74735-2_5.

[GMW12] Tim Güneysu, Igor Markov, and André Weimerskirch. Securely sealing multi-FPGA systems. In *Reconfigurable Computing: Architectures, Tools and Applications (ARC)*, volume 7199, pages 276–289. Springer Berlin Heidelberg, March 2012. doi:10.1007/978-3-642-28365-9_23.

[Gol04] Oded Goldreich. *Foundations of Cryptography: Volume 2, Basic Applications*. Cambridge University Press, 2004.

[Gra06] David Grawrock. *The Intel Safer Computing Initiative Building Blocks for Trusted Computing*. Intel Press, 1st edition, March 2006.

[Gün10] Tim Güneysu. True random number generation in block memories of reconfigurable devices. In *International Conference on Field-Programmable Technology (FPT)*, pages 200–207, December 2010. doi:10.1109/FPT.2010.5681499.

[Gut01] Peter Gutmann. Data remanence in semiconductor devices. In *Proceedings of the 10th conference on USENIX Security Symposium - Volume 10*, SSYM'01, pages 4–4, Berkeley, CA, USA, 2001. USENIX Association. URL: https://www.usenix.org/legacy/events/sec01/gutmann.html.

[Hel09] Helion Technology Limited. *Helion Technology - High Performance AES (Rijndael) cores for Xilinx FPGA*, September 2009. Data Sheet, Revision 2.4.0. URL: http://www.heliontech.com/downloads/aes_xilinx_helioncore.pdf.

[Hel11] Helion Technology Limited. *Helion Technology - AES-CCM Core family for Xilinx FPGA*, August 2011. Data Sheet, Revision 1.2. URL: http://www.heliontech.com/downloads/aes_ccm_8bit_xilinx_datasheet.pdf.

[HKT11] Simen G. Hansen, Dirk Koch, and Jim Torresen. High speed partial run-time reconfiguration using enhanced ICAP hard macro. In *2011 IEEE International Symposium on Parallel and Distributed Processing Workshops and Phd Forum (IPDPSW)*, pages 174–180, May 2011. doi:10.1109/IPDPS.2011.139.

[HMK12] Gernot Heiser, Toby Murray, and Gerwin Klein. It's time for trustworthy systems. *Security Privacy, IEEE*, 10(2):67–70, march-april 2012. doi:10.1109/MSP.2012.41.

[HT09] Helena Handschuh and Elena Trichina. Securing flash technology: How does it look from inside? In Norbert Pohlmann, Helmut Reimer, and Wolfgang Schneider, editors, *ISSE 2008 Securing Electronic Business Processes*, pages 380–389. Vieweg+Teubner, 2009. doi:10.1007/978-3-8348-9283-6_40.

[HUS99] Ilija Hadžić, Sanjay Udani, and Jonathan Smith. FPGA Viruses. In Patrick Lysaght, James Irvine, and Reiner Hartenstein, editors, *Field Programmable Logic and Applications*, volume 1673 of *Lecture Notes in Computer Science*, pages 291–300. Springer Berlin / Heidelberg, 1999. doi:10.1007/978-3-540-48302-1_30.

[Hut12] Christopher Huth. *Design und Implementierung einer transparenten Verschlüsselung für SATA Festplatten*. Master Thesis, Technische Universität Darmstadt, August 2012.

[Hwa09] Seong Oun Hwang. Content and service protection for IPTV. *IEEE Transactions on Broadcasting*, 55(2):425–436, June 2009. doi:10.1109/TBC.2009.2020446.

[IBM12] CryptoCards – IBM Systems cryptographic hardware products, 2012. URL: http://www.ibm.com/security/cryptocards/.

[IEE12] IEEE Standard for Information Technology–Telecommunications and Information Exchange between Systems Local and Metropolitan Area Networks–Specific Requirements Part 11: Wireless LAN Medium Access Control (MAC) and Physical Layer (PHY) Specifications. *IEEE P802.11-REVmb/D12, November 2011 (Revision of IEEE Std 802.11-2007, as amended by IEEEs*

802.11k-2008, 802.11r-2008, 802.11y-2008, 802.11w-2009, 802.11n-2009, 802.11p-2010, 802.11z-2010, 802.11v-2011, 802.11u-2011, and 802.11s-2011), pages 1–2910, 2012. doi:10.1109/IEEESTD.2012.6178212.

[IHS12] IHS Inc. Top 5 most counterfeited parts represent a $169 billion potential challenge for global semiconductor market, April 2012. URL: http://press.ihs.com/press-release/design-supply-chain/top-5-most-counterfeited-parts-represent-169-billion-potential-cha [cited August 4th,2013].

[Inf05] Infineon Technologies AG. *Cooperation Between VeriSign and Infineon – Infineon Trusted Platform Module connected to the VeriSign Certificate Infrastructure*, October 2005. White Paper – V1.0. URL: http://www.infineon.com/dgdl/TPM+Reference+to+Verisign+Certificate+Chain.pdf?folderId=db3a304412b407950112b408e8c90004&fileId=db3a304412b407950112b416601c2053.

[Inf06] Infineon Technologies AG. *Trusted Computing use for embedded platforms*, July 2006. White Paper – V1.1. URL: http://www.infineon.com/dgdl/Trusted+Computing+for+embedded+platforms.pdf?folderId=db3a304412b407950112b41656522039&fileId=db3a304412b407950112b4165ee0204f.

[Int02] Intel Corporation. Intel Low Pin Count (LPC) Interface Specification, August 2002. Revision 1.1. URL: http://www.intel.com/design/chipsets/industry/25128901.pdf.

[Int11a] Intel Corporation. *Going Beyond Exceptional Computing Performance – Intel® vPro^{TM} technology gives an edge to embedded developers*, 2011. URL: http://download.intel.com/embedded/technology/325564.pdf.

[Int11b] Intel Corporation. *Intel® Trusted Execution Technology – Hardware-based Technology for Enhancing Server Platform Security*, 2011. URL: http://www.intel.com/content/dam/www/public/us/en/documents/white-papers/trusted-execution-technology-security-paper.pdf.

[ITU08]   ITU-T, International Telecommunication Union. *X.509 : Information technology - Open Systems Interconnection - The Directory: Public-key and attribute certificate frameworks*, November 2008.

[Jac11]   Joab Jackson. IDC: embedded systems market to double by 2015. http://www.networkworld.com/news/2011/090911-idc-embedded-systems-market-to-250716.html, September 2011. last access: 2012-08-21. URL: http://www.networkworld.com/news/2011/090911-idc-embedded-systems-market-to-250716.html.

[KAE12]   Kari Kostiainen, N. Asokan, and Jan-Erik Ekberg. Credential disabling from trusted execution environments. In Tuomas Aura, Kimmo Järvinen, and Kaisa Nyberg, editors, *Information Security Technology for Applications*, volume 7127 of *Lecture Notes in Computer Science (LNCS)*, pages 171–186. Springer Berlin / Heidelberg, 2012. doi:10.1007/978-3-642-27937-9_12.

[Kau07]   Bernhard Kauer. OSLO: improving the security of trusted computing. In *Proceedings of 16th USENIX Security Symposium on USENIX Security Symposium*, pages 1–9, Boston, MA, 2007. USENIX Association. URL: http://usenix.org/events/sec07/tech/full_papers/kauer/kauer.pdf.

[KBC97]   H. Krawczyk, M. Bellare, and R. Canetti. HMAC: Keyed-Hashing for Message Authentication. RFC 2104 (Informational), February 1997. Updated by RFC 6151. URL: http://www.ietf.org/rfc/rfc2104.txt.

[Kea02]   Tom Kean. Cryptographic rights management of FPGA intellectual property cores. In *Field Programmable Gate Arrays Symposium*, page 113–118, New York, NY, USA, 2002. ACM Press. URL: http://www.algotronix.com/content/securityfpga2002.pdf.

[KG04]   Paul Kohlbrenner and Kris Gaj. An embedded true random number generator for FPGAs. In *Proceedings of the ACM/SIGDA International Symposium on Field Programmable Gate Arrays*, pages 71–78, February 2004. doi:10.1145/968280.968292.

[Kil10a]   Kilopass Technology Inc. *Comparison of Embedded Non-Volatile Memory Technologies and Their Applications*, April 2010. White Paper. URL: http://www.kilopass.com/wp-content/uploads/2010/04/comparison_of_embedded_nvm.pdf.

[Kil10b]   Kilopass Technology Inc. *XPM Register & XPM Memory*, May 2010. Product Brief. URL: http://www.kilopass.com/wp-content/uploads/2010/05/XPM_Product_brief.pdf.

[KJJ99]   Paul C. Kocher, Joshua Jaffe, and Benjamin Jun. Differential Power Analysis. In Michael J. Wiener, editor, *Proceedings of CRYPTO 1999*, volume 1666 of *Lecture Notes in Computer Science*, pages 388–397. Springer, 1999. doi:10.1007/3-540-48405-1_25.

[KKR+12]   Stefan Katzenbeisser, Ünal Kocabaş, Vladimir Rožić, Ahmad-Reza Sadeghi, Ingrid Verbauwhede, and Christian Wachsmann. PUFs: myth, fact or busted? a security evaluation of physically unclonable functions (PUFs) cast in silicon. In Emmanuel Prouff and Patrick Schaumont, editors, *Cryptographic Hardware and Embedded Systems (CHES)*, volume 7428, pages 283–301. Springer Berlin Heidelberg, Berlin, Heidelberg, 2012. URL: http://link.springer.com/chapter/10.1007/978-3-642-33027-8_17.

[KMK09]   Krzysztof Kepa, Fearghal Morgan, and Krzysztof Kosciuszkiewicz. IP protection in partially reconfigurable FPGAs. In *International Conference on Field Programmable Logic and Applications (FPL)*, pages 403–409. IEEE, 2009. doi:10.1109/FPL.2009.5272250.

[KN08]   Adam B. Kinsman and Nicola Nicolici. An energy-efficient architecture for mpeg-2 audio/video decoding. In *Microsystems and Nanoelectronics Research Conference, 2008. MNRC 2008. 1st*, pages 149–152, 2008. doi:10.1109/MNRC.2008.4683400.

[KST07]   Tom Kevenaar, Boris Skoric, and Pim Tuyls. Introduction. In Pim Tuyls, Boris Skoric, and Tom Kevenaar, editors, *Security with Noisy Data*, pages 1–17. Springer London, 2007. doi:10.1007/978-1-84628-984-2_1.

[KV07] Markus Kucera and Michael Vetter. FPGA-Rootkits hiding malicious code inside the hardware. In *Fifth Workshop on Intelligent Solutions in Embedded Systems (WISES)*, pages 262–272, June 2007. doi:10.1109/WISES.2007.4408497.

[Lat12a] Lattice Semiconductor. *LatticeECP2/M Family Handbook*, February 2012. HB1003, Version 05.3. URL: http://www.latticesemi.com/documents/HB1003.pdf.

[Lat12b] Lattice Semiconductor. *LatticeECP3 Family Overview*, April 2012. Data Sheet DS1021EA, Version 02.2EA. URL: http://www.latticesemi.com/documents/ds1021ea.pdf.

[Lat12c] Lattice Semiconductor. *LatticeECP4 Family Overview*, April 2012. Data Sheet DS1037A, Version 01.2. URL: http://www.latticesemi.com/documents/DS1037A.pdf.

[Lat12d] Lattice Semiconductor. *LatticeXP2 Family Handbook*, January 2012. HB1004, Version 03.2. URL: http://www.latticesemi.com/documents/HB1004.pdf.

[Lee06] Edward A. Lee. Cyber-Physical Systems – Are Computing Foundations Adequate? In *NSF Workshop On Cyber-Physical Systems: Research Motivation, Techniques and Roadmap*, volume 2, October 2006.

[LHA+12] Arjen K. Lenstra, James P. Hughes, Maxime Augier, Joppe W. Bos, Thorsten Kleinjung, and Christophe Wachter. Ron was wrong, whit is right. Cryptology ePrint 064, International Association for Cryptologic Research (IACR), 2012. URL: http://eprint.iacr.org/2012/064/.

[LKLJ09] Ming Liu, Wolfgang Kuehn, Zhonghai Lu, and Axel Jantsch. Run-time partial reconfiguration speed investigation and architectural design space exploration. In *International Conference on Field Programmable Logic and Applications, 2009. FPL 2009*, pages 498–502, September 2009. doi:10.1109/FPL.2009.5272463.

[LSS+12] Vincent van der Leest, Erik van der Sluis, Geert-Jan Schrijen, Pim Tuyls, and Helena Handschuh. Efficient implementation of true random number generator based on SRAM

PUFs. In David Naccache, editor, *Cryptography and Security: From Theory to Applications*, volume 6805 of *Lecture Notes in Computer Science (LNCS)*, pages 300–318. Springer Berlin / Heidelberg, quisquater festschrift edition, 2012. doi:10.1007/978-3-642-28368-0_20.

[LTRHDP06] Emmanuel López-Trejo, Francisco Rodríguez-Henríquez, and Arturo Díaz-Pérez. An fpga implementation of ccm mode using aes. In Dong Won and Seungjoo Kim, editors, *Information Security and Cryptology - ICISC 2005*, volume 3935 of *Lecture Notes in Computer Science*, pages 322–334. Springer Berlin / Heidelberg, 2006. doi:10.1007/11734727_26.

[Max12] Maxim Integrated. *DS2432 1Kb Protected 1-Wire EEPROM with SHA-1 Engine*, September 2012. 219-0003; Rev 9/12. URL: http://datasheets.maximintegrated.com/en/ds/DS2432.pdf.

[MBKP11] Amir Moradi, Alessandro Barenghi, Timo Kasper, and Christof Paar. On the vulnerability of fpga bitstream encryption against power analysis attacks: extracting keys from xilinx virtex-ii fpgas. In *Proceedings of the 18th ACM conference on Computer and Communications Security (CCS)*, pages 111–124, New York, NY, USA, 2011. ACM. doi:10.1145/2046707.2046722.

[Mic03] Microsemi Corporation. *Implementation of Security in Actel's ProASIC and ProASIC^{PLUS} Flash-Based FPGAs*, September 2003. Application Note AC185. URL: http://www.actel.com/documents/Flash_Security_AN.pdf.

[Mic11a] Microsemi Corporation. *IGLOO FPGA Fabric User's Guide*, December 2011. User Guide, Revision 2. URL: http://www.actel.com/documents/IGLOO_UG.pdf.

[Mic11b] Microsemi Corporation. *iRNG*, August 2011. URL: http://www.actel.com/documents/IID_iRNG.pdf.

[Mic11c] Microsemi Corporation. *ProASIC3 FPGA Fabric User's Guide*, December 2011. User Guide, Revision 2. URL: http://www.actel.com/documents/IGLOO_UG.pdf.

[Mic11d] Microsemi Corporation. *Quiddikey on Microsemi ProASIC3 FPGAs*, August 2011. URL: http://www.actel.com/documents/Quiddikey_FPGA.pdf.

[Mic12a] Microsemi Corporation. *IGLOO Low Power Flash FPGAs with Flash*Freeze Technology*, March 2012. Data Sheet, Revision 20. URL: http://www.actel.com/documents/IGLOO_DS.pdf.

[Mic12b] Microsemi Corporation. *SmartFusion Customizable System-on-Chip (cSoC)*, September 2012. Data Sheet, Revision 9. URL: http://www.actel.com/documents/SmartFusion_DS.pdf.

[Mic12c] Microsemi Corporation. *SmartFusion2 System-on-Chip FPGAs*, October 2012. Data Sheet, Revision 0. URL: http://www.actel.com/documents/SmartFusion2_DS.pdf.

[Mic12d] Microsemi Corporation. *TRRUST-Stor MSD064/MSD128 SATA SLC SOLID STATE DRIVE*, 2012. URL: http://www.whiteedc.com/pdf/SSD1000_MSD064-MSD128_SATA_SLC_SSD_rev10.pdf.

[MKD11] Mehrdad Majzoobi, Farinaz Koushanfar, and Srini Devadas. FPGA-based true random number generation using circuit metastability with adaptive feedback control. In *Cryptographic Hardware and Embedded Systems (CHES)*, volume 6917 of *Lecture Notes in Computer Science (LNCS)*. Springer, September 2011. doi:10.1007/978-3-642-23951-9_2.

[MKP11] Amir Moradi, Markus Kasper, and Christof Paar. On the portability of side-channel attacks – an analysis of the xilinx virtex 4, virtex 5, and spartan 6 bitstream encryption mechanism. Cryptology ePrint 2011/391, International Association for Cryptologic Research (IACR), November 2011. URL: http://eprint.iacr.org/2011/391/.

[MKP12] Amir Moradi, Markus Kasper, and Christof Paar. Black-box side-channel attacks highlight the importance of countermeasures. In *Topics in Cryptology – CT-RSA 2012*, volume 7178 of *Lecture Notes in Computer Science (LNCS)*, pages 1–18. Springer Berlin, Heidelberg, 2012. doi:10.1007/978-3-642-27954-6_1.

[MLF12]	Tilo Müller, Tobias Latzo, and Felix C. Freiling. Hardware-based Full Disk Encryption (In)Security. Talk at 29C3: 29th Chaos Communication Congress, Hamburg, December 2012. URL: http://events.ccc.de/congress/2012/Fahrplan/events/5091.en.html.
[MM09]	A. Theodore Markettos and Simon W. Moore. The frequency injection attack on ring-oscillator-based true random number generators. In *Cryptographic Hardware and Embedded Systems (CHES)*, volume 5747 of *Lecture Notes in Computer Science (LNCS)*, pages 317–331. Springer, 2009. doi:10.1007/978-3-642-04138-9_23.
[MMO85]	Stephen M. Matyas, Carl H. W. Meyer, and Jonathan Oseas. Generating Strong One-Way Functions with Cryptographic Algorithm. *IBM Technical Disclosure Bulletin*, (27), 1985.
[MMS10]	Sergey Morozov, Abhranil Maiti, and Patrick Schaumont. An analysis of delay based PUF implementations on FPGA. In Phaophak Sirisuk, Fearghal Morgan, Tarek El-Ghazawi, and Hideharu Amano, editors, *Reconfigurable Computing: Architectures, Tools and Applications*, volume 5992 of *Lecture Notes in Computer Science*, pages 382–387. Springer Berlin / Heidelberg, 2010. doi:10.1007/978-3-642-12133-3_37.
[Moc09]	Mocana. *Best Practices for Testing Embedded Devices*, April 2009. URL: https://mocana.com/pdfs/testing-embedded-devices-whitepaper.pdf.
[MPP+08]	Jonathan M. McCune, Bryan J. Parno, Adrian Perrig, Michael K. Reiter, and Hiroshi Isozaki. Flicker: an execution infrastructure for tcb minimization. *SIGOPS Oper. Syst. Rev.*, 42(4):315–328, April 2008. doi:10.1145/1357010.1352625.
[MSV12]	Roel Maes, Dries Schellekens, and Ingrid Verbauwhede. A pay-per-use licensing scheme for hardware ip cores in recent sram-based fpgas. *Information Forensics and Security, IEEE Transactions on*, 7(1):98–108, 2012. doi:10.1109/TIFS.2011.2169667.
[MV10]	Roel Maes and Ingrid Verbauwhede. Physically unclonable functions: A study on the state of the art and future research

directions. In Ahmad-Reza Sadeghi and David Naccache, editors, *Towards Hardware-Intrinsic Security*, Information Security and Cryptography, pages 3–37. Springer Berlin Heidelberg, 2010. doi:10.1007/978-3-642-14452-3_1.

[MVHV12] Roel Maes, Anthony Van Herrewege, and Ingrid Verbauwhede. PUFKY: a fully functional PUF-Based cryptographic key generator. In Emmanuel Prouff and Patrick Schaumont, editors, *Cryptographic Hardware and Embedded Systems (CHES)*, volume 7428 of *Lecture Notes in Computer Science (LNCS)*, pages 302–319. Springer Berlin / Heidelberg, September 2012. doi:10.1007/978-3-642-33027-8_18.

[NESP08] Karsten Nohl, David Evans, Starbug, and Henryk Plötz. Reverse-engineering a cryptographic rfid tag. In *Proceedings of the USENIX Security Symposium*, pages 185–193, San Jose, CA, USA, July 2008. USENIX Association. URL: http://usenix.org/event/sec08/tech/full_papers/nohl/nohl.pdf.

[NIS99] National Institute of Standards and Technology (NIST). *Data Encryption Standard (DES)*, October 1999. FIPS46-3. URL: http://csrc.nist.gov/publications/fips/fips46-3/fips46-2.pdf.

[NIS01] National Institute of Standards and Technology (NIST). *Announcing the Advanced Encryption Standard (AES)*, March 2001. FIPS197. URL: http://csrc.nist.gov/publications/fips/fips197/fips-197.pdf.

[NIS02] National Institute of Standards and Technology (NIST). *Data Encryption Standard (DES)*, December 2002. FIPS140-2. URL: http://csrc.nist.gov/publications/fips/fips140-2/fips1402.pdf.

[NIS08] National Institute of Standards and Technology (NIST). *The Keyed-Hash Message Authentication Code (HMAC)*, July 2008. FIPS198-1. URL: http://csrc.nist.gov/publications/fips/fips198-1/FIPS-198-1_final.pdf.

[NIS10] National Institute of Standards and Technology (NIST). *Introduction to the NISTIR 7628 Guidelines for Smart*

Grid Cyber Security, September 2010. NISTIR 7628. URL: http://csrc.nist.gov/publications/nistir/ir7628/introduction-to-nistir-7628.pdf.

[NIS12a] National Institute of Standards and Technology (NIST). *Secure Hash Standard (SHS)*, March 2012. FIPS180-4. URL: http://csrc.nist.gov/publications/fips/fips180-4/fips-180-4.pdf.

[NIS12b] National Institute of Standards and Technology (NIST). *SHA-3 Selection Announcement*, October 2012. URL: http://csrc.nist.gov/groups/ST/hash/sha-3/sha-3_selection_announcement.pdf.

[NR08] Jean-Baptiste Note and Éric Rannaud. From the bitstream to the netlist. In *Proceedings of the 16th international ACM/SIGDA symposium on Field programmable gate arrays*, FPGA '08, pages 264–264, New York, NY, USA, 2008. ACM. doi:10.1145/1344671.1344729.

[Par05] Milind M. Parelkar. *Authenticated Encryption in Hardware*. Master thesis, George Mason University, December 2005. URL: http://ece.gmu.edu/crypto_resources/web_resources/theses/GMU_theses/Parelkar/Parelkar_Fall_2005.pdf.

[Par08] Bryan Parno. Bootstrapping trust in a "Trusted" platform. In *Proceedings of the USENIX Workshop on Hot Topics in Security (HotSec)*, July 2008. URL: http://usenix.org/events/hotsec08/tech/full_papers/parno/parno.pdf.

[Par10] Bryan Parno. *Trust Extension as a Mechanism for Secure Code Execution on Commodity Computers*. Phd thesis, Carnegie Mellon University (CMU), April 2010. URL: http://repository.cmu.edu/dissertations/28.

[PB61] W.W. Peterson and D.T. Brown. Cyclic codes for error detection. *Proceedings of the IRE*, 49(1):228–235, January 1961. doi:10.1109/JRPROC.1961.287814.

[PC10] Shari L. Pfleeger and Robert. K. Cunningham. Why measuring security is hard. *Security Privacy, IEEE*, 8(4):46–54, july-aug. 2010. doi:10.1109/MSP.2010.60.

[PCI12]   Pci express: Performance scalability for the next decade, 2012. URL: http://www.pcisig.com/specifications/pciexpress/.

[PGV94]   Bart Preneel, René Govaerts, and Joos Vandewalle. Hash functions based on block ciphers: a synthetic approach. In Douglas Stinson, editor, *Advances in Cryptology — CRYPTO*, volume 773 of *Lecture Notes in Computer Science*, pages 368–378. Springer Berlin / Heidelberg, 1994. doi:10.1007/3-540-48329-2_31.

[PNNM09] Miodrag Potkonjak, Ani Nahapetian, Michael Nelson, and Tammara Massey. Hardware trojan horse detection using gate-level characterization. In *Proceedings of the 46th Annual Design Automation Conference*, DAC'09, pages 688–693, New York, NY, USA, 2009. ACM. doi:10.1145/1629911.1630091.

[PP10]   Christof Paar and Jan Pelzl. *Understanding Cryptography – A Textbook for Students and Practitioners*. Springer, 2010. doi:10.1007/978-3-642-04101-3.

[Rad11]   Jerome Radcliffe. Hacking Medical Devices for Fun and Insulin: Breaking the Human SCADA System. Las Vegas, February 2011. URL: https://www.blackhat.com/html/bh-us-11/bh-us-11-archives.html#Radcliffe [cited July, 28th 2012].

[Rav01]   Pappu Sirnivasa Ravikanth. *Physical one-way functions*. Phd thesis, Massachusetts Institute of Technology, 2001.

[RKM08]   Jarrod A. Roy, Farinaz Koushanfar, and Igor L. Markov. Circuit cad tools as a security threat. In *IEEE International Workshop on Hardware-Oriented Security and Trust (HOST)*, pages 65–66. IEEE, 2008.

[RSA78]   Ronald L. Rivest, Adi Shamir, and Leonard Adleman. A method for obtaining digital signatures and public-key cryptosystems. *Commun. ACM*, 21(2):120–126, February 1978. doi:10.1145/359340.359342.

[RSS09]   Ulrich Rührmair, Jan Sölter, and Frank Sehnke. On the foundations of physical unclonable functions. Cryptology ePrint 2009/277, International Association for Cryptologic

Research (IACR), 2009. URL: http://eprint.iacr.org/2009/277/.

[RSS+10] Ulrich Rührmair, Frank Sehnke, Jan Sölter, Gideon Dror, Srinivas Devadas, and Jürgen Schmidhuber. Modeling attacks on physical unclonable functions. In *Proceedings of the 17th ACM conference on Computer and communications security*, CCS '10, pages 237–249, New York, NY, USA, 2010. ACM. doi:10.1145/1866307.1866335.

[SA03] Sergei P. Skorobogatov and Ross J. Anderson. Optical fault induction attacks. In Burton S. Kaliski, Çetin K. Koç, and Christof Paar, editors, *Cryptographic Hardware and Embedded Systems (CHES)*, number 2523 in Lecture Notes in Computer Science (LNCS), pages 2–12. Springer Berlin Heidelberg, January 2003. doi:10.1007/3-540-36400-5_2.

[SBE11] Sal Stolfo, Steven M. Bellovin, and David Evans. Measuring security. *Security Privacy, IEEE*, 9(3):60–65, may-june 2011. doi:10.1109/MSP.2011.56.

[SCG+03] G.Edward Suh, Dwaine Clarke, Blaise Gasend, Marten van Dijk, and Srinivas Devadas. Efficient memory integrity verification and encryption for secure processors. In *36th Annual IEEE/ACM International Symposium on Microarchitecture, 2003. MICRO-36. Proceedings*, pages 339–350, December 2003. doi:10.1109/MICRO.2003.1253207.

[SD07] G. Edward Suh and Srinivas Devadas. Physical unclonable functions for device authentication and secret key generation. In *Proceedings of the 44th annual Design Automation Conference*, DAC '07, pages 9–14, New York, NY, USA, 2007. ACM. doi:10.1145/1278480.1278484.

[SE08] Frederic Stumpf and Claudia Eckert. Enhancing trusted platform modules with hardware-based virtualization techniques. In *Second International Conference on Emerging Security Information, Systems and Technologies, 2008. SECURWARE '08*, pages 1–9, August 2008. doi:10.1109/SECURWARE.2008.23.

[SFH11]   Marc Stoettinger, Thomas Feller, and Sorin A. Huss. A Side-Channel hardened IP-Protection Scheme for FPGA-based Platforms. In *International Conference on Field-Programmable Technology (FPT)*, December 2011. doi: 10.1109/FPT.2011.6269382.

[SH09]   Abdulhadi Shoufan and Sorin A. Huss. High-Performance Rekeying Processor Architecture for Group Key Management. *IEEE Transactions on Computers*, 58(10):1421–1434, 2009. doi:10.1109/TC.2009.88.

[Sha49]   Claude E. Shannon. Communication theory of secrecy systems. *Bell system technical journal*, 28(4):656–715, 1949.

[Sim91]   Gustavus J. Simmons. Identification of data, devices, documents and individuals. In *Security Technology, 1991. Proceedings. 25th Annual 1991 IEEE International Carnahan Conference on*, pages 197–218, oct 1991. doi:10.1109/CCST.1991.202215.

[Sko02]   Sergei Skorobogatov. Low Temperature Data Remanence in Static RAM. Technical Report UCAM-CL-TR-536, University of Cambridge, Computer Laboratory, June 2002. URL: http://www.cl.cam.ac.uk/techreports/UCAM-CL-TR-536.pdf.

[Sko05]   Sergei P. Skorobogatov. *Semi-invasive Attacks – A new Approach to Hardware Security Analysis*. Phd thesis, University of Cambridge, Computer Laboratory, April 2005. URL: http://www.cl.cam.ac.uk/techreports/UCAM-CL-TR-630.pdf.

[Smi11]   Ned M. Smith. Method and apparatus for virtualization of a multi-context hardware trusted platform module (tpm), October 2011. US Patent 8032741.

[Sol12]   Leonardo Solis Vasquez. *A novel Set-Top Box Architecture providing dynamically reconfigurable Security Components*. Master Thesis, Technische Universität Darmstadt, October 2012.

[SPvDK04] Arvind Seshadri, Adrian Perrig, Leendert van Doorn, and Pradeep Khosla. SWATT: SoftWare-based ATTestation for embedded devices. In *Security and Privacy, IEEE Symposium* on*, pages 272–282, Los Alamitos, CA, USA, May 2004. IEEE Computer Society. doi:10.1109/SECPRI.2004.1301329.

[SS99] Bruce Schneier and Adam Shostack. Breaking up is hard to do: modeling security threats for smart cards. In *Proceedings of the USENIX Workshop on Smartcard Technology*, WOST'99, pages 19–19, Berkeley, CA, USA, May 1999. USENIX Association. URL: http://static.usenix.org/events/smartcard99/full_papers/schneier/schneier.pdf.

[SS06] Eric Simpson and Patrick Schaumont. Offline hardware/software authentication for reconfigurable platforms. In Louis Goubin and Mitsuru Matsui, editors, *Cryptographic Hardware and Embedded Systems (CHES)*, volume 4249 of *Lecture Notes in Computer Science (LNCS)*, pages 311–323. Springer Berlin Heidelberg, 2006. doi:10.1007/11894063_25.

[SS08] Mario Strasser and Heiko Stamer. A software-based trusted platform module emulator. In Peter Lipp, Ahmad-Reza Sadeghi, and Klaus-Michael Koch, editors, *Trusted Computing - Challenges and Applications, TRUST*, volume 4968 of *Lecture Notes in Computer Science*, pages 33–47. Springer Berlin / Heidelberg, August 2008. doi:10.1007/978-3-540-68979-9_3.

[STP08] Dries Schellekens, Pim Tuyls, and Bart Preneel. Embedded trusted computing with authenticated non-volatile memory. In Peter Lipp, Ahmad-Reza Sadeghi, and Klaus-Michael Koch, editors, *Trusted Computing - Challenges and Applications*, volume 4968 of *Lecture Notes in Computer Science (LNCS)*, pages 60–74. Springer Berlin / Heidelberg, 2008. doi:10.1007/978-3-540-68979-9_5.

[SW12] Sergei Skorobogatov and Christopher Woods. Breakthrough silicon scanning discovers backdoor in military chip. In Emmanuel Prouff and Patrick Schaumont, editors, *Cryptographic Hardware and Embedded Systems (CHES)*, volume 7428 of *Lecture Notes in Computer Science (LNCS)*, pages 23–40. Springer Berlin / Heidelberg, September 2012. doi:10.1007/978-3-642-33027-8_2.

[SWS+11]   Neil Steiner, Aaron Wood, Hamid Shojaei, Jacob Couch, Peter Athanas, and Matthew French. Torc: towards an opensource tool flow. In *Proceedings of the 19th ACM/SIGDA international symposium on Field programmable gate arrays*, FPGA, pages 41–44, New York, NY, USA, 2011. ACM. doi: 10.1145/1950413.1950425.

[Tar10]   Christopher Tarnovsky. Hacking the smartcard chip. In *Black Hat, DC*, 2010. URL: https://www.blackhat.com/html/bh-dc-10/bh-dc-10-archives.html#Tarnovsky [cited August 7th,2013].

[TCA11]   Abhay Tavaragiri, Jacob Couch, and Peter Athanas. Exploration of FPGA interconnect for the design of unconventional antennas. In *Proceedings of the 19th ACM/SIGDA international symposium on Field programmable gate arrays*, FPGA '11, pages 219–226, New York, NY, USA, February 2011. ACM. doi:10.1145/1950413.1950455.

[TCG07]   Trusted Computing Group, Incorporated. *Architecture Overview*, August 2007. Version 1.4. URL: http://www.trustedcomputinggroup.org/files/resource_files/AC652DE1-1D09-3519-ADA026A0C05CFAC2/TCG_1_4_Architecture_Overview.pdf.

[TCG10]   Trusted Computing Group, Incorporated. *Mobile Trusted Module Specification*, April 2010. Version 1.0, Revision 7.02. URL: http://www.trustedcomputinggroup.org/resources/mobile_phone_work_group_mobile_trusted_module_specification.

[TCG11a]   Trusted Computing Group, Incorporated. *Mobile Trusted Module 2.0 Use Cases*, March 2011. Version 1.0. URL: http://www.trustedcomputinggroup.org/resources/mobile_trusted_module_20_use_cases.

[TCG11b]   Trusted Computing Group, Incorporated. *Protection Profile – PC Client Specific Trusted Platform Module –TPM Family 1.2; Level 2*, May 2011. Specification Version 1.2, Revision 116. URL: http://www.trustedcomputinggroup.org/files/static_page_files/36B214D7-1A4B-B294-D0F4C985F728EB0D/PP_TPM_spec12_rev116_final.pdf.

[TCG11c] Trusted Computing Group, Incorporated. *TPM Main Specification Level 2 Version 1.2*, March 2011. Revision 116.

[TCG12a] Trusted Computing Group, Incorporated. *Storage Security Subsystem Class: Opal*, February 2012. Specification Version 2.00, Revision 1.00. URL: http://www.trustedcomputinggroup.org/files/resource_files/B15F1F8F-1A4B-B294-D03F09D5122B21F6/Opal_SSC_200_rev100_final.pdf.

[TCG12b] Trusted Computing Group, Incorporated. *TCG PC Client Specific Implementation Specification for Conventional BIOS*, February 2012. Specification Version 1.21 Errata, Revision 1.00. URL: http://www.trustedcomputinggroup.org/files/resource_files/CB0B2BFA-1A4B-B294-D0C3B9075B5AFF17/TCG_PCClientImplementation_1-21_1_00.pdf.

[TCG12c] Trusted Computing Group, Incorporated. *TPM MOBILE with Trusted ExecutionEnvironment for Comprehensive Mobile Device Security*, June 2012. White Paper. URL: http://www.trustedcomputinggroup.org/resources/tpm_mobile_with_trusted_execution_environment_for_comprehensive_mobile_device_security.

[Tex05] Texas Instruments, Incorporated. *SN74CBTLV3245A Data Sheet*, August 2005. SCDS034M. URL: http://www.ti.com/product/sn74cbtlv3245a.

[TI11] TI achieves first Netflix HD certification, brings new streaming capabilities to Android devices, July 2011. URL: http://newscenter.ti.com/index.php?s=32851&item=123263 [cited July, 26th 2012].

[TK10] Mohammad Tehranipoor and Farinaz Koushanfar. A survey of hardware trojan taxonomy and detection. *IEEE Design & Test of Computers*, 27:10–25, January 2010. doi:10.1109/MDT.2010.7.

[Tom08] Allan Tomlinson. Introduction to the TPM. In *Smart Cards, Tokens, Security and Applications*, pages 155–172. Springer, 2008. doi:10.1007/978-0-387-72198-9_7.

[Tri07]   Steve Trimberger. Trusted design in FPGAs. In *44th ACM/IEEE Design Automation Conference, DAC'07*, pages 5–8, June 2007. doi:10.1145/1278480.1278483.

[Tru07]   Trusted Computing Group, Incorporated. *TCG Software Stack (TSS) Specification Version 1.2 Level 1 - Part1: Commands and Structures*, March 2007. URL: http://www.trustedcomputinggroup.org/files/resource_files/6479CD77-1D09-3519-AD89EAD1BC8C97F0/TSS_1_2_Errata_A-final.pdf.

[TWW12]   Erik Tews, Julian Wälde, and Michael Weiner. Breaking dvb-csa. In Frederik Armknecht and Stefan Lucks, editors, *Research in Cryptology*, volume 7242 of *Lecture Notes in Computer Science*, pages 45–61. Springer Berlin Heidelberg, 2012. doi:10.1007/978-3-642-34159-5_4.

[VD10]   Michal Varchola and Milos Drutarovsky. New high entropy element for FPGA based true random number generators. In *Cryptographic Hardware and Embedded Systems (CHES)*. Springer, 2010.

[Vit67]   Andrew J. Viterbi. Error bounds for convolutional codes and an asymptotically optimum decoding algorithm. *Information Theory, IEEE Transactions on*, 13(2), 1967. doi:10.1109/TIT.1967.1054010.

[VS07]   Ingrid Verbauwhede and Patrick Schaumont. Design methods for security and trust. In *Design, Automation Test in Europe Conference Exhibition, 2007. DATE '07*, pages 1–6, april 2007. doi:10.1109/DATE.2007.364671.

[vT05]   Henk C. A. van Tilborg, editor. *Encyclopedia of Cryptography and Security*. Springer, September 2005. doi:10.1007/0-387-23483-7.

[Wag12]   Mathias Wagner. 700+ Attacks Published on Smart Cards: The Need for a Systematic Counter Strategy. In Werner Schindler and Sorin Huss, editors, *Constructive Side-Channel Analysis and Secure Design (COSADE)*, volume 7275 of *Lecture Notes in Computer Science*, pages 33–38. Springer Berlin / Heidelberg, 2012. doi:10.1007/978-3-642-29912-4_3.

[Wav12]	Mobile World Congress Opens Window to Trusted Security on Any Device – Security Matters, March 2012. URL: http://blog.wave.com/burke/mobile-world-congress-opens-window-to-trusted-security-on-any-device/ [cited August 4th,2013].
[WFM+07]	P. Wilson, A. Frey, T. Mihm, D. Kershaw, and T. Alves. Implementing embedded security on dual-virtual-CPU systems. *IEEE Design Test of Computers*, 24(6):582–591, December 2007. doi:10.1109/MDT.2007.196.
[WGP04]	Thomas Wollinger, Jorge Guajardo, and Christof Paar. Security on FPGAs: state-of-the-art implementations and attacks. *ACM Transactions on Embedded Computing Systems*, 3(3):534–574, August 2004. doi:10.1145/1015047.1015052.
[WHF03]	D. Whiting, R. Housley, and N. Ferguson. Counter with CBC-MAC (CCM). RFC 3610 (Informational), September 2003. URL: http://www.ietf.org/rfc/rfc3610.txt.
[Wil]	John A. Williams. PetaLinux for Microblaze. Version 0.40 final. URL: http://www.petalogix.com/univ/documentation.
[Win08]	Johannes Winter. Trusted computing building blocks for embedded linux-based ARM trustzone platforms. In *Proceedings of the 3rd ACM workshop on Scalable trusted computing*, STC '08, pages 21–30, New York, NY, USA, 2008. ACM. doi:10.1145/1456455.1456460.
[WP03]	Thomas Wollinger and Christof Paar. How secure are FPGAs in cryptographic applications? In Peter Y. K. Cheung and George Constantinides, editors, *Field Programmable Logic and Application*, volume 2778 of *Lecture Notes in Computer Science (LNCS)*, pages 91–100. Springer Berlin / Heidelberg, June 2003. doi:10.1007/978-3-540-45234-8_10.
[WW05]	Ralf-Philipp Weinmann and Kai Wirt. Analysis of the dvb common scrambling algorithm. In David Chadwick and Bart Preneel, editors, *Communications and Multimedia Security*, volume 175 of *IFIP — The International Federation for Information Processing*, pages 195–207. Springer US, 2005. doi:10.1007/0-387-24486-7_15.

[WYY05] Xiaoyun Wang, Yiqun Yin, and Hongbo Yu. Finding collisions in the full SHA-1. In Victor Shoup, editor, *Advances in Cryptology – CRYPTO 2005*, volume 3621 of *Lecture Notes in Computer Science (LNCS)*, pages 17–36. Springer Berlin / Heidelberg, 2005. doi:10.1007/11535218_2.

[Xil97] Xilinx, Inc. *Configuration Issues: Power-up, Volatility, Security, Battery Back-up*, November 1997. Xilinx Application Note XAPP092 (v1.1). URL: http://www.xilinx.com/support/documentation/application_notes/xapp092.pdf.

[Xil06] Xilinx, Inc. *Spartan-3 Generation Configuration*, October 2006. User Guide UG332 (v1.6). URL: http://www.xilinx.com/support/documentation/user_guides/ug332.pdf.

[Xil07a] Xilinx, Inc. *Advanced Security Schemes for Spartan-3A/3AN/3A DSP FPGAs*, August 2007. White Paper WP267 (v1.0). URL: http://www.xilinx.com/support/documentation/white_papers/wp267.pdf.

[Xil07b] Xilinx, Inc. *Virtex-II Platform FPGA*, November 2007. User Guide UG002 (v2.2). URL: http://www.xilinx.com/support/documentation/user_guides/ug002.pdf.

[Xil07c] Xilinx, Inc. *Virtex-II Pro and Virtex-II Pro X FPGA User Guide*, November 2007. User Guide UG012 (v4.2). URL: http://www.xilinx.com/support/documentation/user_guides/ug012.pdf.

[Xil08] Xilinx, Inc. *Security Solutions Using Spartan-3 Generation FPGAs*, April 2008. White Paper WP266 (v1.1). URL: http://www.xilinx.com/support/documentation/white_papers/wp266.pdf.

[Xil09] Xilinx, Inc. *Virtex-4 FPGA Configuration*, June 2009. User Guide UG071 (v1.11). URL: http://www.xilinx.com/support/documentation/user_guides/ug071.pdf.

[Xil10] Xilinx, Inc. *FPGA IFF Copy Protection Using Dallas Semiconductor/Maxim DS2432 Secure EEPROMs*, May 2010. Xilinx Application Note XAPP780 (v1.1). URL: http://www.xilinx.com/support/documentation/application_notes/xapp780.pdf.

Bibliography

[Xil11a] Xilinx, Inc. *Data2MEM User Guide*, October 2011. User Guide UG658 (v13.3). URL: http://www.xilinx.com/support/documentation/sw_manuals/xilinx14_2/data2mem.pdf.

[Xil11b] Xilinx, Inc. *Developing Tamper Resistant Designs with Xilinx Virtex-6 and 7 Series FPGAs*, December 2011. White Paper WP1084 (v1.1). URL: http://www.xilinx.com/support/documentation/application_notes/xapp1084_tamp_resist_dsgns.pdf.

[Xil11c] Xilinx, Inc. *Spartan-6 FPGA Configuration*, July 2011. User Guide UG380 (v2.3). URL: http://www.xilinx.com/support/documentation/user_guides/ug380.pdf.

[Xil11d] Xilinx, Inc. *Virtex-5 FPGA Configuration*, November 2011. User Guide UG191 (v3.10). URL: http://www.xilinx.com/support/documentation/user_guides/ug191.pdf.

[Xil11e] Xilinx, Inc. *Virtex-6 FPGA Configuration*, November 2011. User Guide UG360 (v3.4). URL: http://www.xilinx.com/support/documentation/user_guides/ug360.pdf.

[Xil12a] Xilinx, Inc. *7 Series FPGAs Configuration*, February 2012. User Guide UG470 (v1.3). URL: http://www.xilinx.com/support/documentation/user_guides/ug470_7Series_Config.pdf.

[Xil12b] Xilinx, Inc. *LogiCORE IP MicroBlaze Micro Controller System*, April 2012. Version 1.1. URL: http://www.xilinx.com/support/documentation/sw_manuals/xilinx14_1/ds865_microblaze_mcs.pdf.

[Xil12c] Xilinx, Inc. *Partial Reconfiguration User Guide*, January 2012. User Guide UG702 (v13.4). URL: http://www.xilinx.com/support/documentation/sw_manuals/xilinx13_4/ug702.pdf.

[Xil12d] Xilinx, Inc. *Security Monitor IP: Unprecedented Ease of Integration for Industry-Leading Programmable Device Security*, June 2012. URL: http://www.xilinx.com/publications/prod_mktg/CS1140_AD_SecMonIP_ProdBrf_Update_June_2012.pdf.

[Xil12e]   Xilinx, Inc. *Zynq-7000 All Programmable SoC Overview*, August 2012. Data Sheet DS190 (v1.2). URL: http://www.xilinx.com/support/documentation/data_sheets/ds190-Zynq-7000-Overview.pdf.

[YN00]   Kun-Wah Yip and Tung-Sang Ng. Partial-encryption technique for intellectual property protection of FPGA-based products. *Consumer Electronics, IEEE Transactions on*, 46(1):183–190, February 2000. doi:10.1109/30.826397.

[YWK04]   Bo Yang, Kaijie Wu, and Ramesh Karri. Scan based side channel attack on data encryption standard. Cryptology ePrint 2004/083, International Association for Cryptologic Research (IACR), 2004. URL: http://eprint.iacr.org/2004/083/.

[ZAT06]   Daniel Ziener, Stefan Aßmus, and Jürgen Teich. Identifying FPGA IP-Cores based on lookup table content analysis. In *Field Programmable Logic and Applications, International Conference on*, FPL'06., pages 1–6, 2006. doi:10.1109/FPL.2006.311255.

MIX
Papier aus verantwortungsvollen Quellen
Paper from responsible sources
FSC® C105338

If you have any concerns about our products,
you can contact us on
ProductSafety@springernature.com

In case Publisher is established outside the EU,
the EU authorized representative is:
**Springer Nature Customer Service Center GmbH
Europaplatz 3, 69115 Heidelberg, Germany**

Printed by Libri Plureos GmbH
in Hamburg, Germany